Also by Ivanka Di Felice:

A Zany Slice of Italy

*A Zany Slice of Tuscany: La Bella Figura and Other Italian Concepts
That Elude Me*

For Steven

My Zany Life

Growing Up in a Rooming House

IVANKA DI FELICE

AND

ANICA BLAŽANIN

"Look for the ridiculous in everything and you will find it."

— *Jules Renard*

TABLE OF CONTENTS

LIVING LOW IN HIGH PARK

By Ivanka Di Felice

MANY PEOPLE THINK IT'S TRAGIC to grow up in a poor neighborhood, but I can assure you it is equally tragic growing up in a rich neighborhood, when *you* are poor.

I watch the quaint cafés and the chic restaurants close for the evening. Well-heeled patrons head to their expensive homes. Spotlights illuminate their yards, sparkling in the dark night. Mature oak trees and well-appointed gardens encircle the stately dwellings. I imagine handsome couples ensuring that the nannies have tucked in their children. The privileged parents undress, slip into bed, and kiss each other goodnight.

Yet among these regal residences, there stands a lone house that defiantly refuses to blend in. Welcome to our home.

I grew up in the swanky west-end neighborhood of High Park—except our house and those who lived in it were anything but swanky. My dad, or Tata, as we call him, started his "real estate empire" after my younger brother, Steven, was born. If there was a skill in renting out rooms, knowing how to read people, and letting only the good ones in, then my parents did not possess it. Hence, we shared our home with a host of colorful tenants: some good, some bad, some funny, and some sad. Yet we survived, and I fondly recall the humorous memories even now.

My childhood trials were only compounded by my father's unfortunate taste for primary colors. His version of "mix and match" resulted in multicolored toilets throughout the house: one color for the base, another for the tank, and, for that extra flair, a baby blue seat. Tata's taste, according to him, was "timeless": the tiles he chose in the bold oranges and browns of the seventies would never need replacing.

In all fairness, though, Tata had spent time, effort, and money "upgrading" the house. He painstakingly painted most of the original oak doors a shiny brown to give them a more authentic oak look.

Yet perhaps a woman who was conceived almost exclusively thanks to a 1964 Ford Galaxy XL has no right to expect much. I'm a dreamer, though—always was and probably always will be. I can't help it. Admittedly, it's not bad, because the cycle is continuous. When one dream fails, I just move on to the next, with never any time to dwell on disappointment in between. I recently found out I'd inherited this trait from both of my parents. I didn't stand a chance.

I was born in Toronto, Canada, in 1967. I am just over thirty-nine years old. It's best not to think about it too hard.

In search of a good life, my dad left Croatia (then called Yugoslavia) and came to Canada. Then, in search of a good wife, he returned. My mom entered the picture at that point. She came from the village of Mučna Reka. If you haven't heard of it, no worries. Only .0001 percent of the people in Croatia have, and all of them live there. Mučna Reka means "Sickening River." Legend has it that a czar exploring his domain first visited the nobly named "Lepavina" (meaning "Good Wine"). Given that the wine was so good, he could not help but indulge too much, and when he arrived at the next village, he threw up like a river, christening it Mučna

Reka, "Sickening River." Hence, my mom always tried to avoid revealing the town in which she lived.

It was rather fortuitous for me that the townspeople, in their attempt to be cosmopolitan, built their homes only a few feet from the heavily trafficked main street. Trucks thundered by, giving the impression that a major earthquake had hit—and leaving you with a feeling of good fortune that your house had remained standing.

Featherbed linens that my grandma faithfully slung across her windowsill to air had a rare combination of aromas that still eludes perfumers: country grass and diesel. Living so close to the road also enabled residents to greet the few people who strolled by each day and ensured an effective neighborhood watch program.

So, while my grandparents and my mother must have endured rattling and shaking, I will always be grateful for the pretentious inclinations of the folks of Mučna Reka. If it were not for that unobstructed view of the main road, I never would have been conceived.

In the Japanese movie *After Life*, a group of people must choose one memory they want to save for eternity. A film will then be made, enabling them to re-enact that recollection, and they will forget everything else. They will spend eternity with their happiest memory.

How does one even choose the happiest memory? Happiness to a five-year-old is ice cream; to a sixteen-year-old, finding your first love; to a fifty-year-old, waking up and still loving the person you said, "I do," to, many years ago; and to an eighty-year-old, like my dad, true happiness comes from catching another raccoon. So, as I age, I redefine what happiness is.

These are my mom's and my memories, mostly happy, some sad, and many funny—even about not-so-funny incidents. Yet in the end, I cannot complain, for the overall result is a happy life, despite some sorrow.

Let's start by going back to my mom's village. I'll let my mother give you her version of "Once upon a time, in a land, far, far, away . . ."

1964 FORD GALAXY XL

by Anica Blažanin

TRY TO PICTURE AUTUMN IN 1964, in a small village in Croatia (formerly Yugoslavia).

We lived like everyone else in the village, about ten feet from the main road. Anyone residing farther away, we called *hillbillies*. The close proximity of the road, formerly dirt but now gravel, gave us a feeling of superior standing, of almost being urban dwellers.

And once in a while, that road was blessed with the vision of a Ford Galaxy XL, zooming past.

We couldn't even dream of such a car, because we had never seen anything like it. The Ford Galaxy, XL Class, was one of the first to boast power windows and front and back lights the size of barrels. It drew more interest than a spaceship landing on Times Square would today. It had followers, stalkers, and even worshippers.

Our road was not exactly smooth sailing. Most of the traffic consisted of horse-drawn wagons, which people occasionally used as transportation, but mostly they hauled heavy loads of wood or field produce. The wagons would drag practically an entire tree with only the branches chopped

5

off, leaving big grooves in the road that filled with water when it rained. It was not a road worthy of the Ford Galaxy XL.

Regardless, the driver traveled through our village a number of times, because this was the closest route to the capital of Croatia: Zagreb.

Those who were blessed with a view of the car said it snuck up on them, for it didn't sound like any car they'd ever heard. Other cars, few and far between on that road, sounded like revved-up motorcycles—you heard them way before you saw them. With the Galaxy, however, the only noise you really heard was when the wheel hit a rut and the back of the car scraped along the gravel. People agreed that this elegant car was not made for our mundane world.

Because everyone focused on the car and not the driver, he was left to everyone's imagination. Naturally, this meant he was over six feet tall, dark, handsome—and rich. Undoubtedly, a very wealthy American, with oil fields galore.

None of us asked why he had spent months in the neighboring village. We knew he was visiting family, but for four months? What was the attraction? We were so excited and entertained by our romantic fantasies about this man that the truth didn't really interest us.

Little did I know that I would soon meet the biggest dreamer of us all.

"REALITY IS ACTUALLY STRANGER THAN FICTION"

by Anica Blažanin

NEEDLESS TO SAY, EVERY FEMALE from fifteen to eighty wanted to meet the man in the car. I myself had tried and failed to execute many "cute meet" strategies. His sister went to the same school that I did, and although I didn't know her personally, I started hanging around her crowd, hoping that when her brother came to pick her up, he would notice me.

When that didn't work, I spent my lunch money on Plan B—a bottle of peroxide. Always a proponent of "more is better," I sat in the sun and kept slowly pouring peroxide on my head, combing it through until I had used up almost the whole bottle. Only then did I notice my black smock streaked with different shades of orange highlights, similar to my hair. My parents also noticed, and you can imagine their reaction!

My mother insisted that I go to a real hairdresser in the morning and dye my hair back to its natural color. But I decided to go to school first and to the hairdresser afterward. I was determined to use my highlights for their intended purpose. I covered the peroxide burns on my neck with a scarf, and to ensure being noticed, I teased my hair in the school bathroom and sprayed it with a sugar water combination for maximum height and volume. For the final touch, I lit a match, blew it out, and, with the carbon tip, filled out my eyebrows. Then I prayed that the mystery man in the Galaxy XL would come to pick up his sister, Marija, that day.

And he did.

So I hovered on the outer edge of the tight circle around Marija, standing on my tiptoes. To get myself noticed, I spoke in a loud, animated manner to the girl next to me. However, her eyes, like mine, kept straying to the real object of our interest. I managed to catch his eye, and when his gaze lowered from my hair to my face, I shook my head in the manner of movie stars with long flowing blonde hair, forgetting that all of my orange hair was fastened on top of my head.

Minutes later, his sister and some chosen friends sailed past me in the Ford Galaxy XL, but it didn't matter. He had spotted me. Granted, how could he not? Vivacious, animated, and with that hairdo, I was obviously a sophisticated young woman.

Now all I had to do was wait for Marija to introduce him to me.

A week went by, and nothing happened. My hair now matched my mood: brown with tinges of yellow and green.

I developed a serious root canal infection that couldn't be treated in our little town, so I was sent to a dental clinic in Zagreb to have oral surgery. Dispirited, sad, and a little swollen, I walked into the waiting room and, lo and behold, who was sitting there? The car owner and his sister. Of all the misfortune that anyone could have, this topped it.

I decided that if Marija didn't recognize me, I would pretend I didn't know them. But she did, and she introduced me to Steve. He didn't look anything like he did when he was in the car. He appeared a lot shorter and not glamorous at all.

That was fine, because I certainly wasn't at my most alluring either.

To my great disappointment, they hadn't driven *the* car but had taken the train, just like me. I'd lost my only chance to experience the ride of a lifetime. They insisted they would wait for me, and I *almost* rudely demanded that they shouldn't. I already looked bad and guessed I would only look worse after surgery, so, to buy some time, I suggested meeting them at the train station.

My morbid premonition proved true, because the swelling gave me a Miss Piggy nose. So I slinked to the train station, got on, and locked myself in the bathroom until the train was well on its way. I gave Steve and his sister a chance to walk through the entire train, then I surreptitiously emerged, staying close to my hiding place in case I spotted them.

The next day at school, Marija said they had searched for me everywhere, throughout the train. Then she dropped a bombshell: "My brother Steve has sent me to ask if you would consider marrying him."

I thought, *This must be some kind of joke*, but I soon realized it wasn't. He wanted to meet me, and if I agreed, he would pick me up in the car after school so we could discuss it.

Reality is actually stranger than fiction, because I had engaged in only ten minutes of unremarkable conversation with Steve at the dentist's office, and the dialogue had none of the brilliance of the orange highlights.

Bewildered, I asked, "But what did he like about me? I was so swollen and blotchy and miserable."

Marija replied, "He thought you had nice legs."

Well, after that, of course, I agreed to meet him.

TRUTH BE TOLD

by Anica Blažanin

SOME PEOPLE BELIEVE THAT EVERY now and then, fortune smiles on us. If that were true, my fortune noticed me at the most awkward time. After it smiled at me, it had the biggest belly laugh, starting in the dentist's office all the way to when I was locked in a smelly train washroom, trying so hard to run away from the very occasion I had so wished for.

So, he thinks I have nice legs. I stared at them now, shod in clunky Russian-made boots that not only hid them well but would make even the legs of Miss Universe appear deformed. I contemplated removing the boots and going to meet Steve in my stocking feet, if I could come up with a story that wouldn't make me sound insane. I could say that my feet were hot in the classroom, so I took off my boots, and somebody stole them. But I refrained, certain that the missing boots would steal the show, possibly involving the police and making me miss the much-anticipated rendezvous. My excitement at getting into the car now mingled with great trepidation.

My face had not changed much since yesterday. The swelling had subsided a bit, but my nose still looked as if it belonged on something that "oinked." Plus, I now had colorful bruises under my eyes. Apparently, my legs were my best physical trait, and they were well hidden. So, with my hideous face, there was only one attribute I could work on to improve my appearance: my hair.

Teasing was at its height, literally. The higher, the better, regardless of whether it complemented one's features or not. Most girls' hairdos gave them the appearance of wearing different-colored pumpkins on their heads—with bangs.

The next step was to inform as many fellow students as possible about the great event, so they could become spectators when I entered the coveted vehicle. After school, at the assigned time and place, a large group huddled around me. Many skeptics came to see whether I was telling the truth.

Right on time, the car turned the corner and headed toward us. My excitement and tension were almost unbearable. It was like the scene from the movie *High Noon*, when the sheriff and the villain meet at twelve noon for the final showdown, while the crowd waits for the outcome.

The car stopped, and the window miraculously slid down. Steve searched the crowd, having difficulty identifying the right beehive hairdo. Finally, with a smile of recognition, he leaned over and opened the door for me. The top of my hair hit the door but bounced back intact.

"Hi," I said.

"Hi."

Then silence. He kept staring at me, grinning, without saying anything.

Did he forget what he said to his sister? Or maybe he was joking, and she took it seriously. More uncomfortable quiet filled the Galaxy.

I wasn't going to tolerate any game playing and messing with my head, so, as the silence became unbearable, I bluntly said, "Your sister, Marija, told me that you might want to marry me, and I'm here to talk about it."

11

He kept smiling and even blushed. At this point, in absolute horror, I felt convinced this was a terrible mistake. Marija had misunderstood, and I got it wrong. I started back-pedaling, apologetically.

"I'm so sorry. I probably got things mixed up. Don't worry, you don't have to marry me. I don't care much for marriage anyway. I'm happy you took me for a ride, really happy. You can drop me off anywhere. I'll walk back to the train station, no problem."

If he had been driving slower, I would have jumped out of the car.

Suddenly serious, he said that he had indeed told Marija that he liked me, and, because he had to leave for Canada soon, he wanted to marry. He suggested we talk first to get to know each other, and I could see whether I liked him and would marry him.

We drove to a coffee shop and sat in a quiet corner, where I got all of the answers to my questions, with none of the replies being as I had fantasized. Why did he come to visit? Why did he stay so long? Why did he come in such luxury? And why did he have to leave so soon?

We all say we want to know the truth. Why do we keep insisting, since the truth often brings us disappointment and pain? Because we are creatures who thrive on hope. We think that the truth will one day deliver what we hoped for.

None of the realities I heard that evening were kind to me. They stripped me of my dream of living like a princess and instead offered me the life of a long-term Cinderella. Maybe beyond that, I'd have a better life than I had now, but I would have to work for it, without the help of a Fairy Godmother.

He had left the old country, as they say, *"trbuhom za kruhom"* ("the belly searching for bread"). His family had lost everything they had during World War II. They had lived in Udbina, Lika, in a valley between the forested mountains of central Croatia. They loved their home and their land. Among other animals, they had three horses. Steve was always small for his age but had developed a mutual friendship with the oldest and biggest horse. In the morning, before they took the cows to pasture, Steve's horse always patiently waited at a spot beside the fence where it was easy for Steve to climb on its back and then would deposit him at a convenient place to slide off.

The news came that enemy armies would soon arrive in their village and that in previous villages the armies had killed many people and burned the homes. Steve's family had only a few hours to get ready to escape. They decided to hitch the cows to the wagons, because they could get milk from them. They piled up everything they could in the wagon and tried to make a comfortable spot among the household items for their mother, who was almost due to give birth. (Later, she did give birth on the wagon to her fourth boy.) With many fears, tears, and prayers, Steve and his father, mother, and brothers, along with other villagers, started the exodus. Hours later, from a hill they watched as their village was engulfed in flames.

What about the horses? It was winter, and the horses needed to be fed, but there was no room to carry all of their hay. In desperation, anger, and helplessness, Steve's father took him to the horses' paddock and explained that they absolutely couldn't take the horses, because if the horses were left behind, the Partisans would either kill them for food or ride them to catch up with the fleeing families.

He said, "We have no choice but to shoot them."

And he did, right in front of nine-year-old Steve. It left a wound in his young heart that would fester the rest of his life. Listening to Steve tell the story was like watching a splinter slowly and painfully be pulled out, but even then, I knew the wound would never heal.

Thus, they had moved as unwanted refugees to another part of the country—Podravina, near the Hungarian border. One would think they would be welcomed and sympathized with, for the residents, too, were Croatians and staunch Catholics. Yet the political divisiveness and the lack of hospitality and compassion made the newcomers' arrival hard to bear. Ten families were provided with a big house to share, with a little furniture but no beds. Instead, they were given bales of hay, which they spread over the floor to sleep on and in the morning bunched it up against the walls.

All of the males in Steve's family immediately started to look for work. Steve's father and eldest brother found jobs in Zagreb, which was a three-hour journey on a slow train with wooden benches. Traveling to and fro each day was impossible and financially prohibitive, so they found cheap lodgings and subsisted on dry food, with the occasional treat of a hot meal.

To help the rest of the family, some wealthier villagers took in Steve and his younger brother as house servants. Steve's brother was employed by kind people, while Steve got the opposite side of human nature. He ate well but had to sleep in a barn with an old wooden wheat chest as his bed and a horse blanket as his bedding. In such unsanitary conditions, it wasn't long before he ended up full of lice. When his teachers became aware of this, they ordered that he have his head shaved. Unfortunately, Steve's head was not perfectly round but had many bumps and indentations, which the local children found amusing. They even tried to write the names of valleys and hills on his head, using it as a globe.

Life was very hard, and the family suffered many deprivations, even of necessities.

The poverty continued, and Steve was especially aware of this while in school.

The village they settled in was 7.5 miles from his school in Koprivinica. At twelve years of age, Steve walked back and forth each day, barefoot. In the late fall, despite the cold, Steve still had to walk this distance barefoot. One day the class collected money to buy the most needy child a pair of shoes. Many arguments broke out over who was the neediest, because every student had his or her favorite poor person. The president of the class, who was also the most beautiful girl in the region, cast her vote for Steve.

He didn't know whether he should shout for joy or die of shame, because he was madly in love with her. Enough of the other students agreed that he was the poorest child in the class, so he got the new pair of shoes. He loved and cherished his pristine shoes so much that he tied the two pairs of shoelaces together, put the shoes around his neck, and proudly carried them, as he continued to walk home barefoot.

One day, when Steve was halfway home, an elderly man on a battered bicycle stopped and warned him not to display his shoes like that but to put them on his feet, because someone passing by could steal them from him. Given all of the hardships at the time, this was a very real possibility.

His fear of the shoes being stolen was greater than his fear of their being ruined while he wore them, so he put them on and carefully marched home.

As he walked, he tried to imagine that he had been given the shoes not because he was the poorest of the poor, but instead that the beautiful girl had voted for him because she was in love with him, too.

The humiliation he felt because of such poverty made him determined to leave the country, despite it being illegal at the time. His first attempt failed, and he ended up in jail. A few years later he succeeded, and, from a camp in Austria, he was accepted by Canada.

The reality in Canada did not live up to his dreams, as he went to work in the bitterly cold north, first in the mines, then on the upkeep of the railroads, and next at logging. He was paid by how much wood he could cut, clear, and stack. Loggers lived in barracks and ate in canteens. He was not a gambler or a drinker, and there wasn't much he could spend his hard-earned money on, so he saved it. After working the obligatory amount of time up north, he went to Toronto, where he got a job in his profession as a machinist.

15

Some of his family members also escaped and reunited in Toronto. After work, they usually gathered together, and that was his entertainment. He kept saving and dreaming of returning to his homeland—not as a broken refugee, but as a man of means, to amend for his painful poverty.

So, after years of diligent saving, he was able to put a large down payment on the 1964 Galaxy XL, and he boarded, together with his car, the *Queen Mary*. He disembarked in Le Havre, France, and in the springtime arrived back in his village, more than a knight in shining armor. The armor he came in was worthy of a king. Hardly anyone was more popular than he, and his family, driving in his car, immediately became elevated to his rank.

He had the means to support the grand show for three months, but he tried not to dwell on that. There were so many important people to entertain and so many pretty girls to date. He enjoyed being seen with the city's lawyers, doctors, politicians, and certified beauties that his armor attracted. Who would give all of that up, if it could be sustained for a while longer?

And it could. He thought of a way. Members of his family in Canada were savers, so he asked them to lend him some money. He asked again, and they did. Once, twice, and then they said, "No more," because it dawned on them that Steve would have a difficult time paying back all of the money he'd borrowed. They insisted he marry, because he was already thirty years old, and two salaries would repay their loans faster.

So, right after the ultimatum from the West, he met me. What the heck? He liked my legs, and, aside from my mashed-up face, I was young—only seventeen—and appeared healthy.

Then I got the math. With two wages, it would take us three years of work to be scot-free. Jacob had to work for Rachel for seven years in the Bible, so I figured I would work for my guy for three. With many adjustments, the dream slowly became a reality. I had to make a decision soon but now on different grounds.

Oddly, when he confessed the state of his finances, I didn't see a man who was irresponsible, delusional, or otherwise unstable. After I got the plain truth, my romantic self twisted it into something more likeable, acceptable, and even admirable.

Nevertheless, if you meet someone, talk for only a short while, and agree to marry him, you are marrying your idea of him. Because I already had plenty of embellished ideas about whom I was marrying and how it would eventually turn out, I said, "Yes"—though perhaps my yes could have been followed by, "Why not?"

REBEL WITHOUT A CLUE

by Anica Blažanin

WHY DID I DO IT? Reminiscing now, I see that a lot of my motives derived from my early education in intrigue and romance, courtesy of Professor Cvitkovich. In reality, she was my elementary school teacher from grade 5 through grade 8, but in her mind she was a professor of literature at the University of Zagreb. And I'm certain she used that curriculum to teach us underage country bumpkins. We studied well-known romantic classics: *Anna Karenina*, *Madam Bovary*, *The Lady of the Camellias*, *Tess of the d'Urbervilles*, and the like.

Prior to this, from age seven to eleven, my literary nourishment had consisted of Zane Grey, Jack London, James Fenimore Cooper, and many more books fed to me by an older family member. So it was no wonder that I became adventurous and reckless, with a strong sense of drama.

What did I feel about leaving school and abandoning my family, whom I loved? The fact that so many girls through history had done this didn't make any one of their situations common. I had read a number of books that dealt with exiled young women, and, for the majority, life began with their arrival to a new country. Yet for a number of us, life, as we knew it, ended on our arrival.

My quick decision to go to Canada was part adventure, part dream. Once you become accustomed to living with dreams, they become closer than family and friends and would be the last things I'd ever give up. They helped me live and hope, and relinquishing them would be like jumping from the tenth floor, hoping that somebody would just perchance spread the net below.

Before I met Steve, my highest aspiration had been to one day have my own room. I was attending a school that would equip me to work as a secretary. If I got a job, which was a big "if," my wages would be so low, I couldn't do much of anything with them. Providing that my father, a bricklayer, would help me, I would have a room of my own. Reality allowed for that and not much else. I would take the excuse for a couch that I now slept on at the foot of my parents' bed and move it to my own room, but beyond that, I wouldn't be able to afford to furnish the room for a long while. My dreams did permit my sewing some cushions and filling them with corn husks. No wonder I seldom visited reality.

I was a good student and Professor Cvitkovich's pet. I wrote essays and poetry, and she praised me endlessly. One of my poems got published in a local newspaper and was read by a well-known Croatian poet, who in turn sent me a note, encouraging me to write. He enjoyed my poem "Triton," saying I described well the destruction of civilization, with only the spirit of their art surviving. He dedicated a poem to me titled "*Škoić*"("Islet"), likewise describing the endurance and resistance of man, despite Triton's savage storms.

It was an enlightening poem, besides being a source of pride and joy—for me, but perhaps more so for my beloved Professor Cvitkovich, who at last had coached a pupil to the first step of greatness. It was enlightening to me for, despite all of the destructive powers I'd assigned to Triton, I really did not know who or what Triton was, when I wrote my poem, but had read about it somewhere and thought it a good word to describe the cause of mayhem.

I was still under the tutelage of Professor Cvitkovich, who filled us with strong emotions that didn't necessarily have sensible outlets, when we were told to gather in front of the school. The teachers informed us that we would demonstrate for Patrice Lumumba, but nobody told us who he was. Older academic high school students initiated the demonstration, having been told to do so by higher powers.

We slowly started to march, led by older students chanting, "Patrice Lumumba!" I found it easy to go along in the beginning, when everybody was relatively quiet, but as the chants got louder I faced a dilemma: if Lumumba was an enemy, then my shouts should be angry, with my face indicating proper disdain, but if he was a friend, then another tone and expression would be more appropriate.

In the end, I concluded it didn't matter, for if he were a friend, then the anger would be expressed toward his enemies. My classmates barely mumbled their chants, because this was our first demonstration, and nobody had instructed us what to do. The older students shouted louder, and, not to be outdone, I raised my voice, yelling, "Lumumba!" Most likely, they didn't understand what they were rioting about either. I waved my hands in the air, inciting my classmates, until we became the most passionate group. We went around town yelling ourselves hoarse, proud that we had done justice to the demonstration.

After protesting with such fervor, I would have been embarrassed to ask who Lumumba was, and because the others felt the same, we dropped the subject. None of us read political newspapers, hence soon forgot about Lumumba and the demonstration.

Yet this shows who I was and how easily I could take up a cause. So, when it came to marrying Steve, my books told me things could turn out okay. And, yes, I would marry him. I would not be a rich, pampered lady in America, but I would be a heroine helping this clever man who was able to spread his dream around and give so many people moments of joy they would never have otherwise experienced—including my family, because their status balloon would be inflated to an unimaginable size.

Now I had to tell my parents that the mysterious man with the fancy car wanted to marry me in three weeks and would like to meet them tomorrow.

MEET THE PARENTS

by Anica Blažanin

I DREADED INTRODUCING STEVE TO my parents as my
future husband until I had a good story to back me up.
Meanwhile, Steve's sister was pleading our case with their
family, aware of all the reasons why Steve needed to be
married soon and to a young healthy woman. They gave us
their blessing, based solely on Marija's description of me. She
undoubtedly left out the part about my flaming orange hair.

Now, how could I convince my parents that leaving
school in the middle of grade eleven and abandoning my
family were the best choices for my future? My rationale
could have nothing to do with the absolute truth. By then,
however, I was good at manipulating reality and presenting it
as truth.

Being born in 1947, right after the war, in grinding
poverty, to two people who understandably got damaged in
the war, I had not exactly been a welcome addition. My
mother was exhausted from caring for my father. He had
acute tuberculosis, and as soon as he finished his prescribed
medical treatment, rendering him noninfectious, he went to

work as a bricklayer, despite his resemblance to a living skeleton. No wonder my mother and I didn't bond much.

So, as soon as I could, I created a better life inside my little head and found existence there much more pleasant. At the time, I didn't know anything was wrong with this arrangement, because most of the children in my town had a similar experience. Whenever we children got together, we helped one another make things more tolerable by inventing games that gave us a sense of belonging. Much later, I learned that those two maimed souls—my parents—did all they were capable of doing, and that what I needed from them just wasn't there.

I told them about Steve's proposal and provided dozens of reasons why my life and theirs would be better. I would send them money, and they could finish the little house; they could come and visit me in Canada or America. The distinction between the two countries wasn't clear to them, and it didn't matter. I needed to be persuasive, because I wouldn't be eighteen for another six months, and I needed parental consent to get married.

None of my elaborate reasoning convinced them, except for the fact that they would become parents of an "Amerikanka" and that I would be the first one in our village to be a space traveler. I would fly by plane, which was almost the same thing. So we worked hard, as much as we could, to improve the appearance of the house, inside and outside, to prepare for Steve's visit.

My father spent all of the next day widening a little walkway so that Steve could park the car in front of our house, though he could have easily parked it at my aunt's next door, who had a wider drive for her cows and wagons. But then the main attraction (the car) would be at their house and not ours. The entire village knew that the car would bring me, Anica, home from school in town about four miles away.

I had three little cousins, two boys, Ivo and Đuka, ten and eight years old, and a girl, Ivanka, six. They also knew that "the car" would be coming to the village. With only one road the car could be driven on, they decided to "ambush" it along the route. So without arousing suspicion by putting on coats and hats, they snuck out of their house and walked all the way to town, barely dressed for the cold November weather. The farther they walked, the longer the ride back in the car would be, hence their little legs trotted almost four miles.

They stood there, shivering, waiting for Steve and me—but in reality for the car, hoping to hitch a ride back. As we approached, they waved and jumped to get our attention—as if we could have missed three half-frozen, scantily clad children with runny noses and bright red cheeks and ears.

Getting in the car was the most exciting event in their lives, and it brought them respect and awe in the eyes of their friends. When we passed their house, their parents were surrounded by other neighbors gathered in the front yard for the occasion, and the three kids waved and yelled through the now miraculously lowered window. They made sure everybody saw them riding in the car, having traded the strong possibility of a good spanking for a moment of fame.

So we arrived. My mom and dad waited in the house, trying not to show their nervousness at the arrival of a famous visitor. After introductions, conversation lagged, so I took it upon myself to explain everything that would get me their signatures, permitting me to marry. To be tactful in front of Steve, I left out the incentive of being "parents of an Amerikanka/space traveler."

Regardless, it worked, and with a three-week deadline, we started arranging the wedding that very day.

THE WEDDING DAY

by Anica Blažanin

AND SO THE WEDDING PREPARATIONS began. Because the blessed event would take place in such a short time, most of the money had to be borrowed. As a result, the neighbors became our bank. Generally, anyone borrowing from neighbors before the fifteenth of the month was considered to be a poor money manager. When we borrowed money, we always repaid on the first of the month, along with a few eggs or some fruit to show appreciation.

The priority was my wedding outfit, because it had to be sewn by the village seamstress. We chose a light cream-colored wool for the suit. We would have a civil ceremony in town, with the idea of later arranging a church wedding in Canada. This was not generally condemned, because Yugoslavia, of which Croatia was a state, vigorously pretended to be populated by true communists—the foremost proof of their allegiance being the constant maligning of God and church.

The entire wedding became a village affair. Some neighboring women who were better off and had some land and cows insisted that they would not accept ingredients such as butter, eggs, milk, flour, or sugar for the batches of cookies and cakes they volunteered to bake. Others offered, but we knew they couldn't afford to buy the baking ingredients, without borrowing money. So we bought these well-wishers everything they needed and thanked them for all of their hard work.

Next came the venue. We had no problem choosing it, because there were no choices. "The venue" for the majority of townspeople came down to the bride's or the groom's own home. The few individuals who could afford to rent a hotel in town to house and cater their weddings were our promoters of equality: the leaders of the Communist Party. The rest of us were not even jealous, for we were used to the fact that no matter what our Red brothers said, it was the same old story: some people had and a lot didn't.

On the day of the wedding, we emptied the house of every piece of furniture. Since the bedroom was the largest room, we cleared out my parents' double bed, my bed, the dresser, and the sizeable armoire. We cleared the little living room and set tables with linens collected from neighbors. We arranged clippings from neighbors' rosemary pots, along with the same ferns as in my bouquet, overhanging the tablecloths, in place of flowers—a humble, yet pretty effect. My sister-in-law made me a beautiful bouquet with white paper carnations, surrounded by asparagus plumosa ferns.

My mother gave me the wedding suit and a green brocade dress with a bolero. Both garments were stunning. Our professionally trained dressmaker had outdone herself. She took great pride that her work would be seen in Canada. I was also provided with a lovely warm flannel nightgown, as well as a pretty nylon one, floor-length with long sleeves, which I would use in Canada next summer, and that constituted my entire dowry. Steve would get me a landing permit for Canada, while I would stay behind to obtain a passport and permission from our government to leave the country. This was still tricky and required almost 200 miles of travel to Belgrade, the capital of Yugoslavia.

On the wedding day, at eleven o'clock, Steve and his family, along with the best man, the maid of honor, and his sister, came to my house. Then, from our little town, we proceeded to the city hall in Koprivnica, where we got married. Then we went back to our house, where my family and guests from my side waited to have dinner. The meal consisted of many courses: the first was wedding chicken soup with homemade hand-cut noodles, as thin as thread, and many meat dishes such as gulaš (goulash), paprikaš, and a variety of roasted meats with potatoes and salad. Assorted tortes and cookies followed dinner, and the neighbors brought homemade strudel with dough stretched thinner than fine gauze, filled with apples and cinnamon, or cheese. That meal was among the most delicious I've ever eaten.

We stayed at my house until seven in the evening. Then the wedding party and my family packed into three cars— Steve's and two other little hunch-backed cars, a quarter of the size of the Galaxy—and we drove to Steve's parents' home. It was bigger than mine and also emptied of all standard furnishings and set with tables and chairs. There we repeated basically the same meal, but afterward, an accordion player accompanied the dancing.

I vividly remember three things from my wedding. Some, such as exchanging vows, taking pictures, or the guests, are just a big blur. The three were the hairdresser, the "bread reception," and the wedding night.

The day of the wedding, I had an appointment at the hairdresser's in town. I had to wake up at 5:30 a.m., when it was still dark, drizzly, and cold. With Steve's village about twenty miles from mine, it didn't make sense for him to drive me to the hairdresser's and back and then back to his village. So I would take the 6:00 a.m. train, then catch the 9:00 a.m. train back home.

I had to walk half a mile to the train station and half a mile from the train station to the hairdresser's. That wasn't a problem, because I dressed warmly and took an umbrella. My problems began at the hairdresser's, when they offered to put a bit of color in my hair to make it brighter, although I had just come to have it styled. What a temptation that was, for I always kept trying to improve my hair. And since it was my wedding day, my hair should look its best. Hence, I agreed. Because blonde hadn't worked so well the last time with my home dye job, I would try red. I had an image of myself in my green brocade dress with red hair—Scarlett O'Hara sans her long tresses.

The hairdresser went to work coloring my hair, and I figured I would have plenty of time to catch the nine o'clock train home.

Probably due to my own attempt to improve my hair a few weeks earlier, the new color didn't take evenly. After half an hour, this mild brightening agent only brought out the orange in my hair. The hairdresser applied something stronger and more permanent. Once rinsed, my hair was the color of tiger fur. The hairdresser applied another color, which worked better but took a long time to process.

Finally, so that I wouldn't miss my train, she had to wash it out and style my hair. The results were not too bad, even if some places were dark red, while others were lighter. The style was complimentary: teased and heavily lacquered to cope with the drizzly weather. I had height and width, and, to protect my hair, the stylist put a shower cap on my head.

I grabbed my umbrella, and off I went, flying to the train station, only to see the tail end of my train disappear into the distance. I was thirty seconds late. There were no phones, no taxis, and no one that I knew nearby with a car. So, I started walking. If I almost ran, it would take me an hour and twenty minutes to get home. My biggest worry was, what would everyone at my house assume when they heard the train arrive and I was nowhere to be found?

It was lightly drizzling, so I sped up. My hairdo was safe under the shower cap and the umbrella. But on the open road, the wind picked up and the drizzle turned to sleet. Against such elements, my "protective armor" was useless. I kept trudging through these inhospitable conditions until I reached home. Everyone was happy to see me, for they'd all assumed I had run away. They reasoned that since I had so impetuously decided to get married, what would stop me from changing my mind?

Then they noticed my hair, and my mom and dad were no longer simply happy to see me alive. My hair changed everyone's mood. I looked in the mirror and cried, knowing that the disaster on my head was my own doing. The wind had kept turning my umbrella inside-out and swept the sleet under the shower cap, flattening my bouffant into a red pancake. Worse, when I took the cap off, a deep red groove remained across my forehead, where the cap's elastic had dug in.

I grabbed a comb and tried to fix my hair, but the red pancake wouldn't budge. It was so well protected by hairspray that it took me fifteen minutes to comb it out, and others helped reassemble it into a much smaller but frizzier style.

Now I had only half an hour to erase the red mark from my forehead before the wedding party would arrive. I kept hoping that Steve would focus on my legs. No such luck, because when Steve arrived with his family and the best man and the maid of honor, my hair was the focal point of their glances. Finally, my future sister-in-law, Marija, plucked a paper carnation from my bouquet and placed it in my hair, directly over a particularly bright red patch.

The second thing I remember was brief and very painful. It took place on my new family's doorstep, where my mother-in-law stood holding a round loaf of bread. I wasn't familiar with this custom but figured I should follow her lead. My mother-in-law recited a welcome speech and then a prayer.

One of my aunts, standing behind me, didn't think I had the brains to know how to react to this ceremony. To help me to do the right thing, she kept pinching me really hard— so hard that I winced. Not knowing the reason she was doing this made me even more nervous. Each squeeze was more painful than the last, and my face involuntarily contorted with agony and tears.

Finally, my mother-in-law thought I was getting overly emotional, so she thrust the bread into my hands and welcomed me into the house. I stepped over the threshold, escaping my pinching aunt. My mother-in-law and I exchanged kisses, and I thanked them for accepting me as a daughter-in-law. Later I asked my aunt, who was known to like alcohol a bit too much, what the pinching was all about.

"I was trying to convey to you that you should accept the bread, then thank and kiss your mother-in-law," she said.

"I figured that out on my own—without the help of your pinches!"

More likely, she was impatient for me to hurry and step over the threshold, so that each guest could be welcomed by a hefty shot of *šljivovic* (Croatian plum brandy).

Once inside, we feasted and danced. After midnight, the curtains on the windows were removed, so that the neighbors could see the new bride—a local custom. The front yard had filled with people peeking in through the window, and my father-in-law, with the help of some guests, took wine, brandy, and strudel out to them.

Their verdict was *"On je išel čez vodu po vodu"* ("He went through water to get water"). Meaning that he could have gotten a girl like me or better in his own village; there was no need for him to travel twenty miles to find a bride.

"KRAUT HOTEL"

by Anica Blažanin

AROUND FOUR IN THE MORNING, the guests started to leave. With the train station two miles away, and the next train not coming until seven, Steve drove my family home—forty miles round trip. As the house emptied, my mother-in-law told me that Steve and I would sleep in a room with one single bed.

The room reeked, and I identified the source: a large wooden barrel covered with a cloth. I then recognized the smell as sauerkraut: fermented cabbage. For anyone familiar with the smell, you know that it resembles the odor of unwashed feet. I hoped this wouldn't be the place where I had to sleep every night.

I put on my flannel pajamas and crawled into bed. Soon afterward, I heard a knock on the door. I thought, *How polite of my new husband to knock*, but it was his sister, Marija, who had nowhere to rest, so she wanted to chat. I moved over, and she crawled into bed with her clothes on. The room had no heat, which was a good thing. If the air had been any warmer, the sauerkraut would have started fermenting faster and bubbling up a dirty yellow foam that would out-do any "bog of eternal stench." Being enclosed in the same space with percolating cabbage might even be lethal.

I realize how different the first night of my wedding was from the norm today and even from the norm then. I don't remember being disappointed, but I do remember not liking the smell. As dawn approached, Steve returned and hurried Marija out of the bed. He then got in, but not before I noticed he had long johns on. I don't know why, but the sight of them upset me. It shouldn't have. After all, it was winter, and nobody had central heating. He had put them on, not to offend me but to keep warm, and besides, I was covered from head to toe in thick flannel. This was supposed to be a romantic night, and all I could think of was those ugly long johns and the awful smell of sauerkraut.

As it turned out, I was saved from any romantic advances, because as he reached over to hug me, we heard a tremendous roar outside, accompanied by screams. Steve seemed to know what was happening and jumped out of bed like lightning. I rushed to the window.

By the early dawn light in the front yard, I saw Steve gently escort his father out of the Galaxy. A few groups of men and women stood a safe distance from the car, while some women repeatedly crossed themselves. Steve's father was very shaky on his feet, partly due to celebrating too much and partly from fear. When I learned what had taken place outside, suddenly the unbearable stench of the sauerkraut and the sight of long johns lost all significance.

Steve had shown his father how to start the car, put it in drive, and slowly move it forward. When Steve returned from driving the guests home, some die-hard guests were still drinking and toasting to our health, Steve's father among them. Steve had parked the car but left the keys in the ignition.

At first, everybody examined the car close up. Then the father bragged that his son had taught him to drive. The neighbors didn't believe him, so, in his celebratory mood, he was going to prove it. He got in and turned on the ignition. People scattered away from the front of the car, in case he succeeded in moving it. He shifted the gears, and the car roared and jolted backward, grazing some people and knocking them to the side. My father-in-law panicked and pressed hard on both the gas and the brake pedal, causing the loud noise.

Nobody was seriously hurt, but the neighbors were concerned that their bodies' contact with the car might have damaged the car. Their bruises would be gone in a few days, but how much would it cost to fix such a luxurious vehicle? Worse, what if they were asked to pay for any dents that their hips, elbows, knees, or other extremities might have made?

I never did sleep in "Kraut Hotel" again. That was reserved for our wedding night. Afterward, we were given a pullout couch in the kitchen, and, by comparison, it wasn't bad. We fed a wood stove a few times during the night, so I was warm and a couple of rooms away from the sauerkraut odor. In its place was the smell of onions and garlic from supper, and that wasn't too bad. The long johns stayed, and I simply got used to them.

New Religious Experience

by Anica Blažanin

THREE WEEKS AFTER THE WEDDING, Steve left for Canada, driving the car over the Austrian and Swiss Alps to the French harbor of Le Havre. It was the end of December, and the car broke down and had to be towed by a sympathetic truck driver. Steve left it in a garage in a small town a few hundred miles from the Le Havre port.

They agreed that after fixing the car, the mechanic would deliver it to the ship headed for Canada. Poor Steve paid a high price for those months of vain living, in which the Ford Galaxy XL played a major role. It, too, took a beating that it never would have, had it stayed in Canada, less admired but honored with much better roads.

I lived with my mother-in-law until I got my visa for Canada. My father-in-law worked in Zagreb and came home twice a month for the weekend. We got along fine. We were both Catholic but couldn't be more different in practicing our devotion. My mother-in-law went to church regularly and occupied herself with rosary beads during most of her free time.

I, however, shared the views of the authors I read at the time. Again, I was too young for these books, but a relative gave me Tolstoy's *War and Peace* and *Resurrection*, along with Dostoyevsky's *Brothers Karamazov* and *The Idiot*.

From what I gathered, those two did not agree with everything that was going on in the church. They felt that we needed much more thinking, understanding, and doing, especially not doing certain things that the churches were. My revelation had not come yet, even though I went to churches when they were empty and waited for instant wisdom. The wisdom in my situation seemed to be "Don't rock the boat. Repeatedly say the verses and don't cheat by skipping the beads, and maybe something will reveal itself in a flash when I pause for a breath." Maybe it did, when I nodded off, but you snooze, you lose.

Six months of waiting is a very long time for a seventeen-year-old, especially when existing on such meager nourishment of mind and soul. However, it leaves you with time to live as you hoped you would. My only outings consisted of going to the village church or the store and making a couple of visits to the doctor.

My mother-in-law and I were always together, and she confided that these were Steve's orders. He worried about me being so young and apparently wild—judging by what I'd done with my hair on our wedding day. So he strongly suggested that I never be left alone. I felt hurt, but if I rebelled, that would prove their point, and I could kiss Canada goodbye. Some have said that I probably married Steve just to get to Canada, but that wasn't true. My "dreams" about my Canadian life always included three years of paying off debts, saving for a nice house, and then visiting Croatia with my husband and maybe an even nicer car, if that were possible.

I did go alone to Belgrade to obtain my passport. Travel would have been too expensive for two people. Because I arrived in Belgrade in the morning after twelve hours on the train, I immediately visited the immigration officials and returned on the 8 p.m. train. So, in thirty-six hours, I was back home, safe and not so sound.

I guess Steve knew this trip would be too much for his mother, who had a bad heart. She felt greatly relieved when I returned in record time, but it didn't earn me any more freedom. Yet it didn't matter. In a few months, I would leave and begin my new life.

WHITE SLAVERY

by Anica Blažanin

FINALLY, I'D GATHERED TOGETHER ALL of the needed documents, and my airline ticket arrived. I received and cherished it as if it were a brick of gold. The date of departure dispelled all notions that the American was pulling my leg or, in Croatian, we say "pulling my nose."

Seeing a departure date hit me hard. Despite all of my bravery, a fear lingered in the back of my mind that I had concocted this entire story on an exceptionally difficult day and then dwelled in it until now. In any event, the plane ticket with the date made me realize the choice I'd made and that I couldn't change my mind. Not only because I had gotten married and caused everyone considerable expense, as well as raised the hopes of myself and others, but I had no other alternative and no reason to stay. If I did, I would become the most notorious person in the country.

The plane ticket with the clearly marked date uncorked tears for everybody, me included. Why did all of these people who were happy to see me go off to a better future now cry when it was time for me to leave? The older ones cried because they were sure they would never see me again. I dared not ask whether that was because they would die before I came back for a visit, or I would die soon after my arrival in a new country. The younger ones suddenly started crying because they had heard that men come from overseas to marry women and then sell them into slavery.

Some had even heard stories about Steve whisking away a few others, in another part of Croatia, before me. The profit he'd made from selling his other wives explained how he'd managed to stay here with such a magnificent car for so long. And this last time, he'd been given specific instructions about the type of woman who'd been ordered, thus explaining his extended stay. There was only one thing they couldn't figure out: what was so special about me that it took him so long to find it?

At first, all of this talk concerned me. My mother, who loved intrigue, mentioned her forebodings and cited every single article she had ever read or heard of, describing women who went overseas and disappeared. My father, the only one lacking imagination, didn't want to hear any such stories. He told me that Steve was a solid, honest man, and if I learned to be a good wife, then we would do fine, much better than he and my mom could dream of.

Lots of prayers were said on my behalf. On my side of the family and village, prayers requested that Steve would turn out to be a good man and would not sell me to who knows who, or, if he must sell me, that at least it be to someone richer than himself, so that one day I could help my family and friends.

On my in-laws' side, the prayers requested that I get on the plane and that it would have enough fuel and working parts to bring me safely to Canada.

As far as I was concerned, neither the threat of slavery nor the passage on the rickety JAT (Yugoslavian Air Transport) gave me the option of staying home. Aside from JAT plunging into the North Atlantic, all other future possibilities were preferable. I was a married woman, and schools did not accept married people. I had finished only up to grade ten, thus I was useless for any meaningful employment. I would have to return to live with my parents and share a bedroom with them. Up to now, I'd slept at the foot of their double bed on a narrow couch. When my father wasn't snoring, he coughed incessantly, due to side effects of a long-standing TB infection.

We had no indoor plumbing and no appliances. The well was in the garden, and heartbreaking poverty surrounded me.

I had to get on the plane, no matter what.

CANADA BOUND

by Anica Blažanin

I STOOD WITH TWO BATTERED, borrowed suitcases. The people who had lent them didn't care if I returned them anytime soon, because they'd only been used to store walnuts in the attic. Originally, I could have fit everything into one suitcase, but at the last minute an old coat was discovered that didn't fit anyone else. The outside of the coat was shiny and threadbare, but a hole in the lining revealed that the other side of the material was perfectly fine. My mother consulted the seamstress, Ljuba, and she took apart the coat and made a dress for me, to ensure that I didn't freeze in Canada. It was the bulkiest, itchiest thing I have ever worn and was the reason I needed a second suitcase.

I was escorted by my family, including my *Teta* ("aunt") Katica and my three little cousins, for whom my mother paid the train and bus fare, so that they could see the planes, as well as see me off. Đuka was sternly warned not to say anything embarrassing on the train. The last time we'd taken him to visit an aunt who lived in the city, he'd asked my mother to buy him a coke from the train trolley. My mother refused, not because it wasn't good for him but because we had no money for such frivolities.

He got angry and yelled, "Then I will never let you pick lice out of my head again!"

Refusing to look at us, he stuck his head out of the train window until he got soot in his eyes. This made them bloody, and he kept crying and rubbing them, so we had to take him to the doctor when we arrived.

As about ten of us left the house, we all cried, off and on, until I clambered onto the plane, fingering my rosary and saying Hail Mary's and the Our Father prayer from Zagreb to Toronto. I must have set some kind of record for piety. I believed that it wasn't the exhausted engines and the visibly tired body of JAT's plane that had transported us to Toronto but the power of my prayers.

During one scary moment, as the plane descended, I peeked out the window and saw what looked like a piece of the wing falling off. I screamed and jumped up, alerting everyone to what had happened.

I got the attention of a harried stewardess, who yelled at me, in what would be the English equivalent of "Shut up! Sit down, and buckle up."

So I did and, in terror, waited for death, until the plane touched down.

Steve met me in the terminal with one of his brothers. I told him that the plane had managed to land with a piece of its wing missing. He explained that I'd seen the wing flap come down, as part of the landing maneuver.

Steve had three brothers living in Toronto, and one was married with three children. A family friend had prepared a lovely reception for me, with about twenty people. Each one gave me a present. I was happy and appreciative, because the gifts here were a lot more valuable than those I'd received back home.

Then we went to my new home: a flat shared with Steve's brother, Walter. We had a large bedroom, filled with new furniture and bedding. The curtains, a bold blue rose print that I loved, were plastic but didn't look it. We had a small but lovely kitchen with a gas stove, a fridge, and, best of all, an indoor toilet with a bath. I was in paradise and could hardly wait to write home.

Steve and I got along relatively well, though we thought about things differently, but I was used to that. I'd had the same problem in Croatia with my family and others. Being mightily outnumbered, I figured the fault was mine and tried to adapt.

THE ROOMING HOUSE IS BORN

by Anica Blažanin

THE DISASTER WITH THE CAR breaking down proved much more costly than initially thought, and it added six months to the loan payments. Eager to start this new dream of paying off the debts, I insisted on working immediately. I got a job at Laura Secord, a famous chocolate factory, and made a dollar an hour.

Back then, you could buy a lot for a dollar, and I was amazed at what we got for ten dollars. I bought meat for everyday meals, all sorts of fruit, and cookies. Steve let me buy cream for my face, and I was introduced to deodorant. The first deodorant I bought, Arid, came in a little metal container, and the first time I used it, the scent brought back memories of my early teenage years.

My girlfriend's family had someone living in the United States, who had sent them a parcel with a similar container. My friend and I assumed it was face cream. The consistency was a little different, but that was likely due to being American, thus good. We lavishly applied it on our faces, being sure to rub a lot of it around our eyes. A few hours

43

later, our itching eyes turned red and teary. We kept rinsing our eyes with chamomile, and after that, my friend used the cream only on her hands.

Finally, I learned the mystery about the cream in the little container and why it wasn't good to use around the eyes. My friend and I had never known about the existence of deodorant.

I now handled the finest chocolates, when, in my previous life, we'd had them only on rare occasions. I worked on the conveyor belt, emptying trays of chocolates, then picking out the broken pieces, and throwing them in large bins. At first, I dared not eat any, certain that it was forbidden. Once I surreptitiously stuffed a piece in my mouth, and my coworker waved her finger at me and said something in Spanish. I took it as a sign that I was guilty of stealing. I found out later that she meant I would get fat.

We struggled to pay off the debt, pretty much living on my wages, with the rest going toward loan payments. I'd come to Canada in June 1965, and in September 1966, I began to feel sick, mainly nauseous and weak. I couldn't stomach any strong smells, such as onions or meat, so I just ate fruit. I felt the same as I had at the age of twelve, when I'd developed hepatitis. I'd been ill for a long time and had the same disgust for food that I felt now.

Steve took me to a doctor, and I told him about my symptoms and my suspicion that the hepatitis had returned. He said that my symptoms indicated pregnancy, because my eyes had no yellow tinge.

And so I was pregnant. I don't know why it hadn't occurred to me. I'd figured that if I didn't get pregnant at the beginning of our marriage, it wouldn't happen at all.

With the debt still looming, we really wanted to pay it off, so I decided to work as long as I could. The nausea slowly subsided, and only occasionally did I feel unwell. So I kept working until I was almost eight months' pregnant.

Then one day, while sorting the chocolates, I had a dizzy spell and fainted. My face hit the conveyor belt, waking me up in time to suddenly vomit all over the chocolates.

The managers stopped production and had to dismantle the machine to thoroughly wash and sanitize every part. They took me to the cafeteria, and, after I revived, they kindly suggested that it would be better for me if I stopped working. Better for them, too—but they didn't say that.

I was almost twenty, and after a long and painful labor, my first child, Ivanka, was born. She was happily expected and, at the same time, feared. I was an only child and had no experience with babies.

Immediately after the birth, the nurse put her in my arms. As I gazed at her, a number of emotions fought for dominance. She looked red, wrinkled, and angry. It seemed as if those little squinty eyes were judging me and found me an unworthy, incompetent mother, which her piercing cry confirmed.

This was worse than I'd thought. She was a lot smaller than I expected, and a deep wrinkle between her nose and forehead seemed to tell me that for months she had listened to what was going on outside and decided it was unfair to have such an unskilled mother. I really felt that she didn't like me much and wished she had a better mother. So I clumsily and with great trepidation tried to prove her wrong.

But she was the stronger one. She made sure she got attention when she wanted it. Her father loved her, once he figured out he could hold her without breaking her. He helped with the bathing and changing. Still bent on paying off the loan, we didn't buy her a crib but instead emptied out a large dresser drawer, rigged it up as the softest, prettiest nest, and kept it on the couch.

My brothers-in-law felt sorry for her and bought her a lovely new crib. However, I'm sure she felt happier and more snug in her chest nest.

She turned out to be a little miracle. And I literally mean *little*. She was the tiniest, cutest blonde baby with the biggest owl eyes, which I still felt were accusing me of doing something wrong. She started walking and had a rich baby vocabulary at eleven months and was toilet-trained at thirteen months. I don't believe that had anything to do with us training her, but she simply didn't like to be soiled.

When Ivanka was seven months old, the hepatitis-like symptoms returned. I looked into my eyes hopefully, but they were not yellow. That meant that I wouldn't be able to work, we wouldn't be able to pay off the debt, and the home we wanted would disappear into the unforeseeable future.

Steve and I came up with ideas on how we still might be able to obtain a family home. We justified our plan of needing a house soon because we would have two children. We took steps to see if my mother would be willing to help us. She agreed, and what followed would become the most painful and shameful experience for Steve and me.

My mother would come and stay with us in Canada to baby-sit, so I could go to work. After Steven was born, we would wait six months and then she would take them both to Croatia. Then Steve and I would move into the cheapest place we could find and work full time, so that in two years we could buy a house.

With Steven on the way, my father brewed his own *šlivovic* (Croatian plum brandy) and, as was the custom, put the bottle away until it would be served at Steven's wedding. Ivanka's batch was already in the cantina, aging, awaiting her matrimony. Perhaps this was why Croatians so enjoyed attending weddings.

My mother came and stayed for almost a year. I worked during the day and went to night school to become a hairdresser, because we had heard that hairdressers make good money. To us, getting rid of the debt and buying a home became the sum of all happiness, and a similar sentiment prevailed among many of our contemporaries in

46

exile. They encouraged one another in the wisdom of getting a home for the children and then bringing them back to enjoy life in their own house. Neither Steve nor I knew how much sacrifice we and the children would have to make or how many regrets I would have until this day.

Of course, we sent my parents a generous amount of money, so that no one would be deprived materially. There was even money for my mother to hire help to wash clothes. Ivanka and Steven not only won the hearts of my family, but my three little cousins, who lived next door, regularly reported to baby-sit, because the rewards were worth it: a piece of chocolate or candy, and the occasional orange. The little Canadians also won the hearts of the villagers, because, as my mother wrote, both children were very outgoing and always smiling.

The villagers usually brought gifts, such as eggs, and those who owned cows brought cheese and butter. My uncle Jandro went to pick wild strawberries every day when in season and brought them to my children.

In return for this kindness and generosity, Steven took the first opportunity, at about one year of age, to show off his little renegade self. While visiting Uncle Jandro and Aunt Štefa, he noticed himself in a two-winged dresser mirror, where the mirror started from the base above the floor. He picked up a hefty piece of firewood and dragged it to the mirror, mumbling in Croatian "Bad child." Then he heaved the wood and shattered the mirror.

Even though that was their most precious piece of furniture, Steven not only was forgiven but became a little hero. The strength he possessed for a little child became legendary. To this day, they have never fixed the glass.

Ivanka, too, was fabled, but for her generosity and care. When she got a treat, she always asked, "What about Steven?" and if there was no more, she carefully saved half of her treat for her brother.

During that time, Steve and I lived for the bi-weekly airmail letters. The reports were almost always good, unless the kids had a cold. Nevertheless, we both cried, even at the happy anecdotes. I had their little clothes around, so as I read the letters I held the clothes and kissed them, crying bitterly.

We both worked and saved, paying one loan at the monthly rate and putting more money into savings.

After a year, we looked for a house and fell in love with a beautiful Victorian home close to High Park, in Toronto. It was three stories, with a huge cultivated backyard. We had to borrow money for the down payment, and in order to afford it, we never had the option of just our family living there. The only way we could keep it would be to rent out most of the house, in the most profitable manner. Thus was born "The Rooming House," which sat among, but apart from, other stately family-owned homes.

Our first priority after moving in was to bring Ivanka and Steven home. Now everyone who'd taken care of them in Croatia, though relieved, wrote how heartbroken they were. The children were brought to Canada by our friends, whom they didn't know. It was a traumatizing experience for all parties involved.

This separation was the most difficult part of my life, up to that point. I had a choice, so it's harder for me to forgive myself. Ivanka and Steven have both assured me that they don't remember anything bad happening to them—as if they could remember good or bad, they were so little.

Those are my recollections, good and bad. I'll let my daughter Ivanka continue with hers. I marvel, for she manages to relate with humor even the not-so-humorous incidents of life and our time in the rooming house and beyond.

THE LITTLE HERO

by Ivanka Di Felice

It PAINS MY MOM TO talk about sending us away, but I always tell her that I don't think it affected us negatively.

"Look how normal we turned out," I say, trying to console her, but then she begins to cry. Either she feels distressed over the degree of normalcy we achieved, or the memories are still too painful. I'm not sure which, but perhaps it's best I not know.

In the photos from that time, my brother and I appear happy and are always celebrating something or other. Granted, this was back when pictures were sacred and taken only on special occasions, as opposed to today, when everyone is his or her own paparazzi. We had the love of both sets of grandparents, along with aunts, uncles, cousins, and a whole village. Even the gypsies loved us.

My grandparents had a small house on a large plot of land, where we would chase chickens, and geese would chase us. On one occasion, I had ventured too close to the goose with her goslings. My grandma yelled across the yard to shoo them away. Yet they kept approaching, and my one-year-old brother, Steven, came to my rescue. He toddled over to

49

protect me, fearlessly waving the geese to shoo, and they did. No wonder everyone viewed him as a little superhero.

Happiness consisted of small things: finding a feather in the yard or the joy of my grandma drawing up a fresh bucket of water from the well to quench our thirst. A communal glass sat by the well, and we all drank from it, passers-by included. Germs were evidently not a concern. Life was simple but good.

Gypsies had their regular routes and often stopped in briefly to visit us and to see what they could glean. My grandparents were of humble means, but, regardless, always found something to give them. My grandma liked to make a production of it, though—going into the house and deeply contemplating what she could part with, making the gypsies aware of the sacrifice. They always saw through her.

Even at a young age, I could tell there was something different about them: their skin was darker, their way of dress exotic, and their voices raspier. They stared at me intently, and, with my big round brown eyes, they probably felt the same way about me.

The four of us slept in one large bed, between cotton duvets filled with feathers. My mom recalled the old tradition of *Čehanje perja* (processing feathers). During the year, as people slaughtered poultry for food, they collected the feathers, then cleaned and stored them until winter. On those dark, frigid evenings, the villagers borrowed tables and benches and held large get-togethers, where women young and old processed feathers for duvets and pillows. Heaps of the stored feathers were distributed, and the women stripped the down from each feather's central quill and discarded the quills, saving the soft down. Everyone would gather at one household each evening for a week or more. On the last evening, with the task completed, the men joined the women—not to help the women but to eat strudel and drink wine and *šlivovic* (Croatian plum brandy).

Mom's uncles played the guitar and the accordion, while everyone danced, disturbing leftover feathers that whirled around like a snowstorm and settled on sweaty faces until people resembled a bunch of mad ostriches. The following week the "only show in town" would move on to the next house, where the cycle would be repeated. This weekly social event was work but also their entertainment during the long winter nights.

We were the grateful recipients of this labor, because we were toasty warm sleeping together, with one comforter on top and one on the bottom. We were happy.

My grandparents never had a car, but we managed, regardless.

I don't know if I missed my parents, and I no longer have the opportunity to ask my grandparents. I could ask my mom, but either answer would probably incite tears, so best to leave it.

After just over a year, we were taken back to Canada. Steven and I were fluent in Croatian and thought baby food was gulaš and paprikaš. We played in our new yard but missed the chickens and the geese—and our grandparents, who also missed us. In Croatia, we had lived in a tiny house, with no indoor plumbing or central heating. We returned to the grand, stately house in High Park that my parents had worked so hard to buy. With their plans to turn it into a rooming house, they would be one step closer to actually owning it—instead of paying ransom to the banks.

In our new home, no gypsies dropped in to visit, but the house itself was filled with people just as, if not even more, astonishing.

LUNCHTIME DRAMA

by Ivanka Di Felice

EVERYONE HAS AN EARLIEST RECOLLECTION. For many of mine, I don't know whether I remember the pictures, the stories, or the actual events. Yet there is one event I will never forget. Neither will my mother.

In the early seventies, I was in junior kindergarten. My teacher, Mrs. Takahashi, was chubby and wore her gray-streaked brown hair in a bouffant hairstyle—a leftover from the sixties. Only years later did I realize her name didn't match her face, because she wasn't Japanese but, rather, had married a Japanese man. In divulging this tale, I hope she is not a fan of memoirs.

I went to Howard Park Public School, where the student body consisted of privileged children of families living in great homes on the tree-lined streets of High Park. We lived in one of those homes, too, only we shared ours with a motley crew of roomers, while non–family members living with my classmates were mainly nannies. My classmates' fathers—scientists, lawyers, hockey players, and other professionals—contrasted with my dad, who made an honest living as a machinist and a slumlord.

As I said earlier, many people think it is tragic to grow up in a poor neighborhood, but I can assure you it is equally tragic growing up in a rich neighborhood, when *you* are poor. The homes my friends lived in looked like ours from the outside, but once I stepped inside, I saw that they were different. Most kids in my class had their own bedrooms and had a special room called a dining room, where everyone sat to eat when they had fancy parties. Meanwhile, my parents and we four children slept in one room. Perhaps that explains why my mom and dad never had any more kids.

My mother worked long hours, so we packed our own lunches for school. As other children opened their lunch bags and either complained about their meals or were overjoyed by them, I realized that someone other than the kids had prepared them.

Trying to fit in, I, too, acted surprised by the contents of my bag, squealing with delight or bitterly grumbling. Considering I had packed it the night before, my look of astonishment deserved an Academy Award. My mother must have felt sorry for me, and so, to my great delight, she sacrificed and spent a small fortune on the loveliest, most fashionable lunch bag ever. It was beige patent leather, hung on a long strap, and had Holly Hobby illustrated on the front. I was the envy of all of the rich children. I don't imagine a child has ever been happier with a gift.

Back when four-year-olds could walk themselves home without a care in the world, we had the option of going home for lunch. I had heard my friends inviting their teachers to lunch at their houses, so, to keep up, I did the same. I made sure that Tony, a handsome boy in my class, heard me.

To this day, I vividly recall that as the words came out of my mouth, I knew it was a bad idea. My mother wasn't expecting us, and I knew I would be in big trouble afterward. And this is when "big trouble" meant something. "Time outs" were only for sports teams.

But I invited Mrs. Takahashi anyway, and when she asked whether I was certain my mother was expecting us, I lied through my teeth and replied, "Yes."

I had large round brown eyes and always wore a serious expression. When she asked me a second time, she looked straight into my eyes, and again I resolutely answered, "Yes."

So she picked up her handbag, and we walked down the street together. I was proud—my teacher was coming to our house for lunch. But there was not enough pride to mask the trepidation I felt. I had inherited my mother's wild imagination, and even at that young age, I could envision my mother's face when she opened the door to find me and my teacher standing there.

As we approached the house, I hoped that Leo, a second-floor tenant, had not left his false teeth on the porch. He drank what I now realize was cheap beer and smoked what I now realize were strong cigarettes on the front porch and often left his empties, his cigarettes, and his false teeth there. He was unattractive, and his fingers matched the color of his crew-cut hair: yellow. He was probably in his fifties, though, at our young age, he seemed like a hundred.

He viewed us children as a nuisance and as competition for his porch space, where he would "take a nap" and then hours later stagger up the staircase, saying, perhaps to remind himself, "I'm Leo. I'm Roman Catholic, and I'm from Elmville." As if something might have drastically changed from one step to the next, he repeated, "I'm Leo. I'm Roman Catholic, and I'm from Elmville," all the way to the second floor.

My sister, Vesna, and her friend Vladimir often stole his cigarettes and, to pay him back for being mean to us, we sometimes hid his teeth.

He obviously did not think us children very bright, for he often tried to sell us his pizza after, with great relish, he had eaten all the cheese off it. Not only did we not have any money, but we knew that pizza was only good with the cheese still on it. When we refused, he would look at us in disappointment, his eyes glazed over, as he walked away, muttering , "I'm Leo, I'm Roman Catholic, I'm from Elmville . . ."

I was clever enough to know that once on the porch, I could just pretend to ring the bell or I could knock ever so lightly, and my mother wouldn't hear. Yet the same madness that made me invite Mrs. Takahashi in the first place still reigned.

I rang the bell hard, and my surprised mother came to the door. As usual, she had a scarf tied on her head and bright red lipstick. No matter what, my mother always had on bright-colored lipstick. She looked at me and at my teacher, then at me, her eyebrows arching.

I smiled and lied again, saying that she had told me to invite my teacher home for lunch today. Proof that she really hadn't quickly became manifest when I was sent to the corner store to buy some tuna, bread, and mayonnaise.

While I was at the store, they no doubt discussed my serious mental health issues. But when I returned, Mrs. Takahashi was a great sport and kept repeating that she wouldn't have eaten anything better in the staff lunchroom.

It was the first time I wished I were older, in grade one, so I could return to school with Mrs. Takahashi for afternoon classes. Instead, I went as far as I could down the street and waved the longest goodbye ever to my teacher, while my mother waited for me on the porch.

Only while writing this book did I find out that although my mom's first instinct was to punish me, this incident made her suspect I was mentally unstable and that she must have done something wrong. So, to make up for it, she decided she'd better be nice to me instead.

"BABYSITTER 101"

by Ivanka Di Felice

LEO WAS NOT THE FIRST, nor would he be the last, tenant my father omitted doing a reference check on. When a tenant "moved out" (code for *died, went to rehab,* or *sent back to prison*), my dad's first priority was to rent the room. It never occurred to him that anyone who could move in on a day's notice was either on the run from the law, just out of rehab, or fleeing his current landlord. Or that anyone willing to live in a room decorated by my father must really not have other options.

My dad had "unique decor concepts," because he was the first (and probably the last) person not to take the term *wallpaper* literally, applying it to both the walls *and* the ceiling and then, for additional flair, spraying both with white popcorn foam. He never consulted my mother when making these improvements; he just "surprised" her with them.

Hence, the vigorous screening process for our tenants amounted to picking "the best of the worst." This last qualification did not apply, though, when someone was a fellow countryman. That was all Tata required. Besides, he felt that references were a scam. Any landlord would write the most glowing report on a problem tenant, if he thought it would get the person out of his home and into someone else's.

While my father had a job as a maintenance mechanic, my mother worked as a hairdresser during the day, if she had a babysitter, but if not, she worked nights at a drugstore. My brother Steven and I were both in school, whereas Vesna, three years younger than me, required a babysitter. References, it would become evident, were even less stringent for babysitters than for tenants, but, thankfully, back then we children were resilient. The Croatian adage "God cares for drunks and children" proved true.

Blonde and blue-eyed Vesna was cute as a button, which raised suspicions because both of my parents have brown eyes and brown hair—or, should I say, natural brown hair, for my mom was always experimenting, and "improving" her hair color. Regardless, Vesna was an extremely happy child, and no matter how wet or hungry she was, as long as she slept next to someone, she was oblivious to any problems brewing.

Though I was only three years older than her, I lugged her around like a pretty doll. Steven did, too, especially at night, because Vesna's little legs were beginning to bow. The doctor's solution was to put her in a pair of shoes that faced out, secured together with a metal bar. Because she hadn't learned to untie her shoes, if she had to go to the bathroom she would hobble across the floor. So, to help her out, Steven and I would drag her like a rag doll to the bathroom. It was neat to have a sister who wore those odd shoes.

Only decades later would I discover that she knew how to untie them, but she loved us carrying her around and giving her attention. Once, a kind lady from the neighborhood stopped my mother on the street and offered to give us food, because she assumed Vesna suffered from rickets (a childhood bone disorder, in which bones soften and become prone to deformity and which in most cases is a result of long-term malnutrition). With my skinny legs and large, wounded eyes, I probably didn't help my mom's case, as she insisted we had plenty to eat.

One day my mother had to run to work, and because I wasn't home yet to care for my little sister (back then, a babysitter merely had to be older than the child she was watching), she left Vesna with Susan, a tenant on the second floor. To all outward appearances, other than living in a room in our house, Susan seemed normal. Thus, my mother entrusted Vesna to her care for the remainder of the day.

When my mom came home from work, she went up to the second floor to get Vesna. All was quiet inside, so my mother assumed that Vesna, as usual, was sleeping. A more powerful advertisement for "ignorance is bliss" could never be found, as my mother opened the door and saw that Vesna indeed was peacefully napping. Susan, meanwhile, had been very busy—busy knocking over and smashing every item in the room. Tables were overturned, mirrors shattered, clothes thrown from their dressers, the small fridge emptied and its contents strewn across the floor in a mad rage.

Vesna lay on the bed, lovingly tucked into a blanket, smiling and unharmed, with Susan sitting on the bed next to her, holding a big knife she had just used to slice her own legs and arms. There was blood everywhere.

As I peered into the room, my wide eyes grew wider.

Soon thereafter, my parents found out that Susan had recently been released from an institution for the criminally insane, proving that one had to be unconventional to choose to live in a room decorated by my father.

"Crush and Kit Kat"

by Ivanka Di Felice

Life was not easy. My parents still had debts, and my mother was pregnant with one more child. The only part of my mom's dream of "America" that she had realized was living in a large house. However, the bank still owned a considerable portion of it, and it was filled with colorful tenants. The heroines in the classics she'd read had not ended up like this.

Soon she would be twenty-six, with four small children, six years of age and under. Though my parents were less than thrilled, we three kids were ecstatic that she was having another baby. We took turns touching my mom's stomach to feel the baby kick.

My mother returned home with Kathy, a beautiful baby with a lovely complexion and dark hair and dark eyes—the opposite of blonde, blue-eyed Vesna. Though my mom struggled to cope with her reality, the three of us loved having a little baby to hold and play with.

Soon thereafter, Vesna developed pneumonia. My parents took her to the world-famous Sick Children's Hospital, where, at the same time, the doctors discovered that her legs were bowed—not due to any lack of vitamins, but because she had a kidney disorder. The family underwent tests, which showed that she had inherited this illness from my father, who also suffered, but to a lesser degree, from this affliction. This explained why he was small for his age growing up and also much shorter than his very tall brothers. She would no longer have to wear her funny shoes to bed, and any suspicions as to paternity were laid to rest.

We children didn't mind that Vesna was ill, because it meant regular trips downtown to Sick Children's Hospital, which had a very nice play area, with lots of toys and books, and a great cafeteria. We met family and friends there, and Vesna always got us a wheelchair to race around the halls in. As Vesna sat on the bed in the pretty pink robe my parents bought her for the hospital, we saw that being sick wasn't so bad. And while the rest of us shared a chocolate bar, Vesna got one all to herself.

Though we were on a limited budget, my mother occasionally took us to a greasy spoon down the street. She got only two orders, each burger being cut in half, and we split an order of fries. Whoever was sick got a milkshake and didn't have to share it, so being sick never seemed like a bad thing. Perhaps that is why, to this day, I aspire to be a hypochondriac.

At two years old, Kathy found her calling: my mother was a hairdresser, and Kathy clearly wanted to follow in her footsteps. She often woke in the middle of the night and, no matter where my parents hid the scissors, she found them and cut her own hair. In particular, she must have loved the feel of the scissors as she lay them flat on her forehead and cut her hair straight to her scalp. The only "style" my mother could give Kathy to fix her uneven locks was a crew cut. Thus, Kathy sported this look for the first few years of her life, giving people the impression that my mother was not very good at her profession—or at hiding scissors.

Not satisfied with cutting her own hair, Kathy woke in the middle of the night and took snippets of hair from the rest of us. This added to the already tragic style I was sporting, thanks to being the latest victim my mother practiced a new cut on. Between us children and the tenants, it appeared that everyone living in our house had ghastly haircuts, thus ensuring that no neighbors would ever hire my mom to cut their hair.

Kathy's peculiar habits did not stop there, because she had a free spirit's aversion to clothes. Clothing was not a reality she would accept, and she was forever disrobing. Kathy was stubborn, and not even a spanking could stop her. On one occasion, my brother walked to a swimming class several city blocks away, only to turn around and find that two-year-old Kathy had followed him the entire way, buck naked. Worse, he now had to march his nude, barefoot, but smiling little sister home.

My mother worried that perhaps being dropped on her head had had an effect on Kathy's personality—for my father liked to play with us; it's just that he never got it quite right. And sometimes he got it dangerously wrong. He was fourteen years older than my mother, and by the time Kathy was born, he was nearing forty. A man of his generation had never had a chance to play. Poverty had deprived him of many toys; then the war and fleeing as a refugee forced him and his siblings to grow up quickly. So he did the best he could, assuming that small children would like nothing more than to learn the games the chess masters played.

At least, chess was safe. Once when Kathy was not even two, my father was happily playing with her at a wedding. While others danced the polka around them, my father repeatedly threw Kathy high up into the air and caught her on her way down. Each time, she screamed in delight. He caught her safely each time, until he was distracted by someone he hadn't seen for a while and then forgot to catch her.

Kathy screamed again on her way down, but this time in terror. She landed on her head but miraculously didn't seem to be hurt. Yet soon thereafter, she took to cutting hair and streaking in the buff.

As she got older, she eventually abandoned her nudist ways—thanks in part to an elderly Polish lady living in a second-floor room that smelled like a church cloakroom. Her preferred attire, regardless of the weather or the temperature, was a pink tufted housecoat, dangerous to the eye and also highly flammable. She always wore a kerchief on her head and reeked of garlic. Kathy abandoned her nudist ways in favor of following this fashion, giving her the appearance of a miniature Polish senior citizen.

She kept up this style for years, until one day my mother saw a child walking down the street and said to me, "Look at that poor child. She must not have a mother."

As the kid approached, my mother realized it was Kathy. It was time to put her foot down.

Granted, my mother did not have a lot of control over us, because she worked nights at a pharmacy, in its cosmetics department. Beats me who was shopping for beauty products in the middle of the night, but, regardless, my mother worked behind the counter and assisted those in need of a beauty fix at 3 a.m.

My father often attended political meetings in the evenings. He never forgot where he came from and who had stayed behind. Due to the war and the poverty he endured as a result, he had a strong desire to see political change in Croatia. What he had suffered through accounted for the unfortunate bitterness and hatred he felt; thus, he sent money and spent much energy furthering the Croatian cause and dreaming of better times for the average man in his homeland. Fixing an entire country's woes required time, so we played hide-and-seek outside with the neighborhood children, until all of the other kids had been called in by their parents—by 10 p.m. on school nights or by 11 on weekends.

Because the "night was still young," rather than go to bed, the four of us wrote cards of appreciation and made gifts for my mother and left them on the table, along with some dinner we heated up for her. Only years later did I realize that food doesn't stay warm for several hours after it's heated. Though on occasion we got into fights, in general, we looked out for one another and were not of the entitled generation.

We eventually made our way to bed, only to be woken up by my dad when he came home in the middle of the night. He showed us love in his own way and was manifestly not an advocate of "let sleeping children lie." He would enter the darkness of our room and ask us, "Are you sleeping?"

If we dreamily replied, "Yes," then he shook us a bit harder to wake us up completely.

"I got you something," he'd say, as if we couldn't guess what it was. "Kids, I got you Crush and Kit Kat."

We all still slept in the same room, so the four of us would wake up and, in a sleepy stupor, obediently march into the kitchen in our one-piece furry pajamas with feet, the soles covered in plastic. Each pajama was a different pastel color, and we looked like little Easter bunnies, sitting at the table half awake, while my father got the party started. He would excitedly hand us each a can of Crush Red Cream soda and two bars of Kit Kat chocolate to share.

We dutifully sat at the imitation wood table, with stunned expressions, eating Kit Kat and drinking soda. He would place one or two of us on his lap and watch us eat. These were very happy times for him. I knew it was odd to be awakened at 2 a.m. for a sugary snack, but it became part of our normal routine. I watched my siblings, who, once the sugar kicked in and they were fully awake, were delighted to be sharing "quality time" with my dad, and I tried to be as joyful as they were.

After "the party" was over, we were sent back to bed, and my dad would remind us to go straight to sleep, because we had to get up early for school the next day. Off to bed we went, with bright red mustaches and little brown teeth. Dentists across Toronto should be grateful to him for those late-night parties.

Ironically, these are my most vivid childhood recollections of sitting at the kitchen table.

THE HAT, A BRATTY KID, AND ONE PATIENT PILOT

by Ivanka Di Felice

MY MOTHER'S FAVORITE AUTHORS WERE Tolstoy and Dostoevsky, with their alleged deep understanding of human nature. She often carried on intellectual discussions with her friends, while we children watched *Gilligan's Island* in the background. This brings up another memory I vividly remember but wish I could forget. Not that it is painful, just terribly embarrassing.

Twenty-six-years old, with four small children, ranging from six to newborn, my mother understandably had bad nerves. Just after Kathy was born, my mom intended to go back to Croatia for a rest. She couldn't shake off postpartum depression, which was then termed by others and my mom herself as "being crazy and lazy." The doctor was the only one who said that she was ill and needed a few weeks' break from her situation, which she says I have described with more humor than it deserves.

Sometimes, if my parents had an argument, my mom would go for a walk, even in the middle of the night. She often took me along. Perhaps it seemed more respectable if a small child accompanied a woman wandering the streets at 2 a.m. We walked to a nearby greasy spoon that was open and at this hour hosted a motley crew of characters. My mom and I didn't fit in. Regardless, we sat in a booth, and she ordered a Western sandwich, while I chose a toasted Danish or French fries. My mom would try to keep the conversation upbeat, as if we were enjoying a meal together at dinner hour. It seems I was destined to be dining after midnight, and to this day I am a night owl.

Thus, it was only natural that I be the one to accompany her on her trip. As this was her first visit back to the home country, after leaving nine years ago with the "American tycoon," my mother had a lot to live up to. My grandmother particularly wanted to keep the illusion of the fairy tale alive and was disappointed that my mother was returning in such a fragile state.

Though funds were limited, my mom purchased some new clothes for both of us, along with an assortment of gifts for relatives back home. She also bought me the prettiest hat ever made. It was light pink, almost iridescent, with a wide brim. A satin bow completed this perfection. With my round brown eyes and my big ears that normally stuck out but were now hidden, I felt like a princess.

Before I continue, I must plead my case that aside from the indiscretion of bringing my teacher home for lunch—and others I have chosen to forget—I was usually a good child. If I was ever given a chocolate bar, I ate only a quarter of it or less and brought the rest home to share with my siblings.

My mother and I took off on Swiss Airlines and would catch a connecting flight to Zagreb. Proud as a peacock, I wore my pink hat onto the plane. Other passengers smiled at me, and I enjoyed all of the attention. I fell asleep, and my mom removed the hat and put it in the overhead luggage bin.

The plane landed, and we ran to catch our connecting flight. While we were climbing the ramp onto the second plane, I realized I had left my precious hat behind. My mother was disappointed, too, but told me that I would have to forget it. That was the moment when I physically turned from a charming young child into an eight-year-old monster. Tears rolled down my face, and I screamed as if someone had plunged a knife into my little body. I was inconsolable.

The stewardess came over to see about all of the commotion. In between sobs, I told her I had left my new pink hat on the previous plane. Perhaps wishing to spare fellow passengers my tantrum or having empathy because I wanted to keep my big ears covered, she called the appropriate people, and although the plane was waiting for takeoff, she rescued my hat and saved the day. Ever since then, I have had a fondness for Swiss Air.

We reached Zagreb two hours later, just as the swelling of my eyes and face subsided. I pranced outside the gates with my pink hat on, to family waiting on the other side. They warmly hugged us, and I felt like a princess once again.

Everyone was grateful to my mom for all of the assistance she had sent over the years, because at various intervals coffee could not be found in Yugoslavia, then laundry detergent, and so on. My mom sacrificed buying things for herself but sent these rare treats to her parents, aunts, uncles, and cousins back home. Now, she divvied up the presents, much to everyone's delight.

My mom was an only child but had two aunts who lived on either side of my grandmother. My mother was close to their children, and, although they were cousins, they'd grown up together like siblings. The last time they'd seen her was when they'd accompanied her to the airport the day she left for Canada. One aunt, Štefa, was beautiful but was married to a man who had an affinity for alcohol, and she, too, indulged in this intoxicant.

To escape his parents, their son, Đuka, joined the navy. I fondly recall him going on leave to visit my mom, ever so handsome in his white-and-navy uniform. I was fascinated by his official-looking outfit, because in Canada no one wore this type of clothing, other than the police who came to our house on occasion.

Life still wasn't easy in Yugoslavia. With a difficult economic situation, the standard of living was far lower than even a family such as ours was accustomed to in Canada. We took our clothes down to the river and washed them on the stones, then went for a swim afterward. I thought it delightful, but then again I wasn't doing all of the hard work. Most likely, anything I'd washed hadn't turned out very clean. Nor was I doing it in the cold of winter, as women used to.

Yet despite that, there were many happy moments. People were generous with what little they had and appreciated the simpler things in life. My mom's cousin roasted a piglet outside for hours, while I watched the older women make their own strudel dough and stretch it across the entire table, then fill it with either sliced apples or squash and poppy seed.

My mom's uncle Đuro believed that "If you do good, it will come back to you." Hence, despite not being a medical professional, he was always running off, pliers in hand, to pull a tooth or to help birth a cow. He always offered people a place to sleep in the barn's hayloft when passers-by looked for accommodations for the night.

My mother had tried to brief me on the custom of saying, "No," when first offered something. I never did grasp the concept of saying, "Thanks, I cannot," when in fact, "I could." So the minute I was offered something, I forgot this silly custom and eagerly said, "Yes," much to the embarrassment of my mother.

We went to the fairs in various villages, where my mom's cousins always bought me a pretty Licitar heart on a string (a gingerbread heart decorated in bright red and other edible colors). Women sold handmade doilies, carved wooden boxes, and other specialties from the area.

In the evening, there would be food, drink, and dancing, and I watched the adults polka, waltz, and tango. My mom taught me, too, and I wanted to dance with her all night. After enough wine, some people would break into song. Croatians are emotional, so the songs usually had to do with a love of home or devastating heartbreak—without that one person, the sun would never shine again. Regardless, everyone, including those who had not imbibed or had their hearts torn to shreds, eventually joined in.

On other evenings, we all gathered in her aunt's kitchen, and, one by one, the neighbors dropped in. The women chatted, while shelling beans or doing needlepoint, and the men tried to hear the news on the radio and drank wine.

There was only one TV in the village. Viewing was reserved for soccer games, which could be watched only from the front yard, through the living room window. So, when a game was on, the men gathered outside this neighbor's window and peered in to catch glimpses of the match.

We had spent the day with family and neighbors, collecting hay for the cows to eat and for fodder. Despite the heat, the bugs, and the discomfort of the work, everyone joyfully broke into song at the slightest excuse. We sat on a wagon loaded high with hay, with the cows pulling us.

Now it was time for another tantrum, as I decided I didn't like where I was seated. My mother told me to sit down before I fell off the wagon, but the same craziness that had gripped me with the pink hat took over my mind, mouth, and actions. I was helpless.

"I miss my father. I want to go home," I said, sobbing uncontrollably. I didn't miss my father, nor did I want to go home, but I wanted to sit on the precarious edge of the hay wagon. All of the relatives started to adjust their places to accommodate me, when my mother gave me one last chance to do as I was told, or I would be walking back.

I knew I was being unreasonable, but reason did not prevail, so my mother ordered them to stop the wagon. I had to climb down and hike the long distance home. Today, this might be classified as child abuse, but my mom made the right call. I never again fussed over where I sat.

I'm not sure what ever became of the delightful pink hat. And as for Dostoevsky saying, "The soul is healed by being with children," my mom no longer believed he had ever actually been in the company of children, certainly not one who had left her precious hat on a plane or had a conniption on a hay wagon. Thus, in her opinion, he was reduced to being a drunkard and a gambler.

THE BRANDY BUNCH

by Ivanka Di Felice

I HAD JUST DISCOVERED THAT not everything one sees on TV or in the movies is possible in real life. The large black umbrella I opened and held onto did not help me float down from the roof of a neighbor's garage. I landed with a thud and thought I had broken both of my legs. I lay there for a while, crying, as my friends stared, equally dumbfounded that I hadn't gently soared down, as we'd all expected. After a while, I was able to get up and slowly limp home. Back then, foolishness was not rewarded with sympathy, so I kept this secret from my parents.

I came home to find Miss Emily, a roomer from the second floor, dramatically descending the stairs, loud music by Strauss blaring from her room. She had left her door open in her haste. She clutched her heart, insisting she was about to have another near heart attack and could she please be given some brandy to prevent it from coming on? Apparently, this method of warding off an attack was something doctors still hadn't discovered.

Miss Emily's looming heart attacks regularly occurred during what was referred to as "happy hour," when many in the city enjoyed pre-dinner drinks.

My parents took on the role of life-saving physicians, as they thrust into her hands a generous shot of brandy, often followed by another, to stave off a possible second attack. After this, she would wobble back to her room, turn up the volume on the radio, and fill the entire house with Beethoven.

Her elegant clothes and the classical music she listened to led my mother to conclude that she must have been educated. As she headed back upstairs, my mom wondered what circumstances had brought her to live in a room in our house. It saddened my mother, but each month when my dad promptly received her rent on the first, it made his heart glad. My father was generous, and Croatians always offered drinks; thus, he never factored that "saving Miss Emily's life" each evening cost him a good portion of her rent.

Steven came in, anxious to tell us about his after-school adventure with his friend Vladimir. "We found three baby squirrels. A tree had fallen down on the street, and they were lying there. So we took them and were carrying them home when a car stopped. A man asked us "What do you have there?" We showed him the squirrels, and he offered to buy them. We charged him five dollars each!"

Steven was so gratified by this business transaction. He split the profits with Vladimir and contemplated everything he could buy with the money he had left over, after already purchasing several popsicles for 10 cents and a few chocolate bars for 25 cents.

In the meantime, he put his money in the little pink ceramic piggy bank my parents had given us to encourage saving. We had mastered the part where you put money into the little pig. We still needed to refine our resolve to leave it there, because we inevitably took the money out again in a few days, depending on our strong urge for sweets.

This was back when twenty-five cents gave us plenty of options, especially if we went to the store down the street that sold candy by the penny. In the good old days, a child needed only a few pieces of candy to be happy.

Around 3 a.m., we heard uncontrollable sobbing from Steven's bed.

"Why? Why did I do it?" he kept asking.

The loud crying soon woke everyone. My mother ran to Steven, his hair wet from the tears.

"What happened?" she asked. "Why are you crying?"

"What about their mom?" he said, in between sobs.

"Whose mom?" she asked, and we wondered the same. Vesna and I looked at each other and made the gesture for crazy.

He couldn't believe she didn't know who he was talking about. "The squirrels!" he said, breaking down. "How is their mom going to feel when she looks for them, and they're gone, and she finds out we sold them?"

My mom probably wanted to say, "The mother squirrel would never figure out you sold them, she's probably glad to have her freedom, and five bucks apiece is far more than they were worth"—but, as all good mothers do, she refrained. She told him the man who purchased them would care for them. She tried to soothe Steven, while I am sure his friend Vladimir slept soundly.

Poor Steven was inconsolable for days.

Meanwhile, Miss Emily seemed to have been miraculously cured. She had not waltzed down for a shot of brandy to ward off her heart attack for days, nor could any classical music be heard blaring from her room. Soon thereafter, we found out that poor Miss Emily had been run over by a streetcar. She had given her last dramatic performance.

My parents dared not tell Steven, who was still getting over selling the squirrels. As I'd already learned, some things were better off left unsaid.

THE THUNDERBIRD TAKES FLIGHT

by Ivanka Di Felice

MY FATHER'S LOVE OF BIG cars and his disregard for gas consumption were confirmed when he drove up to our house in a brand spanking new 1977 Thunderbird. It was orange brown with a vinyl roof, accent stripes, and concealed headlights, often found on luxury models or muscle cars. We felt like millionaires. At last, I could compete with my rich friends at school. The car was enormous, and the four of us children resembled dwarves standing beside it.

Awestruck, we ran around examining all of the car's features. We begged my father to open and close the hidden headlight covers. He proudly sat in the car, opening and shutting them to our squeals of delight. Even the tenants came out to see what the fuss was all about and to offer congratulations.

On weekends, my parents often took us on little trips. My dad loved soccer, so we would go watch games between Croatians and Serbians that usually ended in mob violence. Sometimes they'd take us swimming in the Credit River or, in the winter, tobogganing on a high hill down the road or other activities for children that I see in retrospect were fairly dangerous. We wondered where we would go in the new car, but the African Lion Safari west of Toronto would be out of the question until the car aged on its own, without monkeys scratching it.

Instead, we would go to Marineland. We could hardly wait to speed down the highway.

We sat in the car, waiting for Steven to get in. He opened the heavy door, and then it immediately slammed shut. Steven, still outside, with his thumb smashed in the door, let out an ear-splitting scream. My dad jumped out of the car, opened the door, and, on examining Steven's thumb, realized he would have to take him to the emergency room. My dad sped off, testing the Thunderbird motto that it "was built for flight."

It seems logical to think an almost 4,000-pound vehicle with less than 200 horsepower wasn't exactly a car ready to "take flight," but when you had a screaming child in the back, it was amazing how fast it could go. Anyone who said it "couldn't fly" had never driven his kid to a hospital in it. My dad wildly swerved around the turns, and, because seatbelts were optional in our family, we all swayed from one side of the car to the other, shrieking with joy.

My dad dropped my mom and us four children off, and we entered the emergency room. We weren't the only ones who would be spending a Saturday afternoon in the hospital. Judging from the characters who occupied the seats in the waiting area, we couldn't escape being with drunks or mentally unstable people, regardless of whether we stayed home or ended up on a family outing in St. Joseph's Hospital.

Steven, incredibly accident prone, was always breaking something: his toe while playing soccer, his finger, or his arm, when the wedge holding up the bathroom window fell and landed on it. While the rest of us avoided being victims of the design flaw in the four-child swing my father had built, Steven found a way to fall under it. He lay on the grass as the wooden platform scraped across his back, removing a hefty layer of skin. My father, horrified, immediately changed the swing's design and reconstructed it, but the deep scar on Steven's back was a grim reminder of the failed toy.

By now, the hospital must have assumed my parents were abusing Steven and didn't even bother to come up with plausible stories to mask the beatings, because each one was more unbelievable than the previous one. Times were different back then, because the doctors never filed any reports, and no one ever came to check up on him.

Yet the implausible stories were all true, and although we did get spankings, none of them hurt much more than our feelings, especially if we put on extra pairs of pants or my mom's wooden spoon broke after only a couple of swats. Steven's hospital visits were all of his own doing. This latest one—closing the car door on his own thumb—confirmed it.

Every week it was something, and we were practically on a first-name basis with the nurses. Due to Vesna's illnesses, my parents carted her to the appealing (by comparison) Sick Kid's Hospital downtown. Since Steven's incidents often involved loss of blood, however, they had to take him to St. Joseph's, which was much closer but was unfortunately near Parkdale, an area in Toronto then home to many a drunk and drug addict. Observing the effects of drug use on a Saturday evening in the waiting area was better than any "Say no to drugs" program the schools could devise.

One woman with thin, scraggly hair and a wild look in her eyes seemed to have escaped from a mental asylum. Another man, with a police escort, yelled while attempting to get away.

As people entered the emergency ward, they didn't know where to sit—beside us four rambunctious kids, with Steven moaning loudly, or next to the bleeding woman who was obviously high on something. They contemplated a long while before finally sitting next to us.

After what seemed like a lifetime to us, but especially to poor Steven, they called his name. The doctor examined his thumb and determined it was broken. The doctor cleaned it up, put on a splint, wrapped it, and prescribed painkillers.

The three unwounded children hopped into the back seat, while Steven got to go home in the front, in between my parents. There were some privileges to being a klutz.

Since my dad felt bad for Steven, and for us, he stopped at the corner store and got what he thought were our favorite treats. Thanks to Steven's injury, we came home and drank Crush Red Cream soda and ate Kit Kat chocolate—at long last, before 2 a.m.

The following morning, we got up early to worship the car. We sat on the porch, ensuring that everyone who walked past would see us with it.

"Get ready, kids! We're going to Croatian Park!" my mom yelled.

We, along with most other Croatians in the city, often went there on Sundays. You left your car in a spot in the park, usually next to a picnic bench, and the men would wander from car to car, drinking beer and discussing politics, while the women caught up on the latest gossip.

As the men went from car to car and from beer to beer, the discussions became more riled. Meanwhile, we children swam with my mom in the Credit River for hours, happily lying on our backs, floating down the rapids, and staring into the bright blue sky. Once the men had visited familiar cars, they went to a bar that also sold roast lamb or roast pig off a spit by the pound. Fresh bread and chopped onions rounded off the meal.

Toward evening, a live band played, and people danced. Sometimes we joined in as well. My parents had taught us polkas and waltzes in the kitchen, to the sounds of clapping and cheering tenants, as they walked past us up the staircase. Sometimes the tenants would show off their own moves, turning our kitchen into a dance hall.

Our family often brought a bucket of Kentucky Fried Chicken to the park: the taste of Sundays. The coleslaw resembled a color a designer might use to paint a baby boy's room, and the macaroni salad instilled no more confidence as a wise food choice. But, thankfully, we were indestructible, and if there were any food labels, no one was reading them. Ignorance was bliss, as the four of us wrestled for the drumstick. We sat on an orange-and-black-patterned blanket on the ground, next to our new car. It didn't take much to make us happy: a bucket of KFC and we were all smiles.

Steven couldn't swim with the bandage on his thumb, so another young boy took him fishing, while we went to the river with my mom and swam alongside her. At the end of the day, we met at the car, and Steven proudly showed us his catch: a large bass. He'd put it in a pail of water, and it slowly splashed around, with less vigor as the hours went on.

Steven brought the fish home and put it in the freezer.

At 1 a.m., we heard whimpers coming from Steven's bed.

"Steven, are you okay?" my mom asked, assuming his thumb must be throbbing.

"I killed it, and we didn't eat it. I killed it for nothing!" he said, in between sobs.

Steven was crying over the fish. He had finally gotten over the baby squirrels, but now the dead fish set him off again. He got out of bed and went to the freezer, pointing and confirming that the fish had died in vain. Another round of sobbing began. At least, my mom knew he did not have the makings of a psychopath.

She got him back into bed and stayed with him a long while until he eventually fell asleep.

Being a parent wasn't easy. You had to protect your children not only from others, but from themselves as well.

THE GROUP OF SEVEN

by Ivanka Di Felice

I IMAGINE THAT THE WOMAN who called in the home invasion incident was virtually blind and named Agatha or something similar, denoting an ancient and decorated member of the neighborhood watch program.

"911, what's your emergency?" asked the operator.

"Suspects seen entering Victorian house," she said.

"Do you have a description of the perpetrators?" asked the operator.

"White male suspect is approximately three feet, three inches, with a light complexion, rosy cheeks. Female suspect is just under three feet, wearing yellow pants with happy faces printed on them."

For a more specific clue, Agatha probably added, "Female wearing vibrant pink Barbie running shoes."

Darn my mother and her love of bright colors! Agatha, having done her duty and at the same time procured some thrilling entertainment for herself, could return to keeping vigil by her window.

It must have been a slow day for crime in the city of Toronto, because the police answered the call and soon stood outside the grand Victorian house. "Roger that, the seven dwarves are in view."

The seven of us, ranging in age from four to ten, with the two eldest being ten and the two youngest being four, had gone out in search of adventure after school. We had disobeyed our parents and cut through the woods in High Park—something we were forbidden to do ever since our Group of Seven had stumbled upon a naked man there and politely asked him, "Sir, do you know what time it is?"

The nude man's gruff response was "Can't you see I'm not wearing a watch?"

He was, however, wearing shoes with socks. Our parents were appalled—not that he wasn't wearing a watch, or that shoes and socks without clothes is a bad look, but, of course, that he was naked. After that, we were prohibited from taking any shortcuts through the forest. Because we had a long walk, more than two miles, to this newly discovered abandoned house, we voted to go through the woods and to keep this our secret. Not under any circumstances were we to tell our parents, nor would we ask any naked people for the time.

Steven led the way, with the two four-year-olds in the rear, trying to keep up. We sang en route and exited the relative safety of the woods at a major crossroad. Not wanting to further disobey our parents, we waited for the light to change. Like a mother duck with her ducklings in tow, we marched along the tree-lined boulevards of High Park Avenue, anxious to reach the abandoned house. We walked several miles until we arrived on Annette Street, to find the grand Victorian mansion with boarded-up windows and overgrown grass.

The front door was locked, so we had to find another way in. We sneaked around the back of the property in stealth mode. The door was secured, but we had come so far and were not about to give up. We had heard tales of a suicide on the third floor and that the body was still hanging. I took a bobby pin out of my hair and tried to pick the lock. When this failed, Steven and Vladimir used brute force by throwing their flimsy bodies against the door. It did not budge.

We were perplexed. These methods always worked on television. We found a long wooden pole, so the seven of us took hold of it and stormed the door several times. This was what probably woke up Agatha. Realizing TV had once again deceived us, we searched for other ways to enter. A small basement window was open, just big enough for us seven dwarves to squeeze through. One by one, we fell into the dark, damp basement. Clinging to one another, we fearfully looked for the staircase.

Steven found it and said he was going up to the third floor to check out the dead body. Now that we were there, I no longer wanted to see the body, nor did I want my four-year-old sister, Kathy, to. She was already traumatized enough after we invented the story that my parents had found her in a garbage can and thereafter adopted her.

Steven went up with Vladimir and quickly returned. Someone had taken the body, and only a noose was left. I acted disappointed, despite being relieved. We took a quick peek around, but there was nothing to see in the empty house. We opened the door and guiltily exited the house, as the police car pulled up.

"Run!" I yelled.

But it was too late—they had surrounded us. Our escape had undoubtedly been thwarted by the meddlesome busybody next door. Agatha must have been pleased, thinking, *Good work, Agatha, suspects apprehended.*

Vesna, who each evening sat with her face pressed against the TV screen watching *Columbo*, became our spokesperson. Apparently, she knew the rights of seven-year-olds.

"You cannot arrest us, we're little children," she said.

Although I figured we could slip our small hands out of any handcuffs they placed on us, I thought it best not to find out. Experience had taught me that tears often worked with adults who were not our parents, so in Croatian I suggested that we all cry.

My brother and sisters led the way, with our neighborhood friends following, and soon all seven of us were bawling. Thankfully, neither policeman spoke Croatian, and either they believed our tears were genuine, or they figured we were Eastern European and concluded that taking us home to our parents would be punishment enough.

We got off with a lecture and a ride home. The thrill of being in a police car soon waned, when we saw my father's car in the driveway.

Unfortunately, he was home, so our tears became genuine, as the "character-building" spanking began. Punishment was doled out according to age, because the oldest should have known better. So, while my parents were still full of energy, I got disciplined.

Steven was next, giving Vesna just enough time to put on several pairs of pants. By the fourth child's turn, our parents were usually worn out, and their anger had subsided. There were perks to being the baby in the family.

We never went back to the "haunted" house. Soon thereafter, it was restored to its original splendor, depriving Agatha of her after-school excitement.

KEEPING UP APPEARANCES

by Ivanka Di Felice

STEVEN WAS ONE YEAR YOUNGER than I was. He had brown hair, and I had blonde, but we both had large brown eyes and big ears that stuck out. My grandma had sent the three girls the most beautiful embroidered dresses, which we proudly wore for our school pictures, but my ears stuck out through my straight, blunt-cut hair and ruined my only chance at a decent school picture.

My mother loved trying out new styles before special occasions—even her own wedding—and she also practiced new hairstyles on me, like just before picture day. Perhaps this was timed so that she never had to purchase any photos, for I inevitably ended up with the latest look, which in the seventies meant a wild perm, a bowl cut, or some other style that would leave me with a face not even a mother could love. As she pulled the final perm roller out from my hair, I heard a barely concealed gasp.

I ran to the mirror, but with my hair still wet, I clung to a small vestige of hope that once it dried, it would be okay. That optimism always vanished in a few hours. And since I had inherited that wild imagination from my mother, my disappointment was always greater than your average person's, for not only was my new hairstyle supposed to render me far prettier, more popular, and smarter, it would change my brown eyes to blue, our family would evict the tenants and live alone in the house, and we would purchase a cottage for vacations.

But alas, as the final roller was removed and my hair dried, all that had changed was that my straight blonde hair had become frizzy, and the perm had given my hair a light orange hue. With this hairstyle, even my imagination proved lacking: the tenants would stay, and my eyes would remain brown.

My mother once gave Kathy what we called the "elf cut," and Vesna felt such pity for Kathy that she couldn't let her bear that burden alone. Vesna requested that my mom give her one as well. A greater deed of self-sacrifice has not been known to mankind.

As we grew, so did our ears. I no longer had my pink hat to conceal them, and Steven refused to wear any hat. Finally, my mother took Steven and me to a doctor to get them "pinned." He appeared to be close to a hundred years old, but my mom figured that at least by now he must have done several of these surgeries, even if his hands shook. Steven and I both had the procedure done and left his office with large white casts around our heads, as if we had undergone major brain surgery.

I felt embarrassed by the cast and spent the next few weeks hiding in the basement, in a room my father had reclaimed from the tenants and turned into a family room. He furnished it sparsely, with a couch, a chair, and a bright orange carpet.

Meanwhile, Steven thought the cast on his head looked cool. He went out in public often, weaving elaborate tales about the illness he had and remarkable stories of his recovery. Saturday afternoons he went rollerblading, where he had the attention of the whole rink, as he rode in circles with his cast on his head. It was deeply disappointing for him when his ears healed enough to have it removed.

I returned to school with straight hair and no ears sticking out. My timing was off, though. It was school open house, which was something I tried to avoid.

I went to school with several children whose fathers were professional hockey players, and, naturally, I felt quite important knowing them, even though I'd never been to a hockey game in my life, nor did I even care about the sport. But they were famous, and that was all I needed to know. My father could be quite charming but on occasion showed up after enjoying a glass of wine and was a bit too merry, so I told only my mother about open house and swore her to secrecy. After all, with my fancy lunchbox, I had a reputation to maintain.

So, as the evening approached, we got dressed and walked the couple of blocks to the school. My mother mingled with the other parents and discussed what I assumed was my utter brilliance with the teachers, while I strolled around the school, examining the displays and the exhibits. There would be coffee and donuts, and, with my imagination, the evening might as well have been a diplomats' ball.

Until I heard the words "Ivanka, your father is looking for you."

I made my way to the next room, hoping he would find my brother first and could visit his teachers instead. Yet it wouldn't be long before the entire school was on the alert, yelling, "Ivanka, your father is looking for you!"

I had no chance to flee, as my dad unmistakably approached. My brother and sisters accompanied him, thrilled he had found us all. Four children, same parents, same upbringing, yet they obviously had no appearances to keep up. They were happy my dad had found us and thought it hilarious that I didn't feel the same way. I don't know how he discovered every open house, despite my efforts.

Now that my friends had met my father, I figured it was safe to bring them home. So I invited Karen, who lived a couple of streets over. Her life was like a fairy tale. Her dad worked, while her mom stayed home, and whenever I went there after school to play, her mom was cooking dinner. Their family lived in the entire house. They had a piano, a dog, and a cottage on an island. But Karen was lonely. Her brothers and sister were all much older, and she was jealous of my life, with all of the children I had to play with.

As we approached our house, I saw Leo's crew-cut head on the porch. I whisked Karen to the side entrance and brought her into the kitchen through the backyard. We made it safely into the house without running into any tenants. Perhaps I could keep up appearances after all.

It seemed that no one was home, but strewn across the table lay individual pages that had been torn out of a pornographic magazine. I had never seen anything like that before, but I knew they were bad and that they weren't something one adorns one's kitchen table with. Horrified, I couldn't have Karen think my parents had left the pages, so I devised a plan to blame it on a crazy tenant. The flaw in my scheme was having to tell Karen about our living arrangements.

I crumpled the papers and threw them in the garbage, acting indignant. I took Karen to the front porch to introduce her to Leo, who would become my scapegoat. Moments after Karen had met Leo, Vesna and Vladimir marched out of the kitchen, panicked and yelling that someone had taken their show-and-tell items.

"We found pictures in the garbage, and now they're gone! We wanted to take them to school for show-and-tell," Vesna said.

My sister had no clue what she had found. Appalled, I could imagine the expression on the teacher's face when Vesna and Vladimir stood in front of the class, flashing pornographic images. Because show-and-tell was designed to provide children with a forum for speaking publicly, I still cannot fathom what Vesna and her friend had planned to say.

Still, worse for me, I had introduced Karen to Leo for no reason. Had I known the photos belonged to Vesna, perhaps I could have kept up appearances after all.

Following that incident, not surprisingly, Karen's parents preferred that I play at her picture-perfect house.

DELIVERY "BOY"

by Ivanka Di Felice

OUR 2 A.M. SNACK OF CREAM soda and Kit Kat chocolate was still digesting when the buzzer went off a few hours later. The loud ringing of the double bell alarm clock filled the room. Perhaps it was a mistake. Steven glanced at the glow-in-the-dark hands, but they, too, indicated it was time to get up. I was now fully awake and urged him, saying, "This was your idea."

Steven had ambitiously answered an ad to deliver newspapers. He liked the idea of making "lots of money" in his spare time and a picture of a happy, smiling kid on a bike balancing a large canvas bag atop his shoulder no doubt inspired him.

Yet one short week later, he had lost his inspiration. The money aspect was still appealing, but the actual work involved in earning it brought him back to reality. And so the alarm continued to loudly ring, until everyone but Steven was up. He would finally awaken as the rest of us hovered over him, yelling. Each morning Steven inevitably conned one or more of us into assisting him, and we marched out into the cold to deliver the papers, muttering that this would be our last time helping. If we all slept in, then several of us had to go, to ensure the papers got delivered on time.

In his quest to make lots of money, Steven had taken on a route far greater than was manageable, and as we dragged the heavy metal shopping cart behind us, our degree of unhappiness increased.

If any child labor laws existed in the seventies, the newspaper was indifferent to them. Nor was there any concern about the safety of unescorted children wandering the dark streets of Toronto at 6 a.m.

The ad stated, "You can earn lots of money every week delivering newspapers," adding, "All that is required is reliable transportation, a willingness to rise before dawn and be done before breakfast, the ability to work on your own, and dedication, dedication, dedication." It was soon apparent that although Steven wanted to earn lots of money per week, the only other requirement he possessed was the willingness to be done before breakfast.

Judging by our clothes, toys, and room, we were not demanding children. Despite this, my parents still thought it would be good for us to learn the value of money. They believed that delivering newspapers would "build character" and teach responsibility. They felt that Steven should not give up so easily; thus, despite Steven's pleas to quit, they suggested he keep trying.

So each morning the alarm buzzed at an ungodly hour, followed by bickering as to who would go that day. Then several of us children, and sometimes even my parents, would scurry to deliver the newspapers. Whether it rained, snowed, or froze us with sub-zero temperatures—and even when we were sick—those papers had to be delivered on schedule every day. Toronto winters are a horrible time to be out on the pre-dawn streets and the un-shoveled sidewalks.

After school, we had to collect the money from wealthy patrons we delivered the newspapers to. Although some were generous, not everyone possessed this quality, and a few misers paid in pennies, forcing us to count every one.

When it came to tips, none of us fared much better than the others. We were convinced that sending Vesna, with her bowed legs and coke bottle glasses, would result in more generous tips, but she received nominally more than did Steven with his large brown eyes. Not even my scrawny self, coupled with my big, sad eyes, could get certain neighbors to part with much. They planned to keep the wealth in the family.

This "enterprising" adventure came to an end, before we killed one another, when we did the math and realized this wouldn't be our route from rags to riches.

We took the little profit we had made and chose to go to a movie as a family reward for our labors. We children, who ranged from five to eleven years old, wanted to see a cartoon that had just been released, but my mother, having perused the entertainment section of the newspaper, saw an intriguing ad for Invasion of the Body Snatchers—a science fiction film about a group of people who discover the human race is being replaced, one by one, with clones devoid of emotion.

We drove downtown to the theater, with its comfy red velvet seats, and with a large container of buttered popcorn in hand eagerly awaited the movie. But as the movie progressed, the four of us children became frightened, began to cry, and begged our parents to leave the theater.

"We can't leave now. We have to wait for the happy ending," my mom insisted. Either she really believed that, or she couldn't stand the idea that we had spent a small fortune to see the movie, only to leave partway through.

As more and more people were taken over by clones, we again pleaded to go. Yet my mother again assured us that this was a Hollywood movie and, unlike the foreign films she usually took us to, which were true to life, Hollywood films always had happy endings.

We obediently sat there with our hands covering our eyes, waiting for the good people to prevail. Instead, the humans were powerless to defeat the pods. The final scene in the movie, with Donald Sutherland's open-mouthed scream, leaves no doubt that the pods have won and that humanity is doomed for extinction.

We left the theater, screaming, and cried all the way home. We blamed my mother for insisting it would have a happy ending. It left us with nightmares, severely traumatized. My parents were also traumatized, as the four of us climbed into bed with them every night for weeks.

Next time around, we were allowed to choose our own movie, a Disney cartoon.

"DONNA"

by Ivanka Di Felice

IF WE EVER OBJECTED TO some of the colorful tenants, my father would insist that he liked living with other people— although his greatest enjoyment came on the first of each month when he separated them from a portion of their government checks.

Tata was always devising ways to bring in more income. The pretty sunroom on the second floor had a third of its square footage stolen to become a bathroom. Blue must have been the fashionable color at the time, or it was to my father, because every fixture was baby blue: toilet, sink, tub, and tiles. It took the guesswork out of mix and match. And evidently blue was timeless, because that bathroom remains that way to this day. This became an actual apartment with its own kitchen, bedroom, and bathroom; hence, it would be for higher-class tenants only. A very tall woman with long blonde hair seemed to fit the bill and rented it.

Donna soon became not just a tenant but a friend of the family. My mother often gathered her girlfriends together for lunch and would invite Donna as well. They spent the afternoon laughing and having intellectual discussions. On occasions when my mom had to work nights, Donna baby-sat us. She was very strong and was able to wrestle all four of us at once. She did have a peculiar smell, something I now realize was glue. At that age, however, I had no idea that glue, along with other controlled substances, could be used for recreational purposes.

If Donna was going out for a special occasion, my mom would lend her clothes. Donna, extremely modest, always went into another room to undress, rather than changing in front of us small children.

We liked Donna. She was probably our favorite tenant and our best babysitter, though, after Susan, this was not a difficult honor to achieve. She let us do whatever we wanted. We hung outside until late at night and then came in and jumped on her, but she didn't mind. She simply lay there, and because she was strong, she fought us off, sending us into fits of laughter.

Eventually, Donna moved and we lost contact with her, as we did with all of our other tenants, some for justifiable reasons.

A few years later, on a Tuesday, Donna called my mother at work at the hairdresser's down the street. She wanted to meet up the following day. My mom went to the arranged place, but Donna never showed up. My mother tried to contact her but to no avail.

Then my mother received a phone call from the police, stating that they wanted to meet with her. She wondered what it could be about. They picked her up from work and took her back to the station. The police had found a date book with my mom's name and number scribbled in it.

"Do you know a Peter H___?

"No. But I do know Donna H___ ," my mom said, assuming Donna might be Peter's sister. This was my mother's first introduction to transvestites. Good thing she was sitting down when the police told her that Donna *was* Peter and that Peter had been murdered when the perpetrator found out that Donna was a Peter. Apparently, though, Donna had stabbed the perpetrator first.

This was a shock for our entire family, and I don't think we kids quite understood the situation. At this point, my parents stopped asking tenants to baby-sit us.

SUPERHERO GONE BAD

by Ivanka Di Felice

MY GRADE SIX TEACHER, MR. Slobodian, looked like a more well-fed version of Mr. Kotter, with a mustache and wild, curly hair styled in an Afro, back when that was not a look. Even worse, I suspected it was a man perm.

Anyway, one day Mr. Slobodian assigned us a project: to invent a superhero for a comic book (that I could understand). He subsequently asked us to write what we thought about doing the project (that I did not understand). I'm not sure what prompted him to ask, but I took his request to mean two things: (a) that he *wanted* my opinion, and (b) that he wanted my *honest* opinion. I quickly discovered that he wanted neither, and so would my mother, when she was called in for an emergency meeting.

One could assume that someone who looked as if his hero was Mr. Kotter had more pressing issues to attend to. But no, his foremost issue seemed to be calling my mother in, who had four children and who had to take time off work, losing precious money.

Always thinking outside the box, when asked to pick a superhero I opted for something fresh, a new superhero.

Hence, Super Shoe emerged. Though a plain brown (for the ordinary among us), Super Shoe had a colorful cape and funky laces, and, more important than physical appearance, this superhero could really solve world issues, stomping them out, one crisis at a time.

I never did like homework, so I did as little of it as possible. Yet I worked really hard on this project and had Super Shoe solve as many real or contrived problems as a twelve-year-old could imagine. To say that I had never been a very good artist was a total understatement, so perhaps it wasn't always clear from the drawing alone what Super Shoe was battling. Based on the balloon above, however, it was evident that Super Shoe was embroiled in important world issues.

I tried to maintain my original enthusiasm, but so much effort was required to simply draw the basics that by the end of the project I had missed several episodes of *Happy Days* and had sacrificed seeing the Fonz apologize. Given that this was not an art class, I thought an essay would have been a better use of my precious TV viewing time.

Anyhow, Mr. Slobodian asked—so I answered. I'd hoped my brutal honesty at such a young age would inspire the teacher to believe I was destined for great things. If I could figure out this was a dumb project, imposed on us by someone who simply had the power to do so, then I was destined to lead the people, to stand up for the lowly, the poor, and those without a voice. Instead, my writing prompted his concern about my mental health and whether I had the makings of a psychopath.

I left that parent teacher meeting, stunned. It changed the world for me. Could honesty not always be the best policy? Do you really want to teach someone about to enter her teen years that it's better to lie than to tell the truth? To this day, I'm puzzled by the emergency meeting he called with my mother. And since my mental health is just fine (according to my honest self-diagnosis) and I haven't killed any small animals or humans (small or large), I think his assessment of me was wrong. Thank heavens, he didn't ask me what I thought about his hair—I might have ended up in even worse trouble.

I'm not sure what my mom thought of that meeting years ago. After I had brought home my kindergarten teacher, she had worried about my mental health, and perhaps this now confirmed her suspicions.

DODGING ROGER

by Ivanka Di Felice

WHILE MY MOM WORKED, I would heat up dinner, lovingly made by the people at Chef Boyardee. After my brother and sisters ate, we went back outside to play. My father had purchased a motocross bike for Steven, and the boys on the street built a ramp and would lay us kids on the ground, one next to the other, to see how many bodies they could jump over. I was always on the end with the tires landing on me, leaving skid marks on my back. Just before my lungs collapsed, a strange-looking man stepped onto our porch.

Even at a young age, I knew the "Room for Rent" sign could signal trouble. Our house was meant to be filled with a happy family, the grand oak staircase leading up to children's bedrooms and the attics turned into playrooms filled with toys. Meanwhile, our staircase led to a string of rooms filled with—charitably speaking—sometimes bizarre people. With each new arrival, it became more difficult for me to "keep up appearances."

A website now boasts that High Park "is home to a *wide range* of people." Forty years ago, I already knew that, because many of them lived with us.

As if watching Leo attempt to climb to the second floor was not enough entertainment, my father arranged for our lives to be enriched by musical interludes in the basement apartment. The tenant he referred to as *Mali Mile*, "Little Mike," a short fellow countryman, like Leo, sported a crew cut, which made me presume there was a direct correlation between choice of hairstyle and one's affinity for alcohol. No sober person ever got a crew cut.

Little Mike played the Hawaiian guitar for hours while drinking. We dutifully sat through these performances for what seemed like ages. Thankfully, the "entertainment" sometimes came to an abrupt end, when Little Mike blacked out and fell over. The clapping after that was genuine.

When Little Mike was not putting on a concert, he engaged in deep conversation with the devil.

Perhaps because of these recitals, I never did well in music. I took piano lessons from a kind lady up the street at a discounted rate. It might have been her way of keeping us off the street, but one day after my lesson, she said, "You either need natural talent or the drive to practice, if you ever want to be good at the piano. You have neither." She took my hand and returned the crumpled bills I had given her, adding, "It breaks my heart to see your parents wasting their hard-earned money."

And that was the end of my musical career.

Now, an elderly man with a white crew cut, only one good eye, and the look of a professional maniac stood on our porch, asking to speak to my parents. As he stuttered, I didn't know which eye to look at, and it took him ages to tell me he had seen the "Room for Rent" sign in the window.

We already had enough strange people in our house. Even our pet was weird. My parents had brought home a cat named Morris. This cat hated us four children and stood guard, hissing and refusing to let us use the stairs leading to our basement. His only redeeming quality was that he could pee into the toilet and would wipe the seat with his paw afterward.

Although I knew that leaving a room empty for any given time was terribly painful to Tata, I took matters into my own young hands, based on Roger's haircut alone.

"Oh, that sign, that's a mistake," I told him. "The room has already been rented. Sorry."

I grabbed the sign and took it inside with me, waving goodbye.

Roger was tenacious, for soon the doorbell rang again, several times.

"I'll get it!" I quickly yelled to my dad.

Sure enough, it was Roger. Again, I didn't know which eye to look at, as he took a long while to say in a loud voice that the sign was in the window, so there must be a room for rent.

I kept insisting, but so did Roger.

My father heard the commotion and came out onto the porch. Roger began to plead his case. My father looked at me, and I knew I was in trouble for lying.

Later, I got a long "character-building" lecture from my dad on how I shouldn't judge people by their outward appearance and, more important, how I'd almost lost a month's rent.

Not surprisingly, Roger was able to move in quickly, much to my dismay and my father's delight. He came with just one suitcase—where, I was convinced, the body was hidden. After that, Roger treated me much as the cat did, except he let me pass on the stairs.

Roger, long retired, had nothing to do. His days revolved around his next meal at the greasy spoon up the street and weekly phone calls to Debbie, far younger and whom he called his girlfriend, but who conveniently lived a distance of several thousand miles away. Roger always sent her money, and each time she mailed him a new picture of herself, which he was quick to share with us.

As the years went on, with still no sign of Debbie, I began to wonder whether the letters were coming from prison. Whenever Roger walked past our kitchen door, he peeked in and lingered under the guise of asking a question that inevitably drove my dad insane.

My father grew tired of Roger's lurking and insisted we keep the kitchen door closed. We were not in the habit of closing it, because the other tenants usually just staggered up to their rooms. Thus, we often forgot, only to find Roger lying in wait for us. Sneaking in and out of the house without getting caught by one-eyed Roger, as he was christened, became the norm.

As we got older, my parents first tried to give Steven his own bedroom on the second floor—the same floor as Roger's room. While most children would have jumped at the chance to have their own room, we had grown accustomed to sleeping in the same one, on two sets of bunk beds, and Steven refused to move. Then they tried to give me that bedroom, while the other three kids slept downstairs. Each night my parents threatened to spank Steven or me if we didn't go up to that room. Steven and I would fight, and finally one of us would go. We acted as if my parents were sending us to a torture chamber. None of the tenants had ever harmed us, and some were even nice to us, but, regardless, I usually stayed awake all night, frightened, my imagination running wild, as I waited for daybreak so I could escape.

My parents eventually gave up. We gladly took our few belongings from the room, and my father immediately put the "Room for Rent" sign back up.

My mother reminded us that whoever moved in now, it would be our fault.

PLAN B

by Ivanka Di Felice

MY MOM HAD VISION, AND no matter what situation she found herself in, if things didn't work out, she imagined a Plan B, as vivid to her as reality. Her dreams had already led her to faraway places. Only half of her dreams needed to be true; the other half she could invent.

Because things were unfortunately not working out with my father, she would need a Plan B. Yet at thirty-three years of age, with four children, eight to fourteen, with very little money, and with her experiences in life, a pleasant Plan B was far harder to imagine than in her youthful days. Hopefully, she could dig down deep to find that same vigor and optimism about better days ahead, which she had once believed in.

So, after sixteen years of marriage, my parents planned to separate. Each assumed the divorce would be easier if some "dirt" could be dug up on the other party—or, at the very least, the divorce would be far more interesting. My mother became a private investigator and not a very good one, partnering with a housewife from around the corner. They disguised themselves and drove around for hours, chatting away, assuming they were in stealth mode, yet all the while my father was completely aware of what they were up to.

My father, conversely, thought himself more clever, because his spying did not require leaving the comfort of his home, being cooped up in a car for hours, or expensive gas bills. He had the phone bugged. Yet after taping hours of costly recordings, all he learned was that Vesna was enchanted by the echo the phone currently made and would pick it up and hum into it for hours, on occasion changing the tone.

He also discovered that my mom possessed never-ending patience, as she listened to an elderly lady recant hours of uninteresting gossip. Worse yet, this woman was a modern day Norma Desmond, of *Sunset Boulevard*, and lived in the past. Hence, she reminisced and described bygone events in terrifying detail, making it sheer torture for my father to sit through hours of the minutia of her life.

When my mom's amateur investigations didn't succeed in catching my dad *in flagrante delicto*, she then spent a small fortune to hire a professional. She had enough money to hire the private detective only for a weekend but felt that if my dad were doing any wining or dining, it would be then.

Meanwhile, my dad's hours of listening to the minutia of the elderly lady's life paid off, because my mom had hired the detective and made all of the arrangements over the phone. So that weekend, my father got dressed up, and, though he wasn't in the habit of going downtown, he went, figuring he would make the detective work for his money. He made himself very obvious and cruised from bar to bar, and when he thought my mom had gotten her money's worth—time-wise, at least—at 2 a.m., he drove back home.

My poor parents. They'd had a lot going against them from the start. The happy endings of the many books my mother read were not her reality. Had she stuck with learning her life lessons from operas, she would have been more

103

prepared for the difficulties and tragedies of existence. To top it off, so many people were living vicariously through my mother that she feared disappointing them, as well as herself.

My father kept the house and the tenants and handed over an agreed-on amount of money to my mother. She made do. My father was heartbroken that my mom would take all four of us. He had hoped that the children could be split up like assets, so he asked for two, leaving my mother two. His lawyer wisely instructed him that judges usually don't break up children, thus my father dropped his case, and the four of us went to live with my mom. We were all saddened to leave my dad, our neighborhood, and our childhood home, despite all of the eccentric tenants.

My mother found a small house and made a deal with the real estate gods to give it to her for what she could afford. They heard her prayers, and soon this little house, one and a half stories, high up on a hill, was ours.

Our lack of funds taught us new endeavors; thus my mom, and her four children, ages eight to fourteen, learned but never quite mastered how to assemble and stain furniture, deliver catalogues in the harsh winters, and love the bright red shag carpet that came with the house. We learned to duck under the low ceilings in the two bedrooms in the attic, and if we occasionally forgot, we quickly remembered when our heads hit with a loud thud.

Moving to this neighborhood—far northern High Park, as it might be termed by zealous real estate agents—also taught us another valuable life lesson: how to be poor in a *poor* neighborhood. Some of my classmates had even less than we did. Although I felt embarrassed to be the only one of my old neighborhood friends whose parents were separated, living here introduced me to the concept that children of the same family could have different fathers. While our new area did not boast a large park or quaint shops, it did have its own "conveniences": quick and easy access to an arsenal of drugs and weapons, as well as a fine furniture shop that was curiously manned by half a dozen fellows playing cards.

My mother had never learned to drive. She had attempted it, but after a few erroneous turns that put her going west in an eastbound lane on the highway, my father ended his career as a terrible driving instructor and hers as an equally bad student.

She still worked in High Park, and when she rode the bus home, she cried to leave the stately homes with towering trees, as the bus weaved farther north into our new neighborhood. Growing up poor, we had always tried to believe that riches did not bring true happiness, but even the Bible said, "Give me neither poverty nor riches." Regardless, after riding past the elegant homes of High Park and arriving at our little house, with the "relative peace" one had with four children inside, she was nonetheless grateful.

Despite the problems between them, my mom always remained civil to my dad and encouraged us to visit him on the weekends. I thought it was kind of her, but now I suspect she may have wanted a break from four rambunctious children.

We could also visit my dad during the week, even on school nights. On one occasion he called, saying he'd had a bad dream. I hadn't known my father was superstitious, but he must have been, because he asked my mom to please send him the children to care for. This dream had indicated something bad was about to happen. Not convinced of such things herself, but probably wanting a well-deserved break, my mom had my dad pick us up.

Later, while my dad was inside the house, we ran loose outside, playing hide-and-seek in the neighborhood with our old friends. Suddenly, a gate opened and a pit bull charged at us. We all ran, but Kathy, being the youngest and slowest, got caught in the grips of the dog. We tried to get him off her, but he wouldn't let go, ripping the flesh on her legs.

Our screaming attracted the owner, who came out and accused us of teasing the dog, all while Kathy lay bleeding on the sidewalk. She needed thirty-six stitches. My poor dad felt awful, but he consoled himself with the idea that perhaps something worse would have happened to us had we stayed at my mom's.

To supplement her income from what my father gave her and from working as a hairdresser/psychologist (that is, lending a sympathetic ear to customers with their own problems), my mother rented out our basement. While the tenants in our last home walked or staggered up the impressive staircase, here the ceilings were extremely low, with ducts and doorways you had to stoop under. Thus, my mother was surprised when a tall man not only answered the ad, but subsequently rented the apartment.

We soon discovered that he and the tenants at my dad's house were kindred spirits, whose main objective in life was to drink. He boasted that he loved music and was musically inclined. Our vision of him listening to the sweet sound of classical music abruptly ended, when he unpacked his drum set and spread it across the entire kitchen.

As he pounded away at the drums, it became brutally obvious that our house lacked good insulation between floors, and that this lone man could make more noise than four boisterous children. Thankfully, a tall man, regularly drunk, in a basement with low ceilings and jutting ductwork, was not a good combination, and he eventually moved out—while he still could.

My mom realized it was time to screen her tenants more thoroughly. She ensured that the next tenant did not drink or smoke, hence we felt substantially more at ease with him—until we noticed that he never went anywhere without a large gym bag, and that concealed inside this bag was a large machete. We discovered this when we came home to find a pile of trees chopped down and his trusty machete bringing down the last beloved one.

He felt our house would be "safer" with no trees around. As he put the machete back into his gym bag, we tried to come up with various "reasonable explanations" one might have for carrying a large hatchet-like knife. Yet he soon provided the answer for us, when he explained the finesse required to chop off a head in one easy blow.

He shared this "classified information" with me because we needed to be open with each other—since, after all, I was his girlfriend.

"What do you mean, I'm your girlfriend? We're not dating," I said.

"Yes, we are. We're dating telepathically," he said.

My mom's life finally resembled a novel, only this time a thriller.

I had to move out of the house for a while, until he left and my mother devised a better screening process.

One would assume that my mom would give up on tenants, but economics dictated she could not, and she still believed in mankind. So she took out another ad in the newspaper, hoping a woman would call. However, only men responded to the ad, so she had no choice but to agree to let a man with a thick Spanish accent come and see the basement "apartment" for rent. She figured he was probably South American and hence most likely not tall, so he might not kill himself on the protruding ducts.

Soon thereafter, a Spanish god walked up the many stairs to our house. He had piercing blue eyes and longish, dark curly hair. His chiseled features completed his model-like appearance. He was unlike any tenant we had ever seen.

Although my mother usually had us wait upstairs and be quiet when prospective tenants arrived, this time the four of us wanted to see this man, so we came down and introduced ourselves. He was even more handsome close up. We could have gotten used to a tenant like this.

We were on our best behavior and pointed out features of the house that my mom might not have mentioned: how the ancient, somewhat crumbling shower that resembled a cave could accommodate four people, bathing at once. Or how the large protruding duct, which sneakily awaited at the bottom of the landing, potentially decapitating someone, was not that hard to get used to, as long as you were careful and sober.

Despite meeting us four children, who couldn't stop talking at once and who would be living above him, and although he was told that the hallway separating his kitchen and bedroom led to the mutual laundry room, he still, miraculously, took the place.

He was handsome, nice, and had a gentle manner. The only peculiar flaw we could detect was that he willingly moved in with us and into our neighborhood. This, in itself, raised suspicions. Was he a convict on the run? Was he evading a jealous, hot-tempered Latin ex-girlfriend? If so, our basement would be the perfect place to hide and was ideal if one ever needed a shower for four.

We discovered he had a job and wasn't home most of the time, which perhaps made living below us far easier.

"MAHNA MAHNA"

by Ivanka Di Felice

WE SOON MET A FAMILY who lived a few homes north of us. They had a small bungalow, with no tenants, and Ed worked as an executive at Esso, while his wife, Alice, was a stay-at-home mom. They had one daughter left at home, Lesley, who was two years younger than Vesna and one year older than Kathy. She could be friends with both of them.

We were fascinated by this family, and they were equally fascinated by us. Alice affectionately referred to us as the Gypsy Kings. Their lives revolved around structure, whereas we did not know the meaning of the word. Lesley had her own bedroom and, something unheard of to us, a bedtime. They had what appeared to be peculiar rules: Lesley had to come in at a precise time, and everyone ate meals together, around a table. Even more preposterous, Lesley had to excuse herself if she got up. Despite this regimen, I liked this family and longed to live like them, while their daughter longed to live like us.

Though Alice had raised Lesley to be prim and proper, she loved it when we weren't. Vesna would drop in, open their fridge, and yell, "Alice, what you got to eat?" Lesley would

109

have been grounded for a week had she done that at someone else's home. She knew it, and so did we.

Because of Vesna's size and the shape of her legs, she often got teased, but she was tough. After school, she went over to Ed and Alice's and proudly reported, "I hit a boy right in the mouth today in the schoolyard."

Alice, rather shocked, asked, "What happened?"

Vesna explained that the boy was making fun of her, so she made a fist, ran up to him with her arm stretched out, and planted her fist on his mouth. He never made fun of her again, nor did any other boys dare to, either. Lesley would have been grounded for life, but they laughed it off because it was Vesna.

They took us under their wing, often had us over for dinner, and drove us everywhere. One evening they introduced Kathy to a buffet restaurant. With wide eyes, she looked at the endless selection of food. Unable to decide, she took a bit of everything. Her plate was piled high by the time she returned to the table. Her eyes, though, proved bigger than her stomach, for after sampling a bit of each item, she could eat no more. She stood up and went back to the buffet. She walked back and forth, searching for the spot she had taken each item from, and scraped the remainder off her plate back into its bowl.

By the time Ed and Alice realized what was happening, Kathy had returned to the table with her empty plate. Lectures my father had given us about children starving in Africa evidently had made an impact on her. Meanwhile, Ed and Alice paid the bill in a hurry and snuck out of the restaurant.

Whenever they drove us anywhere, for the first few years, we all fit into one car. The three of them were in the front, with the five of us in the back. Seatbelts for children were apparently optional during this period. As they pulled up to our house, we all quickly hopped out of the car and inevitably left a virtual wardrobe of possessions littering the back seat.

On reaching home and discovering this, Ed had to drive back down the street, and we ran down the steps to gather our things.

Then Ed devised a plan. As he pulled up to our house, he put on a recording that said, "We are approaching the runway and soon landing. Please remain in your seats till we come to a complete stop. Before disembarking, please look around and take all of your belongings as you leave. Thanks for flying Ed's Travel."

This worked, and we left behind only a quarter of the junk we normally did.

Ed owned an eight-track system and always played the song "Mahna Mahna" from *The Muppet Show*. Alice had a beautiful voice and loved opera music but proved to be a good sport, as she lowered her standards, joining us to belt out the tune at the top of our lungs. With the car windows open, we were so noisy that everywhere we went, people stared to see where the racket was coming from. We loved to see onlookers' astonished faces when they saw this rambling blue car, full to the brim with happy children and adults, singing away. As we got older, Ed and Alice used two cars to accommodate all of us. To this day, I appreciate the love and care they showed us.

Ed provided very efficient directory assistance. Instead of paying for this service, we called Ed to ask for the phone number of a mutual friend. By the following day, we would have lost it and had to telephone Ed again.

"I gave it to you yesterday," he said.

"I lost it," was our obvious reply.

They never could understand our modus operandi or, rather, lack of one.

Though my mom was a single mother, barely scraping by with a mortgage and four children, she never took people's kindness and generosity for granted. She cut their hair (albeit not always in the styles they asked for) and, in her little time off, transformed her kitchen into a factory to make cabbage rolls by the dozens, stuffed peppers, homemade cheese or apple strudel, and other Croatian delicacies. She then delivered them to neighbors and friends. If anyone asked for a recipe, she could never provide one, because each time she made it differently.

This made Alice chuckle, for even in this area our families differed. Alice followed her printed recipes to a tee, whereas my mother used a pinch of this and a big dash of that. In general, my mom's motto, when it came to cooking, was "more is more," but her meals were always tasty and greatly appreciated.

She believed and lived the concept that "there is more happiness in giving than in receiving," and she gave to others whether they had far more or far less than us. It worked. Although she never gave to get back, somehow it played out that way, and everyone felt richer for it.

So many wonderful people, despite their orderly and organized ways, weaved their way into our lives and we into theirs. I suppose another family, the Daveys, to this day wonder how we not only weaseled our way into their lives but became the best of friends.

I don't know whether the "opposites attract" theory applies to friendships, but if there ever were an "odd couple" of friendships, then ours with the Davey family would be it.

We were from the Balkans, which had started two world wars. They were from Switzerland, synonymous with neutrality, nor had it been involved in military conflict for two hundred years.

They lived by rules, and we lived to break them.

They made their beds every morning, while we waited for special occasions to make ours, such as when expecting guests. They washed their dishes after every meal, while we felt there was no need to wash them more than once a day.

They were organized, and my mom could not even spell *organized*.

They were private, and we were not. We believed that only serial killers might want to keep a secret or two.

They were quiet about money, and we openly spoke of how we had none.

Yet somehow they adopted us and one day even bravely asked a single mom with four rowdy children to their beloved cottage.

This proved to be a "vacation" unlike any they'd ever had before. As they sat peacefully with my mom, attempting to read a book by the fire and discuss Victorian times, we kids got into a boisterous wrestling match on the nearby couch. The Daveys nevertheless managed to keep an imminent heart attack at bay.

In the end, we discovered they were far more resilient than we'd ever imagined, for they kept inviting us over and they kept surviving—admittedly, if only barely.

In many ways, life couldn't have been better—nor, despite being relatively poor, could we have been any happier.

"Weeping for Joy"

by Ivanka Di Felice

IT HAD RAINED ALL NIGHT, and Saturday morning we heard a knock at our side door. Carlos's gentle voice alerted my mom that "There is a bit of water on the floor."

My mother had never dealt with home repair problems at our old house on High Park; my dad did all of that. Nonetheless, she assured Carlos, "I'm on my way down. I'm getting a mop."

"Okay," Carlos said, in his usual mild manner. His smile must have confirmed that he was pleased to have dispensed of the body with no one the wiser.

On entering the basement, my mother immediately realized she needed rubber boots and waders, rather than a mop and a pail. Water had flooded the basement, ankle deep.

Despite her limited knowledge of plumbing, my mom realized something was seriously wrong. Being on top of a hill and climbing all of those stairs each day should have had its privileges; water should have run down the hill, not down into her basement. Worse, she feared the solution might be very expensive. She had spent all of the money my dad had given her, placing as much of a down payment as possible on

114

the house, with a bit left for furnishings. She could barely keep up her mortgage payments, so although she hoped it wouldn't be serious, she dreaded that it was.

She called Ed, and he arrived immediately. After much consultation with professionals, it was determined that the weeping tile around the house would need to be replaced. It would be prohibitively expensive, because a ditch had to be dug out.

My mother's mouth dropped, and her expression grew dim, as they discussed her options—all of them very costly.

"Don't worry, we'll figure out something," said Ed.

My mom forced a smile.

Soon thereafter a solution was reached. It would cost my mom a minimal amount for the parts, but the labor would be free. She would just need to provide food for the workers Ed was gathering, who would arrive in a few days to do the work. The food she could do, no problem.

In no time, dozens of men converged on our hill and began digging. The neighbors lent a hand, and a human chain formed to bring all of the materials from the trucks up the many steps. We children joined in, too, not sure whether we were useful or in the way, but the men allowed us to stay and "help."

Inside, my mom had the food factory fully operable. Other women assisted, and everyone practiced "more happiness in giving than in receiving." Everything around the house was dug up; mud was everywhere and on everyone. It was a total disaster but also a beautiful sight.

We didn't know why, but soon thereafter Carlos moved out. Perhaps he feared another flood, or his ex-girlfriend had calmed down (we never did find out whether anything like that were true, but we liked to imagine the intrigue). He restored our faith in tenants—or, at least, he left before anyone discovered the body.

In place of the Spanish god came a short, eccentric Caribbean lady who tried to make the place home. "Home," being Jamaica. She painted the kitchen in bright colors and wallpapered the combination living room/bedroom. She thought "out of the box" as she applied the patterned wallpaper both vertically and diagonally, something previously unbeknownst to designers. She called us down to proudly display her handiwork, and we collectively told our first lie, as we all said it looked great.

She must have longed for her homeland, because she'd attempted to recreate the Caribbean atmosphere with bright plastic flowers and a profusion of hot air, keeping several space heaters running. My mom probably spent more on electricity than she earned in rent.

I suspected the Jamaican woman would have brought home palm trees had the ceiling height allowed. She had a thick accent and "ask" became "ax," so when we children were naughty, we imitated and teased her. Regardless, she eventually became like family to us—albeit, Jamaican family. We learned to live with the smell of curry permeating in the air, which helped us fit in with our classmates at school.

Though she had her peculiarities—we almost never saw her without rollers in her hair—my mother appreciated the fine qualities she possessed of being kind and generous. When she laughed, she did so uncontrollably, patting her hands up and down on her knees. Because Kathy had a penchant for imitating tenants, my mom hoped Kathy would emulate the woman's fine attributes, rather than take to wearing the colors of Jamaica and sponge rollers all day.

OCCUPATIONAL HAZARDS

by Ivanka Di Felice

My mother worked long hours as a hairdresser in the Crossways Mall on Bloor Street, not far from where we had grown up. Each day she bought a coffee at Midway Donuts and chatted with the owner. One day my mom noticed a HELP WANTED sign and inquired about it. After all, I was fourteen, and surely a part-time job would teach me innumerable life skills. More important, the extra money would come in handy.

The discount department store across the aisle from where she worked had also asked whether she knew of anyone seeking employment. They probably didn't have my eleven-year-old sister in mind, who was short for her age, due to her bowed legs, thus looked only about seven—or Steven, who was only a few years older. Perhaps the kids' eager faces convinced the manager, so he hired them. Thus, Vesna and Steven spent their free time before Christmas lugging heavy boxes out of the storeroom, much to the surprise of customers, who up until then had assumed Canada had stringent child labor laws.

Kathy, at the age of eight, perhaps not wanting to feel left out, became "self-employed." One weekend while we were visiting my father, Kathy disappeared. We hadn't really noticed as we played hide-and-seek with our friends from the neighborhood, while Tata attempted to teach Steven chess. But as evening drew closer, we realized Kathy was nowhere to be found.

As we sat on the porch, we saw a small figure coming down the street, who appeared to be carrying a large object. As she approached, we noticed the ratty clothes, the baggy white sweater, and the torn red pants. With matted hair, a clown-like face, round red cheeks having been drawn on, it was as if a tiny clown had become homeless. The object being carried was a large white drum that the child beat with a wooden spoon.

As the clown approached, we were shocked to realize it was Kathy.

"Look how much money I got!" she said.

With great pride, she held out a pouch full of cash and a note that the funds were for poor children. The neighbors in High Park were either naive or sympathetic and generous. Unbeknownst to us, Kathy had spent the afternoon begging from door to door—and apparently it had worked.

This time my parents were a united front, and they took the drum away, insisting she give up her entrepreneurship. They explained that it was both unsafe and wrong to solicit funds in this way. After that, though, I never doubted Kathy would be able to take care of herself, if necessary.

With my mom having already secured work for my younger siblings, and Kathy for herself, I was next. My mother arranged for an interview with Bertha—and the lady lived up to her name. She was a burly, no-nonsense woman who ran an honest business selling coffee, donuts, muffins, and ice cream: no easy feat. She was tall, and her teased hair put her over six feet. Her hands and wrists were twice the size of mine. Though I was only fourteen and had never held a job before, other than being an assistant in Steven's not very successful newspaper delivery scheme, she was willing to give me a chance.

Bertha lived in the same lower-class neighborhood that we did, confirming that one doesn't make a fortune with a business such as hers, so we arranged for her to pick me up at 6:00 a.m. the following Saturday morning.

At 5:30 a.m., when the alarm went off while it was still dark outside, and cold air blew in through the cracks of the windows, I realized that working might not be as much fun as I'd initially thought. For a brief second, I contemplated crawling back into bed. But my cursed, yet vivid imagination pictured what Bertha might do to me if I kept her waiting, and this proved highly motivating.

I got dressed in what I assumed was donut shop attire and went downstairs to wait for Bertha.

My mother had worked full time most of my life, so she hadn't been around much to teach me the basics in a kitchen. I was still scrawny and had large, round eyes that always appeared startled. Once, a friend's father had told me, "Ivanka, you have such big eyes," at which I batted them playfully, as I waited for the remainder of the compliment. He continued, "Like a cow."

I stood next to Bertha, wide-eyed, struggling to grasp all of the instructions. She was training me today, but in a few weeks, I would open the shop on my own.

I was entrusted to prepare the egg salad sandwiches, when suddenly she shrieked. Evidently, Bertha could multitask, because she kept a watchful eye on what I did while she prepared the muffin mix.

"You never put the bread knife back into the mayonnaise. You will contaminate it, and people could get very sick!" She quickly took out the miniscule breadcrumb, as if her quick reflexes had averted a national disaster.

Her customers were apparently more sensitive than my family, because we had been "contaminating the mayo" for years. By the time the mayonnaise jar at home was half empty, it was speckled with an even ratio of breadcrumbs to mayo.

As she gave me further precise instructions, it occurred to me that Bertha must have had some military training. Everything had an order, a system, a label, and a rule. Based on everything I was doing wrong, my family should have been dead years ago. I wondered whether someone like me, one of four children who were nicknamed the Gypsy Kings and who had a "five-second rule" when things fell on the floor, could live up to Bertha's exacting standards. After catching several more of my culinary infractions, Bertha must have wondered the same. I feared this might be the end of her charity work, but perhaps Bertha felt sorry for my mom, knowing we needed the extra money, so she kept me on.

Aside from trying not to poison and consequently kill the customers, I would be entrusted with other intimidating things, such as a key. Apparently, it could not be left under a planter in the mall. I would have to remember to take it with me and then, when needed, to find it. I'd never grown up with keys. With all of those tenants, we furiously rang the doorbell until someone staggered up or down the steps and opened the door. A key was never needed, only patience on occasion.

Bertha explained the process, and soon it was time to open the security roller shutters. I waited in the background as she greeted the first customer. She poured the coffee and handed the man a donut, then collected his funds. She carefully counted the change before handing it to him.

After I went through several more weeks of boot camp, Bertha either felt I was ready to open on my own or else she couldn't bear to spend another day with me, the one-person food-wrecking crew.

On Saturday morning, I rode my bike the several miles from our house to the donut shop in the Crossways Mall. This strange plaza had all of the makings of a good mall: a prominent location, free parking, a grocery store, and two tall buildings above it. It should have been thriving, but all of the stores hung on by a thread. In North America, it's actually a feat to have an unsuccessful mall, and this one proved it could be done.

My customers were mostly older people who lived in the bachelor apartments above and spent a good part of their day wandering the mall, making small talk with merchants. Many of the women had their hair done each week by my mom (and had been getting the same hairstyle for the last fifty years), so they stopped by to pick up a coffee for her and confide their latest ailments to me. I learned a lot about rheumatoid arthritis at fourteen. My large eyes always appeared empathetic to their plight; hence, they usually left me a tip.

I tried hard to remember everything Bertha had taught me, and I don't believe I poisoned anyone. I got to take home the day-old donuts, as well as any sandwiches that hadn't been sold. Some didn't look so appealing by closing time, though. Most normal people would have chucked them, but we ate them, proving that everyone in our family had a stomach like a catfish and could digest anything.

To celebrate my job, after both of us finished work, my mother took me to the one classy restaurant in the mall. I was awed by it and by its prices. Whenever we had eaten out in the past, it was at greasy spoons or McDonald's, and we usually shared two plates of food between four children. But here we were, the two of us, each with her own menu, and my mother was so proud. Being here somehow made her feel as if "we had made it."

She insisted I order the fillet mignon, but as my eyes followed the dots leading to the price, I couldn't. She was adamant, but instead of examining the food items on the left, I stared at the prices on the right. I ordered the second cheapest thing on the menu, and to this day I regret it. It would have meant a lot to my mom had I ordered the most expensive meal. It would have confirmed that we were doing all right and that everything would be okay.

On receiving my first official paycheck at fourteen, I understood the satisfaction of work—or, at least, the satisfaction of being paid. The following Thursday, I skipped school and went to the Eatons' red balloon day sale with Alice. Everything was marked an additional 50 percent off already deeply discounted prices. I joined the buying frenzy and spent my entire pay on clothes for my family.

Returning home with large shopping bags filled with garments and shoes, much to the delight of my mom and siblings, I was certain I would be able to master bringing the key with me and to avoid contaminating the mayonnaise.

"EVERYTHING IS UNDER CONTROL"

by Ivanka Di Felice

WE FOUR CHILDREN STOOD VIGIL. As cars approached, one of us ran up the many steps to advise mom that our ride was coming. A silver car slowed, almost undetected with its well-tuned engine. We assumed it was Kevin, driving the "new car" he had recently bought. But alas, as the car drove away, we realized we had induced the driver's lingering, as he stared at four children and enough camping gear and food to make it appear as if we had been evicted and our belongings thrown down the stairs after us.

The four of us sat on the railing like birds on a power line. After a long while, we began playing, twisting, and jumping down each time a car slowed. If Kevin didn't show up soon, one of us would break an arm or a leg falling off our perch. Because we didn't have a car and relied on others for rides, my mother insisted we be ready on time and never keep our chauffeur waiting. So we had woken up hours earlier, lugged all of our gear down the steps, and waited, while my mother, not a morning person, had another coffee, hoping she would soon come out of her zombie-like state.

A group of friends had planned to go camping on a national park island, Beausoleil. Kevin, an old family friend in his early twenties, had offered to drive us. For a man that age to offer to drive a woman and her four children on a two-hour trip, either he was a really good person, or he had done something very bad and believed in hell. As the hours passed and car after car approached, slowing to peer at us nearly crazed children and then speeding off, we realize that punctuality was not a trait possessed by all people, nor was a telephone.

Just as my mother polished off the last cup of coffee, herself now somewhat crazed, and we had given up hope, we heard clanging in the distance. An old Dodge Ram van approached, and as it came closer, it grew louder. We saw Kevin behind the large wheel. Hope was now overtaken by despair. Kevin exited the bright-blue van with a matching blue baseball cap, and the rest of his outfit showed his optimism that people would mistake eccentricity for genius.

"Sorry I'm late. I was trying to find some seats for the van," Kevin nonchalantly said. In my limited knowledge of vehicles that transport people, seats had never before been optional. The van had no windows on the side, so Kevin proudly swung open the back doors as if showing off a valuable prize on *The Price Is Right.*

The open doors revealed several colorful woven web lawn chairs, tied together with a rope, for safety. The lawn chairs looked as if he had discovered them in a dumpster, and I worried about their fitness even on stable ground, never mind with Kevin at the wheel. For additional seating, a wooden bench leaned against the side. If my mother was tired of having four children, this was her chance to rid herself of some of us.

Kevin, like most other twenty-year-olds, was invincible and felt we were as well, because he ignored my mom's—and

Safety Canada's—seemingly unfounded standards and loaded up the van. As we sat on the patio furniture, as usual, my eyes conveyed extreme fear, but the other three children were ready to embark on our adventure. Thankfully, my mother had packed far too many supplies, and in case of an accident, we would be cushioned by sleeping bags and packages of pasta.

As Kevin drove maniacally, we discerned that similar to seats, the front and back suspension was also unnecessary. As the rain poured down, we discovered another standard feature Kevin had overlooked: the defroster. Kevin, a genius in his own mind, having been forewarned, was forearmed and handed each of us a rag to mop down the windows. He recommended that breathing and talking be kept to a minimum.

The only components that proved trustworthy on the van were its brakes, as Kevin took a curve at an unmentionable speed. We swerved and came to a crashing halt as he slammed on the brakes. The chairs almost fell over, testing the resilience of the ropes. Despite our fear, we survived relatively unscathed.

Kevin, meanwhile, exited the van, inspected it for damage, and said, "Don't worry, everyone, the van is okay." He remained a hero in his own mind.

The plummeting gas gauge was in working order; thus, we stopped along the highway to fill up. My mom insisted on paying, despite the gas tank being bottomless. My mother was always very generous and appreciative, even to people putting her and her children's lives in jeopardy.

Undeterred by Kevin's driving, we pulled into Honey Harbour, a small community on the southeastern shores of Georgian Bay. We would rent a boat on the mainland and venture across the open waters of Georgian Bay until we reached Beausoleil Island, to meet up with the rest of our friends. We entered the marina, and if the van could have had a twin in the form of a boat, then we had just rented it.

As we unloaded the contents of the van and transferred them into this motorized rowboat, I wondered how many times we could tempt fate today. We'd packed the boat above its maximum limit, and once we all got on board, only a few inches of the boat remained above water. We chugged away from the dock to the astounded stares of onlookers, who likely assumed our remains would never be found.

Kevin proceeded slowly, and as long as we didn't encounter a single ripple, we would probably make it across the open body of water and onto the island. We felt important exchanging waves with distinguished fellow boaters who sped past us in their fancy boats.

As their wakes reached us and we almost toppled over, we decided to steer clear of other boats, and Kevin headed toward open water. Thankfully, before we got very far, our engine started to protest. Since acquiring the van, Kevin had apparently become immune to clanking sounds, but we knew this wasn't a good sign. As we headed out, the waters became rougher, and a wave gushed over the side and into the boat.

Kevin once again proved unconquerable, as he handed us metal cups from the dish set and ordered us to bail. We faithfully scooped water out of the boat, as Kevin kept aiming for open water. Thankfully, however, the engine had our best interests at heart, because it discharged a final few coughs, gasped, and died. I imagined our end would be the same.

Kevin frantically pulled the rope, but the engine was adamant it was time to return to safety. After several more tries, he grew convinced the motor had broken down. He now made his way to the middle of the boat, grabbed hold of the oars, and started rowing, while we continued to bail.

After a long while, we reached the shore. Despite the marina being closed, Kevin hadn't lost hope. He removed the engine, and he and Steven carried it to a nearby picnic table. After several hours, Kevin felt confident, because he'd managed to take the motor apart.

Though not mechanically inclined, I knew that it took virtually no skill to disassemble something; the difficulty lay in putting it back together in working order. As the pieces remained strewn across the table, it was apparent Kevin had only the first set of skills. I wondered how the community would react to find our tent pitched on their public beach in the morning.

"Don't worry, everything is under control," Kevin said with the confidence that only someone delusional could possess in this situation.

A man emerged from a nearby house. He looked at us, the boat, and the motor and probably wondered when gypsies had taken up camping in the Canadian north. Perhaps he didn't want the likes of us staying on their beach, or he was a very kind person. Regardless, being experienced with boats and motors, he helped us put ours back together.

As he reassembled the engine, he let Kevin in on an important detail—the cause of our problem, in fact: "Always ensure the gas line is completely attached to the tank."

He pushed our boat back out into the lake, and we all waved goodbye.

As we headed into the treacherous open waters, Kevin handed us our bailing cups and triumphantly said, "See, I told you everything is under control."

We arrived at the island and set up the tent. It wasn't standing exactly straight, and though we had many pegs, poles, and strings left over, Kevin insisted they were extras.

Italy had the leaning tower of Pisa, and Italians felt proud of it, I thought, anxiously looking at our tent. It was standing, but not a breath of wind stirred that night.

As we drank our smoked coffee, we realized we had nothing that would make us successful campers. No hatchet, Coleman stove, lantern, bug spray, or other articles smart campers displayed that I didn't even know the names of. Yet somehow we survived, and, thankfully, there was still no wind to test the tent.

We spent the day swimming on the other side of the island. When we returned, we saw from afar a peculiar boat that resembled a small, old battered army ship—another marine equivalent of Kevin's van. It had docked close to the playground, and behind the swings, the monkey bars, and the slides was a field with a group of about twenty-five men playing soccer.

A sandpiper had a nest in a clump of tall grass by the playing field, and the soccer ball almost landed on it. The sandpiper attempted to protect its young by flailing its wings and limping away from the nest, but the men paid no attention. In contrast, most visitors to the island were so eco-friendly that they would avoid stepping on a rattlesnake, not because it might bite them, but so they didn't hurt it.

My mom's motherly instinct of protecting the young kicked in, and she marched into the middle of the soccer field, demanding that the men stop playing so close to the bird's nest.

A tall man nonchalantly replied, "We cannot move. We were told to play right here."

"That was before you saw the bird, but now you have to move, or I will call the warden," said my mom.

"The warden is the one who told us to play here," he said.

A short, scruffy guy joined us and announced, "You don't understand, lady. We are crazy."

"Crazy or not, you're causing distress to the bird."

At which point, we wondered whether my mom was crazy. To help her appreciate what type of crazy, the short man gestured as if slashing a knife against his own neck, while smiling at his cleverness. The rest of the group approached, while a man in a uniform tapped my mom's shoulder and motioned for her to turn around slowly and follow him. Then, suddenly, lots of uniformed men closed in on the soccer players.

The warden explained that the men were inmates from the Penetanguishine asylum for the criminally insane and that mom was fortunate not to have provoked a hostage situation.

The guards formed a corridor, and the convicts boarded their sad ship. Four speedboats guarded the vessel as it left, one on each side and two behind.

It seemed that no matter where we went, each house we lived in, or even which vacation we took, we couldn't escape being surrounded by mentally ill characters or criminals.

Today alone, we'd escaped near capsizing and being taken hostage by the criminally insane. As a strong wind began to gather, we hoped for miracle number three: that our tent would remain standing.

A Man's Shed Is His Castle

by Ivanka Di Felice

At sixteen, Steven wanted to get a motorcycle. My mother feared for Steven's safety, as much as she feared going crazy with worry each time he was a minute late. Hence, she maintained an adamant "No."

But Stephen had divorced parents, a little ingenuity, and an inherited "Plan B" gene from his mom, so, because she continued her objections to his getting a motorcycle, Steven stopped begging her and instead begged my father. My mother encouraged a united front, but divorce was complicated. Having his son come back to live with him was something my father wanted, even if it meant allowing the boy to get a motorcycle, thus giving my father sleepless nights.

Steven moved back in with my father, into the bedroom that at one time had formed part of an impressive front hallway but that drywall and determination to make a buck had transformed into a room. The four of us used to sleep there, so Steven, now alone in the room, must have felt like a king.

My father still had the habit of bringing home people to live in the house, much in the way others brought in stray

130

pets. But my father never asked, "Can I keep him?" He just did.

My father met Mirko in the park where older men liked to gather around and play chess. Minutes after he'd met Mirko, my dad knew that the man could not tell the difference between a pawn and a king but hung out at the chess club only to get the latest Croatian gossip and politics.

Mirko seemed to suffer from attention deficit disorder, because he couldn't finish a sentence without even interrupting *himself*. It was as if he played all of the characters at a cocktail party where everyone shared his syndrome and was on speed. As the jug of wine emptied, Mirko began speaking in two languages, at an ever more dizzying pace. Under the influence of strong homemade wine, my father found Mirko amusing.

Mirko epitomized the Croatian proverb *Djeca, budale i pijani pravdu govore* ("Children, fools, and drunken men tell the truth"). On this occasion, he fell into two categories, as he elaborated on his mostly accurate but not politically correct opinions of everyone and everything. Like my father, Mirko never referred to anyone by his or her given name, and the entire evening's conversation took place in code.

"Fatso regrets she married Stingy. She may have been better off with Wrinkly. Skunk says . . ."

Mirko spoke faster by the glass, discussing a sorry group of people: not one had a complimentary nickname.

The jug of wine completely empty, the two men tottered out to the backyard shed, where my father kept the remainder of last year's wine and a new batch brewing in large barrels.

This ten-foot by eight-foot structure used to be a playhouse where we four children spent many a joyful hour, back when children needed very little to amuse them and make them happy. It was equipped with bunk beds, and a small table with a bench on either side served as our kitchen, where we pretended to dish up lunch. Ironically, we were the envy of the rich children in the neighborhood.

The playhouse had been converted to a shed, reinforced like a fortress. Bars had been added to the windows, so no one would steal the wine. My father and Mirko returned with more alcohol, and one assumed their purpose for going to the shed had been accomplished.

"So, one hundred dollars will be okay?" my dad asked.

"Yes, that's fine," said Mirko.

Anyone placing bets on what cost a hundred dollars would have lost his shirt. My father's mission in visiting the shed was twofold: to procure more wine for them, and also to show his client his rental quarters. Having run out of rooms to let, my father had agreed to rent Mirko the shed. The price was undeniably a bargain—for one hundred dollars, he had electricity and a heater to keep him alive in the minus 22-degree Fahrenheit weather.

The fact that Mirko was willing and able to move into the shed quickly did not faze my dad. And indeed, a few days later, Mirko, who was also known as Sheriff, showed up with a couple of small bags and happily moved in. We told my father the neighbors might not appreciate a man living in a shed in the backyard, but he replied, "I don't care what Raccoon thinks."

That neighbor, too, had been re-christened.

Many a warning was sounded that it might not be safe for Mirko to sleep in a small shed surrounded by vats of fermenting wine, but Mirko proved modern science wrong. Though the wine was horribly bad that year, Mirko devised a method to drink it: by plugging his nose, he found it tolerable. Indeed, he was resilient.

The shed was multifunctional: it served as Mirko's living quarters, it functioned as a cantina where the wine brewed and was then kept, and it also housed barrels of fermenting cabbage. My mother had barely survived her wedding night surrounded by sauerkraut. Meanwhile, each night Mirko wrestled his way in between several bulky barrels of it to get to his bed. He must have been irresistible to elderly Eastern European women, because he reeked of eau de sauerkraut.

My father allowed Mirko to use his kitchen, and Mirko's culinary skills proved limited. Almost every evening, he cracked a dozen eggs into a big pot of sizzling oil, then added sausages and onions. When the concoction was cooked, he added a loaf of bread torn into pieces. To save on dishwashing, Mirko ate directly out of the pot. He truly was indestructible and, defying cholesterol findings, could have been a poster boy for the egg producers of Ontario.

On occasion, he made polenta, whipping up a batch with plenty of sausage for his neighbors, the sparrows outside, for their dining pleasure. He placed the mound of cornmeal outside the door to the shed, proving that the neighborhood sparrows were also indestructible.

One-eyed Roger had been one of our longest tenants. He never seemed to age, perhaps because he already looked eighty at sixty. Mirko despised him and his lurking. Mirko had his flaws, but he was generous, always offering his beer, wine, and food. The beer and the wine, we would accept on occasion; the food, we knew better.

Roger was the opposite, embodying every joke ever made about cheap people. It became Mirko's personal mission to protect my father from Roger, and Mirko came up with several aliases for Roger—none, of course, flattering.

However, Mirko was amusing only if one was under the influence. On the days when my father didn't drink, Mirko's hyperactive personality drove him mad, inspiring my father to rename Mirko. Hence, he became *Šašavi, Munjeni, Ludi,* and *Blesavi,* proving that Croatians have a rich vocabulary when it comes to words for "crazy."

Some evenings Mirko would chat and shadow anyone in the house who would listen, but just as often, he called it an early night and headed out to his blistering cold lair.

My sisters and I worried about finding Mirko frozen to death and the subsequent predicament of explaining unclaimed rental income to Revenue Canada. Yet both he and my father paid no heed. My father's only dilemma arose when he was required to fill out a census form and wasn't sure whether to add Mirko as a person "living in the house."

Although I thought Mirko might have been going through a little slumming phase, he proved me wrong, because he rented the shed for five years. During that time, he ate more than ten thousand eggs, drank copious amounts of undrinkable wine, rechristened everyone he came into contact with, and, miraculously, survived. I hope he left his body to science. Or perhaps the Croatian adage was true, after all: "God looks after drunks and children."

We finally convinced my dad that it might not be kosher to have someone living in his shed, and he moved Mirko into the house. I wasn't sure which was more painful for my dad: giving up the income from the shed or having Mirko rent the room adjacent to his.

We knew that Steven found the latter more painful.

Two Kids in Casts

by Ivanka Di Felice

IN MY OLD NEIGHBORHOOD, AND Steven's current one, the two-month school vacation during the summer was for lounging on the dock at the cottage; going to camp, where one swam or rode horses; or having parents as one's personal chauffeurs, as one signed up for a host of in-vogue sports.

Yet that was for the children who grew up in the single-family homes around us. We had no summer cottage, and the only time we rode horses on school trips, Steven ended up on a mount named Psycho. Though my horse had a more docile name, he proved just as crazy. At least, after that, we no longer dreamed of going to horseback-riding camp. Any sports we were involved in had to be played in our backyard or someplace we could get to on foot. There were no parents driving us around; there were, in fact, no parents around.

This summer, though, my father got Steven a job at the factory where he worked as a maintenance mechanic. My father was brilliant when it came to machinery. He could repair anything and spent much time fixing things in other people's homes, while my entire childhood he promised my mother he would eventually get to the broken items in our house.

Steven worked diligently all summer. After all, he now had a motorcycle to maintain and pay off. Even after he stayed out late, he woke early the next morning to go with my father to the plant that made binders, notebooks, and other school supplies. We thought that perhaps working hard in a factory would also encourage him to do better in school. He spent some money and saved some.

Vesna went into the hospital at fifteen to have surgery to correct her bowed legs. She would have them broken below the knee, then reset. She was used to doctors and hospitals. As a young child, she often went to medical conferences, where they had her strip down to her underwear and stand in front of hundreds of students, while experts explained her condition.

The operation was successful, and we all went to visit Vesna at Sick Children's Hospital. Everyone bore gifts; friends brought some very elaborate ones. Vesna got her first designer sweater and a Sony Walkman—the surgery was worth it for the gifts alone.

Just before visiting hours ended, Steven came to see her. Charming as ever, he gave her a big kiss and handed her a plastic bag.

"Can you keep this here for me?" he nonchalantly asked, then added, "It's a friend's."

Vesna, assuming it was another gift for her, felt slightly disappointed as she opened the bag to find a handgun in it. Though shocked, she agreed to keep the gun for Steven overnight. Hence, they put it in the middle drawer in her nightstand for safekeeping. To ensure no one would find it, they pushed the gun to the back of the drawer.

Steven gave her a kiss goodnight, and off he went, knowing the gun was safe in Sick Children's Hospital. He promised he would come back the following evening.

The gun sat in the drawer all day, none of us the wiser as we put things in the top drawer, until Steven came after work to pick it up. He casually retrieved it and took it away. It would be his and Vesna's secret for years.

Vesna came home after a few weeks, and her leg was still in a cast when we received a phone call. Steven had been in a motorcycle accident. Alive but badly bruised, he had a broken arm that required surgery. The surgeons pinned and screwed his arm in several places.

After being released from the hospital, Steven came to our house while he healed. My poor mother worked full time and had to care for two of her children in casts, lying in the living room.

When Steven recovered, he returned to my father's house. However, he did not go to work in the factory again, because he counted on getting a significant settlement, due to the accident. With all of that money that would soon be his, why work for minimum wage? The elaborate dreams began; one day maybe he, too, would own a house in High Park, but without tenants.

ALL PAIN, NO GAIN

by Ivanka Di Felice

I HADN'T BEEN ABLE TO get in touch with my friend Mary for several days. She eventually called me back and admitted she was in hiding. She'd had a regrettable session with a home-tanning lamp; she had stayed under it too long but had worn goggles. She said she looked like a masked bandit, her oddly colored tanned face in stark contrast to the white skin under the goggles. I couldn't help but laugh, assuming she must be exaggerating.

I hopped into the now-almost-ten-year-old 1977 Thunderbird my father had gifted me. Not trusting automatic windows, he'd also given me a hammer, "just in case." I drove over to Mary's to survey the damage.

I knocked, and she opened the door slowly, ensuring that no neighbors would see her. I tried not to gasp, for she indeed looked bizarre, her dark tanned face with a white mask around her eyes. She was a pretty girl, but her vanity had made her hideous. It would indeed be sometime before she would go out in public. I visited for a while, trying to avert my eyes from staring at hers.

As I left, she asked, "Do you want the tanning lamp? I am done with it!"

Although she might have been done with tanning lamps, Mary was still faithfully doing the *20 Minute Workout* and had taken to sleeping on the hard floor, ever since she'd heard "sleeping on the floor makes you sexy."

Though months had passed, there was no discernable improvement in Mary's sexiness. As far as I could tell, the only thing that had come of her sleeping on the floor was that her back hurt.

Hence, I had no plans to sleep on the floor. The *20 Minute Workout* always turned into forty minutes for me, because I had to take breaks constantly, fearing an untimely death if I continued. So I would take the focus off my body and put it on my face. The tanning lamp would transform me into the Barbie doll that everyone aspired to look like in the eighties. Being too young to fear things such as cancer, and, like most youths, possessing the dangerous combination of invincibility and vanity, I took the lamp.

"Whatever you do, be careful," Mary said. "You don't want to end up like me."

I didn't want to end up like her, but I was tired of using the tanning products from the drugstore that rendered my face an unusual shade of orange, with my nose several hues darker. I would use her lamp, but I would be cautious. I would leave sleeping on the floor to her.

I read the instructions, and although it warned to always wear protective eyewear during lamp operation, I had seen what happened to Mary, so I skipped this stage. I then used my mathematical skills to determine that if I moved the lamp closer, I wouldn't have to sit under it as long.

I stayed under the lamp the required amount of time, according to my special time-saver formula. Afterward, I got ready for bed, eagerly anticipating seeing myself in the morning, when my transformation would take place. Then I would join the ranks of tanned models, with bystanders assuming I had money to go down south for the winter or skiing in Gstaad.

But alas, in the morning I awoke no taller or any bustier than the night before. Nor did my face appear very tanned. I had little to show for my efforts.

I slowly drove the huge Thunderbird to my father's house, because I believed every moving object on the road was out to get me. Perhaps when you drove a car as big as the Thunderbird, you were justified in believing you would hit something eventually. Size alone dictated it.

With my head only slightly higher than the dashboard, people could confirm that I was alive and had a pulse only when they saw me exiting the car. I stopped at the gas station, as was the custom when driving an 8-cylinder car, and filled up the tank one quarter. When the quarter tank seemingly evaporated, I would park the car—which in itself was a nightmare—and walk the rest of the day. Ironically, those were the good old days. The fleeting moments when we could afford to be driving in the car were magical. When you have very little, you learn to appreciate the things you do receive.

I reached my father's house, and as I got out of the car, my face had a tingling sensation. I attributed this to the cold, bitter wind blowing in Toronto. I found the key in the "secret hiding place" that all tenants and their friends knew about, and I entered the house.

Tata sat in his usual chair in the kitchen with his tenant Mirko. I greeted my dad with the customary double kiss and chatted with them, as my face tingled even more.

My father looked at me, suddenly alarmed, as my face became redder and redder.

Finally, Mirko, asked, "What's happening to your face?"

I ran to examine myself in the mirror. My face had not turned the lovely tan color of models in *Vogue* or the long-haired blondes on television, but instead I resembled an old woman who'd had a lifetime love affair with dodgy whiskey.

My nose was bright red and the rest of my face only a shade less intense. It occurred to me that my hypothesis on tanning lamp times needed refining.

The stinging got worse, and I went to lie down on the couch. I took a piece of frozen meat and placed it on my face. The heat radiated from my face as if from a light bulb. I tried to sleep, but the burning prevented it. Worse, my eyes began to hurt, as if I had glass shards in them.

I felt a presence over me and realized it was my father and Mirko, questioning me about why I looked more leprous by the minute. I remained silent. I wasn't giving up my secret, proving George Sand correct: "Vanity is the quicksand of reason."

My father wouldn't have supported my efforts to improve my God-given looks, and I was in too much pain to endure the lecture that would ensue, as my father shook his head in disbelief and tsk-tsk'ed me. It was never easy for a father to find out he had raised such a stupid child.

I drove myself to the doctor's. By the time I got there, I could barely see, which finally justified my propensity for slow driving.

I had to admit the error of my ways to the doctor who examined me and gave me his diagnosis: "You have burned your face."

He fortunately did not—at least, not verbally—also diagnose me as being dim-witted. I would leave that to my father, my siblings, and my friends. He sent me to an eye doctor down the street, who informed me that I had burned my corneas.

I spent the next few days in bed, with my face beet red and my eyes crusted over and in pain. I dared not call Mary, fearing a lecture from her as well. My vanity had indeed transformed me. I went from being a relatively pretty girl with a white complexion to a madwoman with a bright red one. Yet as Croatians said, "Something good comes out of every bad." I learned the lesson of compassion: I suddenly felt very sorry for poor Mary. I also felt a rekindled love for tanning lotion. Although it left me orange, at least it was painless.

"One Size Fits All"

by Ivanka Di Felice

I HAD BEEN WORKING SINCE I was fourteen and had learned quite a bit at the Donut Shop—such as, butter pecan ice cream had lots of calories, and one couldn't eat unlimited quantities of it, even if it was free.

After that, I went to work for the Bata Shoe Company and discovered that I was very good at sales—rather, I was highly motivated by commissions. It wouldn't take me long to convince Chinese men who wore size 7, a size I had run out of, that a pair of size 9 shoes would fit them equally well, aided by a few apparatuses such as insoles and heel grips. I got commissions on sundries, so customers also left with shoe spray, brushes, and a host of other items they couldn't live without, despite having no intention of purchasing originally. When shoes were too tight, too narrow, or too short, I insisted that they would stretch in no time. Size was no obstacle in selling someone a pair of shoes. I'd mastered the never-before-heard "one size fits all" theory in shoes.

I had to give up my lucrative sales job when I developed a conscience and suddenly felt guilty watching the heels of Chinese men bobbing up and down as they walked across the store, in shoes far too big. Suddenly, squeezing a fat woman's foot into a narrow shoe pained not only her but me, and I realized I was doomed. Why the shipments didn't include more shoes of each size escapes me to this day.

I then went to work for Black's photography shop, where I was trained to print pictures. There I discovered that the people frequenting the Dufferin Mall did not lead very exciting lives. Because there were no "delete picture" options, I was forced to carefully examine entire rolls of babies with faces only mothers could love.

I had always been determined to work hard and earn enough money to have a comfortable life, one that would involve a house without tenants. A brokerage firm downtown was advertising for help in the newspaper, so I applied. I had only finished high school—and that, barely—but I did have lots of nerve and practice selling the unsellable. To boot, I had a very nice dark gray suit. So I put it on and took the subway downtown to the financial district, hoping to convince a prestigious brokerage firm to hire me. I felt that if given a chance, I could prove myself.

I hoped they would never ask to see my high school report card, which would confirm my disdain for typing class or, worse, would reveal that I had quit math after grade 10—though I blamed that on Mr. Yan. I assumed he had been interviewed for the teaching job by another Chinese, because, although he was very enthusiastic, unless you were Chinese you couldn't understand a word he said. When he saw that I had trouble with math, he kindly tutored me after class, going to great lengths to explain geometry. Yet his extra lessons only confirmed that I couldn't understand Chinese, even after school.

Because I'd had so much practice selling things, such as size 9 shoes to people who wore size 7, I managed to talk my way into the job. I would begin in a couple of weeks, filing annual reports and other financial information in the

Research Library on the fiftieth floor of one of the towers downtown.

Though all I did was file all day and work along with two eccentric older ladies, who'd probably been banished there, I felt very important. After all, I was working on Bay Street, albeit hidden in a library with strange characters and no windows—but nonetheless.

I found myself in unfamiliar but familiar circumstances, working among the rich and elite of Toronto, while being anything but.

So, while the other assistants and brokers shopped in downtown boutiques on their lunch hours, I, too, shopped—till I dropped. Literally, as I ran to the Goodwill secondhand clothing store twenty-minutes away. I returned with plain white plastic bags. Thank heavens, Goodwill had the decency not to advertise your poverty on their bags. However, being poor didn't mean not being well dressed. I wore many of the same name brands as did the girls in my office, albeit a few years older and perhaps donated by them or their mothers.

Eventually, I "moved up the corporate ladder" and began working as an assistant to stockbrokers. I learned much at the firm, one important lesson being that money didn't always bring happiness. Or that much younger ex-wives could be referred to as "several hundred thousand dollar experiments."

My boss had his own issues, and though he was very clever financially, he couldn't always control his emotions.

"What do you mean, you cannot have the fax fixed in the next hour?" he would yell into the phone, then add, "I can order one hundred pounds of crack cocaine, and it will be here in fifteen minutes."

He reasoned that the fax repairmen should prove they were more efficient than drug dealers in the city of Toronto. The stunned repairman had to listen to a barrage of mankind's accomplishments over the past century, all supposed to entice him to arrive more quickly.

"We have men on the moon, and the fax machine cannot get fixed in an hour?" My boss sometimes went overboard, when he'd brag, "I can get a nuclear bomb here in an hour."

He lived by "It's easier to ask for forgiveness than for permission," but because he was brilliant financially, everyone eventually forgave him.

I got my sister Vesna a job there as well, and my father was very proud that his children worked on Bay Street. I had to laugh, because I had no doubt he told his donut shop buddies that we were both CEOs of prominent firms downtown.

My boss had a generous side and would lend us his cottage and give us his opera tickets. When he lost his cool, he endeavored to make it up to me by sending me to all of the top restaurants. Courtesy of his lack of self-control, I had dinner at the Hotel Crillion in Paris, at the famous Susur in Toronto, and at several other highly rated establishments. Thankfully, he never figured out that it would be far cheaper to stay calm.

I worked for him for years, testing my patience. My salary was referred to as "danger pay," but as Nietzsche said, "That which does not kill us makes us stronger." I survived those years, if barely, but rarely felt stronger.

"DRIVING MISS ANNA"

by Ivanka Di Felice

THE THUNDERBIRD EVENTUALLY PROVED TOO costly to run; parts began breaking, and I couldn't afford to fix them. The gas consumption was prohibitive, and I also thought it might be nice to drive a smaller car, where people could see my head above the dashboard. So I broke the family tradition of having a love affair with big cars and bought an unglamorous Chevrolet Chevette.

The phone rang, and Vesna answered it.

"Can I borrow the Chevette tonight?" asked Steven.

"No, the last time you didn't bring it back on time," Vesna responded. Not "on time" meaning, he returned it several days, not hours, after he had promised. He begged Vesna some more, then, knowing better, said, "Let me speak to Ivanka."

Vesna was reluctant to put me on the phone, knowing I didn't want to lend him the car but was hopeless when it came to saying no. She handed me the phone but gestured for me to be firm. I winked, showing her my resolve this time.

147

Steven was charming and everyone loved him: old women, young women, old men and boys alike, in this country and in every country. While visiting my elderly grandmother in Croatia, he put a cowboy hat on her, and, despite her hefty figure, he swooped her up and carried her as if over a threshold, her legs flailing as she begged to be put down. A photo was snapped, and both of them had the biggest smiles. To this day, it is my absolute favorite picture.

So with this kind of charisma and his zest for life, how could I resist? He knew it was only a matter of time before I said, "Okay. But *this time* promise me you'll bring it back on time."

"I solemnly swear it will be back by 11 p.m.," he vowed.

At 1 a.m., I realized that "solemnly swearing" was a relative term, so I gave up waiting for the phone to ring or for him to return. I wondered where he and my two-toned brown Chevette had ended up, but I tried to sleep, despite worrying. It was probably best I didn't have children.

I wasn't the only one who couldn't say no to Steven. On more than one occasion, he convinced my dad that he had gotten mixed up with the mafia, who were about to kill him if he didn't pay his gambling debts. Fortunately, the debt was always rather small, so my father kept paying to prevent his son's legs from being broken, until we caught on that the sum of money the mafia always requested covered the cost of a couple of cases of beer—just enough for an evening of fun for Steven and his friends. Even more curious, the voice of the mafia boss sounded an awful lot like a friend's from the crowd Steven ran with these days.

Yet somehow Steven always remained one step ahead of us. With his charisma and creative imagination, he came up with ways to avoid work, yet still have some cash flow, albeit mainly thanks to my inability to say no, along with my father's. Steven had done odd jobs but with silly requirements, such as showing up on a regular days and at predetermined hours. He decided this wasn't for him, and besides, with the large settlement coming, his time could be spent more productively. Thinking up ways to extort money from me and my dad was easier and more in line with his free-spirited personality.

John, a ninety-year-old tenant on the second floor, also proved to be a source of income. John kept forgetting to pay his "union dues," but, thankfully, Steven was around to remind him and to collect the $112.50 that John owed. "

And even though John had most likely never signed out a library book in his life, Steven ensured that John's recurring fines for overdue books were promptly paid and that the various collection agencies were also given their money in a timely fashion. When John handed over the cash, Steven actually provided the senile man with a receipt—in Steven's still juvenile handwriting, he confirmed the amount paid and that this covered John's union dues or other fines until further notice.

Steven never viewed these activities as wrong: it was Robin Hood–like to take from those who had more and give to those who chose not to work and had less. Steven was more noble than Robin Hood, for Steven had a settlement coming from the motorcycle accident, and he had full intentions of paying everyone back. Well, maybe not John, but at ninety and in poor health, John didn't need the money. Besides, John was loaded, yet he refused to go to a nursing home, insisting on staying in his room. Thus, my father had to eventually feed him, so those "union dues" were Steven's way of ensuring that John gave a tip to the family for the care he was given. Because he was virtually bedridden, John would no longer need that nice pair of black shoes lying in his closet, so, when Steven went out on special occasions, he would borrow the shoes but always return them. I guess there is some honor among thieves, after all.

Steven did work for a brief period. After an evening of partying, he had fought with a friend, who consequently fell and broke his leg. Steven felt really bad about this, so he temporarily suspended his "collection agency" and took on regular work, in order to provide this friend with a steady income until he was healed. I'm sure that cured Steven of ever fighting with anyone again.

Despite his imposing physical presence—he was over six feet tall and broad—he had a sensitive side. Once we came home to find him watching Arthur Miller's *Death of a Salesman*. He was so touched by the film that he had to stop watching it at regular intervals, in order to get through it without bawling. The two-hour film lasted almost six hours with breaks.

As he got older, Steven was torn; he knew his lifestyle of beer, nightclubs, and, inevitably, fighting would not end well. He tried to break free from his group of "friends." We begged him to spend time with us. When he did, we had fun together, my mom and her four children, watching a movie she had chosen that would supposedly enlighten us on human nature.

She particularly loved foreign films, because she felt they were educational. Her latest one certainly proved to be. She took us to the then decrepit Revue Theatre on Roncesvalles Avenue to see a German film titled *Sugar Baby*. The only part of the advertisement she must have noticed was that the film was foreign and had subtitles. Worse, she organized a group of friends to accompany us, who relied on my mother having checked the movie's content.

The increasingly sexually explicit scenes flashing across the screen were so embarrassing that my mother admitted defeat and forfeited the large sum of her hard-earned money she had paid for all of us at the box office.

"But it was rated PG!" she kept saying in her defense, as we all marched, heads down, out of the theater. We teased her afterward, as we read the review: "*Sugar Baby*: A plump Munich mortuary worker tracks down and seduces a married subway conductor."

From then on, it was back to Russian classics. Her idea of a perfect family evening was watching seven hours of Tolstoy's *War and Peace*. I didn't know how she managed to afford the popcorn during that film. "Fluffier" films would be along the lines of *Brothers Karamazov* by Dostoyevsky, which ran only 147 minutes.

Yet somehow, through her eagerness, she managed to have us believe that we enjoyed these types of movies and that Hollywood films were for less intellectual people.

Maybe watching all of those brooding Russians drinking had taught Steven to be exotic. He was the leader, and wherever Steven went, the party happened. It was like the Italian commercial "No martini, no party," only in this case it was "No Steven, no party."

With as much conviction as I had when saying "no" to him, he, too, tried to say no. Then, caving, he would promise us, "I'll be back in an hour." Since it would "only be an hour," I lent him my car.

Days later, he would casually saunter in as if he were only minutes late. I was happy to see him and that he was okay, his presence dispelling my lingering fears about what had become of him. I repeatedly lectured him on how this was the *last* time he could use my car, he would smile and assure me he would never be late again, and all would be forgiven.

My father's fondness for big cars once again emerged and solved my problem with Steven borrowing my Chevy Chevette. An old man was selling his baby blue 1966 Chevrolet Bel Air, in mint condition. My father bought the vehicle for Steven, with the idea that once Steven got his money, he would repay my dad.

My father and Steven took the car out for a ride. This antique car received its fair share of attention, albeit not nearly as much as when my father had driven the Ford Galaxy XL through my mom's small town more than two decades ago—but then again, this one didn't cost nearly as much.

151

Steven loved the car. He put on John's shoes and painted the town red. He visited everyone, and the car was an instant hit. Steven practically lived in it and was always checking to see whether Mom needed a ride. Since she didn't drive and Steven didn't work, this proved a great liaison. It was also Steven's introduction to the fact that cars ran on gas. My mom helped out, and they went everywhere, even up north for beautiful drives in the Canadian countryside: "Driving Miss Anna."

My mother did notice that Steven always wore the haunted look of a fugitive every time a siren was heard. Only after the police or the ambulance passed could he relax.

And so they spent many days driving, talking, and laughing in the big blue car. Like mother, like son, for after all, my mother, too, had a love affair with big cars.

Night Art

by Ivanka Di Felice

STEVEN GOT HIS SETTLEMENT FROM the motorcycle accident. His pain, his suffering, and the metal pins that would remain in his arms as grim lifetime reminders of the motorcycle accident were somewhat avenged. He didn't receive the amount he and my father had planned on, close to $1 million, but he did receive almost $80,000—an enormous sum of money at that time and particularly for someone in his early twenties to manage. Steven's generosity knew no bounds. He gave me retroactive gas money for all of the times he had returned my Chevette empty, which was probably the only reason he'd brought the car back. With his handsome good looks, his charming personality, and a ton of money, he became even more popular.

My parents advised Steven to use his money wisely. My father, always the dreamer, had spent years envisioning which investments Steven would make with the money. Yet Steven had also spent many years planning and had too great an imagination to simply put the money in a bank. So, among other things, he bought another car: a brand new candy apple red Sunbird. He bought himself a pair of boots but, after bringing them home, realized that each boot was a different color, so he continued borrowing John's shoes.

He leased a large loft space, under the guise of opening an art studio, in a rundown factory. He worked tirelessly to convert the space into a nightclub. He ingeniously named it Night Art, hoping neighbors would assume it was an art studio. Steven, being impetuous, didn't want to take part in any crazy government scheme regarding permits or zoning and thus incited many a neighbor to phone the police, as his club rowdily celebrated opening night.

Steven had everything working against him and the success of his nightclub. Namely, the city of Toronto, the neighbors' quest for peace, and his overwhelming generosity and host-like qualities in doling out free liquor. Probably my parents' prayers were against him as well.

It didn't take long for him to run through all of the money, with little to show for it, except a leased loft painted black, scattered with empty kegs and bottles, and a pair of mismatched boots. To add to his woes, his friend had borrowed the brand new car and totaled it, while insisting someone else had done it. The only other remaining souvenir was his crooked arm with pins in it.

So Steven, along with the rest of us, was back where we always were financially, having just enough to get by. Yet somehow it was a relief. The years of waiting and dreaming were over, and perhaps now Steven could start a real life. He was charismatic and clever and could work hard; maybe now he would.

CLOSE CALL

by Ivanka Di Felice

THE PHONE RANG AND MY mother answered it. "Kathy, why would I throw a video in the garbage?"

But Kathy couldn't find it and inexplicably insisted my mother go search for it in the trash. Tomorrow was garbage day, so my mom had already lugged the bin to the curb. To humor Kathy, my mother walked down the many stairs and checked the bin.

Vesna, meanwhile, had parked the blue VW Fox my father had bought her, also complete with a hammer, on the street and was leaning over into the car to get her purse.

A sports car parked a few feet behind Vesna, and a man stepped out, walked over to Vesna, and was standing behind her, his arms in the air, ready to grab her, when my mother looked up from the garbage and saw him. She screamed, and the man let go and hopped into the passenger side of a car, while the driver peeled out.

Vesna and my mother shook as they ran up the many stairs into the house.

The phone rang seconds later. It was Kathy. She had found the video; in fact, it was right there next to her on the couch at my dad's this whole time.

We phoned the police, who came right over, as there had been a slew of rapes in Scarborough. They wrote down any details my mother and Vesna could offer and advised us to take precautions when traveling home alone.

Yet whoever it was had to be determined, for on several occasions when we came home, I looked into the rearview mirror to see a car parked, and when I honked the horn, alerting my family and the neighborhood, the car furiously pulled away from its spot and peeled out. We began to live in fear.

The neighborhood watch program proved effective, because whenever we came home and madly honked if we saw anyone suspicious, our neighbor, a hefty middle-aged man who was a hunter, would come out with his shotgun. If he wasn't home, then his bulky sons would escort us up to our house.

After another close call, Steven decided to provide a regular male presence. The police warned him not to touch anyone first but added that if they so much as put a hand on him, then it would be self-defense. I wasn't sure Steven would have the discipline to wait.

He took protecting us seriously and sat on the railing for hours, appearing menacing with his current skinhead look. He was tall and strong and perched himself at the bottom of our stairs, smoking, his eyes fixed on any cars that slowed down. Although we felt safe, most passers-by no doubt felt uneasy walking past him. On some evenings he put on his black leather motorcycle jacket and tied a bandana across his head, giving the appearance that a Hell's Angel had taken up residence with us.

Steven had never before taken a responsibility this earnestly. If he came up onto the porch for a break, he would talk loudly, making sure his presence was still known.

My mother cooked him his favorite meals and watched him devour them. As Steven gained weight, he became even more intimidating.

A Croatian proverb that said, *"Svako zlo za neko dobro"* ("From even bad things one can draw out something good"), again proved true. In this case, the stalkers had brought us closer as a family and as a neighborhood, and thankfully no one had gotten hurt learning this lesson.

DASHED DREAMS

by Ivanka Di Felice

STEVEN, NO LONGER EMPLOYED BY his whims and dreams, returned to being Miss Anna's personal chauffeur on her days off, with evenings spent as our personal security guard. They drove vast miles in the gas-guzzling Chevrolet Bel Air, exploring the breathtaking Canadian north and forging a close bond. They both enjoyed relaxing, except for when they occasionally heard a siren, and Steven still got antsy. Yet aside from that, the days were long and peaceful. My mom took many pictures, usually all of the same shot. To her, when something was beautiful, she had to keep shooting. Single-handedly, she kept Kodak in business for years, though our albums were full of virtually the same photo of Steven with a tranquil lake behind him.

With plenty of time on the open road and days spent gazing at lakes, Steven had time to contemplate his lifestyle. He needed a change, but at the same time he recognized that while living with my dad, with all of his friends in the High Park area, it would be difficult. He asked if he could move back in with us and my mom. She readily agreed and made plans to paint the peach room and prepare it as his bedroom.

158

It would be ready in about a week's time, and then he would come and live with us. We were all thrilled.

One day the phone rang early in the morning, as I was getting ready for work. I answered it, and moments later I was ripping hot rollers out of my hair and throwing them across the room. We got into my Chevy Chevette, and shaking, I drove as fast as I could to my father's house. A police car, parked on the curb outside, confirmed the terrible news.

Two police officers in dark navy uniforms stood solemnly above my father, who was slumped over in a chair with his face in his hands, sobbing.

"No! No! No!" he kept yelling.

I had never seen my father cry before. The policemen offered their condolences and confirmed that Steven had been killed in a motorcycle accident. We had lost our only brother and my parents their only son.

The words seemed unreal. This could not be happening. He had planned to move in with us next week, and we were going to be one big happy family.

Steven's voice was on the answering machine last night when I had gotten home from the seamstress's. He was looking for me at 5:30 p.m. He had gotten the time wrong, because I had agreed to pick him up at 6:30, but when I didn't show up at 5:30, he left with his friend instead. I couldn't help but think that had I been home, he would still be alive.

The policeman said that when we were ready, we would need to go to the morgue to identify Steven. Though this would be a horrendous task, until we saw him we still had a remote glimmer of hope that there had been a dreadful mistake. The other passenger on the motorcycle, a friend of Steven's, was alive but in very rough shape. Everything that could have been broken, fractured, and/or ruptured, was, but he was still alive. Steven's strong body was intact, but his aorta had snapped on impact. He had died instantly. Though he hadn't suffered, this news brought us little comfort. He was twenty-four years old.

My father couldn't bring himself to come with us, so my mother and we girls went down to the morgue. As they showed us the TV screen, I closed my eyes, selfishly hoping that when I opened them, it would be someone else. But it was Steven. He lay there as handsome as ever, peaceful, with a baby blue sheet pulled up to his neck over his body. The improbable glimmer of hope was gone forever. The sound of my heart pounding roared in my ears. Steven had been on his way to true happiness and freedom, and now he was trapped in death. The bottle of *šlivovic* my grandfather had put away twenty-four years ago on Steven's birth would never be opened at his wedding.

***

I believe funerals are designed to keep you busy during the immediate days following the tragic news of a loved one's death. You have no time to feel the overwhelming anguish, because you are so busy choosing a coffin and a plot, taking a suit to the drycleaners to bury your dear one in, ordering flowers, and doing a host of other things that will be inconsequential in no time. Plus, the inevitable family battles prove a good distraction from the pain you feel.

Steven's funeral was no different. Somehow the coffin we preferred and that coincidentally cost far less wouldn't be good enough. We upgraded to the Mercedes of coffins, though Steven would have preferred the 1966 Bel Air version. The purple roses I liked were not masculine enough. The green suit . . . The one thing we all agreed on was that he would be buried in John's shoes. We did what we knew Steven would have wanted, and if John were to find out, we were sure even he wouldn't mind.

We walked into the funeral home, and we three sisters almost fell over in shock to see Steven lying peacefully in the coffin. If dying at age twenty-four were not enough of an injustice, his thick dark hair, which he had been particular about, had been combed over and slicked back as if he were a Mafia kingpin from the eighties.

Kathy burst out, "Steven would die if he saw his hair like this!"

Realizing how ridiculous that statement was, we all burst out laughing. Kathy grabbed a small can of hairspray out of her purse, and Vesna dug out a brush from hers. I nervously stood guard while they hunched over the coffin and proceeded to adjust Steven's hair.

The funeral director entered. Taken aback, he asked, "What are you doing?"

We felt like criminals caught in the act, but we had to give Steven a voice. We said that our brother would have hated that hairstyle and we had to change it before anyone saw him.

"I will take care of it," the director said.

We began to explain how Steven had styled his hair, but the director kindly shooed us out of the room and told us not to worry, to leave it to him. Judging by his own hairdo, we had plenty to be concerned about and doubted the director could style it to our satisfaction (or Steven's.) We lingered, hoping to provide fashion pointers, but he obviously didn't appreciate our supervision.

We returned to find it nominally better—at least, the director had parted it on the side—and we felt proud that we had stood up for Steven, one last time.

We had a eulogy in English at a funeral home in High Park, for Steven's many friends, while another would follow in Croatian at the church for my father and the Croatian community. We had two funerals. Steven would have loved all of the attention.

I made a quick trip to my doctor's, and she introduced me to little pink pills that would supposedly help me cope. Unfortunately, this medication had the desired effect, so at the funeral home visitation I greeted everyone slightly lightheaded, in a jovial manner much more suited for a cocktail party than a wake. "Thanks for coming!"

My sister Vesna glared at me, wondering what was going on. I consoled myself that Steven would have laughed over this.

The following day the memorial service was held. People gave their final condolences, and the coffin was closed. I knew Steven was dead, but the final closing of the casket overwhelmed me, and even the little pink pills could no longer mask my despair.

Colin, a good friend, gave a lovely eulogy, after which the pallbearers, Steven's friends, picked up the coffin and carried him outside to the limousine waiting to take him to the church. We followed, devastated and in tears.

A crowd gathered as they hoisted the coffin into the hearse. Just then, some Croatians showed up to pay their final respects, because according to their custom, one unbeknownst to us, the coffin would not be opened in the church. Steven was already in the vehicle, and although we wanted to be respectful of other people's customs, we didn't know what to do. The hearse was blocking the road, so the driver took Steven on a little tour of the area, while we searched for a solution. A heated discussion ensued, and the limo had to keep circling the block. Though it was tragic, all that my sisters and I could think was how Steven would have gotten a kick out of this.

It was decided that the pallbearers would lift him back into the funeral home, the coffin would be opened, and those who had not had the opportunity could give their final respects. Steven's final moments were as outlandish as his life had been.

A thousand people attended his funeral. He had made an impact on so many lives and would be remembered for his charismatic, if occasionally mischievous ways. He was deeply loved and had touched many. He was remembered even by his first-grade teacher, who also attended the funeral.

Soon thereafter, we discovered the reason for Steven's aversion to sirens. Driving Miss Anna had not been as legal as we had assumed. My mother's calm demeanor as she enjoyed peaceful trips up north with her son wouldn't have been that tranquil had she realized Steven had been driving without a license. It had been suspended ages ago for nonpayment of several fines. He acted like a fugitive because he was one.

Yet those trips afforded my mom a special time with Steven just before he died, so Miss Anna wouldn't have had it any other way.

THE BLUE PLATE AND THE FLORAL CUP

by Ivanka Di Felice

AFTER MY BROTHER DIED, WE knew life had to go on, but we didn't know how it could or how it would.

Tata never did get over Steven's death, and the way he coped was by never speaking of it. I guess he didn't want us to see him crying. For us, too, the pain was unbearable, for we were not only brother and sisters, we were close friends. You cannot choose family, but you can choose your friends, and we were both. Though we were surrounded by others, who every day for two months brought us food, we still felt alone. We knew that our suffering was not unique; others had endured perhaps even worse fates, but the emptiness we felt was only ours.

The guilt of missing my brother's phone call that night weighed heavily on me, and I vowed never to have another suit tailor-made.

I moved into Vesna's room and slept in her double bed with her. After several weeks, I flipped over so that my feet were against her face.

"What are you doing?" she asked.

"I need my privacy," I told her. "Needing my privacy" netted me a terse invite to return to my own room.

The room that would have been Steven's still needed to be painted, so my mother asked Steven's friend if he would do it. He assured her it wouldn't be a problem and came to the house to provide an estimate. He gave her a reasonable quote and asked for an advance. My mother handed him $50 and never saw him again.

Though she wasn't yet ready, my mother had to resume work at the hairdressing shop for economic reasons. The funeral had been costly for both of my parents, and the insurance company hadn't even provided enough for the casket. I have hated insurance companies ever since.

A couple of days after returning to work, my mom came home with reddish skin, and I knew she hadn't been using a sun lamp. It resembled a mild rash, so none of us paid too much heed to it. We spent another evening reminiscing and crying, and off we went to bed.

By morning, my mother's face had swollen like a balloon—not a round balloon but, rather, only some parts of her face, thus distorting her beyond human recognition. The rash had become crusty, practically gluing her eyes shut. She resembled the Elephant Man. Fear now mingled with grief. We helped her bathe, for my mother always refused to go to the hospital prior to washing up. She could be having a heart attack, but she would arrive, albeit in a coma, smelling of Irish Spring.

I drove her as fast as my Chevy Chevette could to the hospital, both for her sake and ours, not sure whether what she had was contagious or permanent. I was only twenty-five and had just vowed never to have designer clothes made again, so if I couldn't rely on chic clothing for sex appeal, I needed my face. We had enough to deal with, and the thought of the rest of us waking up with balloon faces tomorrow was too much to bear.

We arrived in record time for a Chevette, and after we waited for what seemed like an eternity, they called us.

The triage nurse calmly asked, "Why did you come to the hospital today, Mrs. Blazanin?"

Either the hospital had implemented a policy to include hiring people with mental disabilities, or this triage nurse was too accustomed to seeing people stagger into emergency rooms carrying their own heads, for she didn't blink when asking that inane question.

"I think it's obvious," my mother said. And it was to all onlookers as we entered the hospital and to those nearby who inconspicuously vacated their seats and scattered when we sat down in the waiting area. Even the "regulars" at St. Joseph's hospital, the drunks and the drug addicts, sobered up enough to know better than to seat themselves next to my mom.

The doctor called us in, much to our relief and the relief of those around us. While trying to look my mom in what was left of her eye, he, too, asked the same absurd question about why she had come to the hospital. I began to have my suspicions whether he was part of the same program as the triage nurse, had forgotten his glasses, or, at the very least, had graduated at the bottom of his class. I wished she'd said that she had broken her toe, to see his reaction.

After further questioning, the doctor was not overly concerned by what he assessed as an allergic reaction. They gave her a prescription and, much to our dismay, sent her home to our care.

We filled the prescription, and on returning home, we took my mom to her room to relax. We fluffed her pillows and brought her books and snacks, making her comfortable, while we secretly hoped she would stay confined to her room until we were confident the diagnosis had been correct and that she was not contagious.

I did all of the cooking and insisted she rest—in her room. We found a tray we had bought her years ago to serve breakfast in bed and hadn't used lately. We wiped the dust off and brought all of her meals to her. Vesna, the really brave one, risked whatever my mom had and made physical contact by putting the eye cream in Mom's eyes.

Meanwhile, I tried to compensate for my cowardly ways by jumping at her every demand, insisting she needed to take it easy and that anything she required could be brought to her (as long as I didn't have to touch her).

All was going well, and I thought she hadn't caught on to her quarantine, but alas, our mismatched dishes gave me away. After several days, she noticed that each of her meals was served on the same blue plate—the blue plate we had only one of. I also erred by serving her coffee and tea out of our one rose floral cup. She was a good sport about it. Maybe she would have done the same—though she never did find out that I used rubber gloves and boiling water to wash her dishes.

Eventually, she began to look human, and I felt it safe to serve her food from our assorted dishes. To my shock, the doctor must have been right. I stopped boiling water for the dishes and gave up using gloves.

My mom saw her family doctor, who agreed with the diagnosis. Apparently, she had been mildly allergic to the chemicals she had worked with as a hairdresser for so many years, but with the stress of my brother's death, her body could no longer cope. My mother also had a very bad back, so the doctor suggested she find a job where she had to neither stand nor sit. I could come up with only one trade that involved neither activity, and although it supposedly paid well, it wasn't a profession that interested my mother.

My mom's difficult life would become harder. It would take real determination to live by her oft-quoted words of Dostoevsky "You have to learn to love life, despite it all." But she'd done it before and, surely, would figure out how to do it again.

HOME IN BEL AIR

by Ivanka Di Felice

THE PHONE RANG AT MY boss's cottage, where I was moonlighting as a nanny. He said, "Ivanka, it's for you."

My mother was on the other line, and it was highly unusual that she would call.

"Is Kathy with you?" she asked.

This was an odd question, because Kathy had never accompanied me on weekend jobs. "No. Why do you ask?"

"I got home, and she isn't here. So I thought maybe she was with Vesna or you or had gone to visit your dad, but now I know she isn't with any of you."

My mother put the phone down and went upstairs. She returned a few minutes later and, in tears, said, "She's gone. She has taken all her clothes and left."

It took a minute to sink in. "Are you sure?" I asked. "Gone for good or gone to sleep at someone's house for the weekend?"

"All of her drawers are empty, and there is a note on the dresser," my mom said.

"Stay calm, Mom," I said. "There must be some explanation."

And there was, but as my mom read the note, there was no explanation we could comprehend. I couldn't ask my boss to drive me the two hours home, and the next two days seemed like an eternity before I could try to find some answers and comfort my mother.

The note explained that Kathy loved my mom, that she was great and had done nothing wrong, but this was simply something Kathy had to do. Kathy was eighteen years old, but perhaps Steven's death had touched her far more than we knew.

Kathy was considerate and called to leave messages whenever she thought we weren't home, letting us know she was okay. We had no idea where she was, and every night the three of us went to bed with an uneasy feeling.

One day while Kathy was leaving a message, assuming our mother was at work, Mom picked up the phone and begged to see her. Though taken aback to be speaking to our mother, Kathy agreed to meet her.

We watched the large baby blue Bel Air slowly approach our house—the car that had brought my mother countless hours of joy, with Kathy's head now slightly visible above the dashboard. My mother ran to the car in earnest to hug her.

Kathy parked and, suddenly panicked, said, "Just a minute please." She then leaned over into the backseat, so that her legs were sticking up, while her head was buried in the high pile of clothes in the backseat. One by one, she threw pieces of clothing into the air, all the while shouting, "Hang on, it will be okay!" as she kept digging.

My mother didn't understand what was taking place, until Kathy emerged with a small, frightened gray kitten in her hand.

"I couldn't find her. She was meowing because she had buried herself pretty deep," Kathy said, relieved.

My mother peered into the car, shocked, as it dawned on her where Kathy had been living these last few weeks. The inside of the car contained things one would normally find in a place of residence: clothes, shoes, bottles, lots of empty cheeseburger wrappings from McDonald's, which was then having a 99 cent sale, cans, bags of cat food, and so on.

The last we knew, Kathy was not mentally ill, on drugs, or an alcoholic, nor did we know of any plausible reason for her choosing to live in a car, as if on skid row. Kathy had always been a free spirit, but this was taking it too far. At least, she was dressed normally, though she did have all of her clothes right at her fingertips.

It pained my mother to see her like this, so she begged Kathy to come home. But Kathy seemed perfectly happy and wasn't worried in the least that she was in any danger, living and sleeping in a car. She insisted that my mom not worry. While Kathy held the kitten, it began to meow, so Kathy released it back to its "play area" in the backseat. The whole scene was surreal. My mother couldn't help but wonder what she had done wrong. The kitten happily jumped and climbed amid the tall piles of clothes, occasionally snagging her claws on a piece of fabric, as Kathy laughed and untangled her.

My mother had just lost one child and couldn't bear the thought of losing another, but Kathy was adamant. She lived in that car for three weeks, and then good news: she had found an apartment and would be moving into it. More good news: the kitten could come with her.

The Bel Air, which had been a source of so many memories, now both good and bad, would be put up for sale, by a real estate agency. Well, okay, I made that part up—but the car was sold, and my mom bought something with the funds in memory of Steven, Kathy, and the kitten.

After living on her own for a while, Kathy moved back to High Park, into the family home, taking the apartment with the blue bathroom on the second floor. My father was happy, as was Kathy for a long while, while my father still took care of the tenants and the house. Eventually, though, as my father delegated more responsibility to her, she would look back on those early days of blissful ignorance with a kind of dreamy nostalgia, perhaps even for life in the Bel Air.

A RETURN TO MY ROOTS

by Ivanka Di Felice

A YEAR HAD PASSED SINCE my brother died, and Kathy moved out, so I embarked on my own adventure, one not involving a car. I moved to Croatia from Canada in 1993. Because Croatia was still embroiled in a war, I will admit to having bad timing. Yet for my father, who was a patriot, my move enabled him to invent elaborate tales about why I went and, depending on who was in political favor at the time, which group I was working for.

I spoke Croatian relatively well, because I'd spent my early days with my grandparents. Later my dad's motto had been "When a Croatian feeds you, then you will speak Croatian. When an Englishman feeds you, then you can speak English." Though I hated his repeating this line over and over when we forgot and spoke English within his earshot, I was now grateful.

I moved in with my grandmother in that small village a half hour from the Hungarian border—the place where my mother had grown up and had escaped to marry my father. She still lived in the same modest three-room house, which was really two, because one of the rooms was a hallway, but

172

since she had a pretty floral couch in it that had come in a container from Canada, she had "made it."

Postcards from my mother's various travels were proudly displayed throughout the house, the tape yellowing, barely holding them to the glass of the credenza in the kitchen. My mom had always sent necessities and gifts over the years, and my grandmother had an armoire full of lovely things that she deemed too good to ever use.

Anything that possibly could, had a pretty doily on it, and, despite the divorce, my mom and dad's wedding picture still hung on the wall, while pictures of us grandchildren were everywhere, the most prominently displayed one of my grandmother in a cowboy hat with Steven. Like my dad, she, too, could not talk about his death. It seemed older people coped by keeping heart-wrenching pains buried deep within.

Though my mother had offered on several occasions, my grandmother refused to get indoor plumbing, claiming that people still stopped by her place to get a drink of "real water." Drawing water from a well seemed like an easy feat, but after several attempts I realized it was not. Hence, I became completely dependent on my aged grandmother for daily water.

The little house had two bathrooms; now one was inside, which made my grandma feel important because it had "running water," albeit in the form of a bucket of water you had to throw into the toilet after use. The other one, an outhouse, stood a few hundred feet from the house, and its toilet paper still came in the form of old but soft-leafed magazines.

A small cantina off the kitchen always housed a small piece of smoked bacon, eggs in a box from her hens, my grandma's homemade butter, and a creamy ricotta-like cheese from the milk the lady up the road brought her. Each evening she made me chamomile tea gleaned from nearby fields and poured in a dash of *šlivovic* (Croatian plum brandy) or a few drops of wine, which she used as a substitute for lemon. She didn't drink much but felt that a bit of alcohol each day would keep you healthy.

Having lived in a cold climate my entire life, I foolishly assumed that even if it were very cold outside, you would still be warm inside. I was wrong. My grandma's house was heated by two wood stoves: one in the kitchen, which she also used for cooking, and one in the bedroom. She always lit the one in the kitchen but didn't mind sleeping in polar conditions. She took pity on me, though, because she kindly heated my side of the bed with hot ceramic tiles prior to my getting in. We shared a large bed with down comforters over and beneath us, courtesy of her fowl. I slept with a hat and no longer needed blush, because I awoke with a rosy complexion each morning.

Sometimes my sleep was interrupted by the echo of gunfire, as nearby villagers practiced shooting in the middle of the night, preparing themselves for what might be inevitable. Other times, I awoke to the sound of my grandma huffing and puffing as she got down to use the potty, which she subsequently slid under the bed. I'm not sure which was worse. My grandma's deafness came in handy, because she slept like a log through the shooting. For both sounds, I wished I were deaf.

I quickly made many friends in the village and became a sort of superstar, due to my Canadian status. Though no one was well off materially, people shared what they had, and even small deeds and gifts did not go unnoticed. We enjoyed meals with friends and family as much as, if not more than, the fancy dinners I had attended with the very rich. Appreciation for the little that one had made everything taste better.

"A night on the town" took on new meaning, as I walked the couple hundred feet to either my relatives' or my friends' houses, who lived nearby. My life had turned 180 degrees—from the sophistication of the financial district on Bay Street to this simple, yet very happy, life. Little did I know, my life would get even happier.

ORANGE IS *NOT* THE NEW BLACK

by Ivanka Di Felice

TWO MONTHS LATER, I GOT a job in translation in the capital, Zagreb, a pretty city with tall plane trees lining the wide boulevard that led to the main square, full of elegant coffee bars and restaurants.

I rented a small, furnished bachelor apartment from an elderly lady. I could have lived with most of the ancient furniture, but not the ugly mustard yellow couch, upholstered with uncomfortable material that felt like fiberglass. Sitting on it convinced me it was stuffed with scrap metal. It would surely give spinal damage to even the fittest people. I asked the landlady whether I could throw it out and get a new one, but she replied, "My son might get married soon and will need the couch."

Her son wasn't even dating anyone, and I had met him. He moved slowly, he spoke slowly, and if he hadn't gotten married by now, it would be a long while before he could talk anyone into it. I felt the risk was low that he would fly to Las Vegas and get married overnight, so I arranged for my mom's cousin Ivo, who lived next door to my grandma, to come under the cloak of darkness and take away this ode to a bygone era. He would store it until my landlady's son announced an engagement.

Ivo came, but the couch weighed a ton, and we could barely lift it. Yet somehow the two of us managed to move it, though we endangered our backs and at one point my life, when it slipped and trapped me under it. We loaded it onto the roof of his car. I worried that it might be too heavy and visualized his untimely demise, as the couch crashed through the light tin roof onto him. He assured me it would be fine, so I waved goodbye to him and the couch, which would remain in his attic until the landlord's son found a suitable bride.

The apartment was near Jarun Lake, and soon after moving in, I met Marko on a streetcar. I was reading an English book when the tall young man sitting next to me, with crew-cut blond hair and green eyes, began chatting, aiming to dazzle me by using all three English words he knew at once. We conversed in Croatian the remainder of the ride home, until I got off at my stop.

After that, I kept running into him, and soon I began to wonder if it was by chance. But since he was several years younger than me and had a crew cut, I never gave it a second thought. I had visited Florence in my early twenties, had bought an exquisite peach-colored swing coat, and from that moment on had fallen in love with Italy. Ever since, I had hoped to marry an Italian, for they were dark, handsome, and stylish beyond any North American's dreams. Marko was nothing like that; hence, I was safe.

He was young, and perhaps that made him impetuous and, in some ways, refreshing. He took it upon himself to drive me to work each day. Having spent the last few years working with the rich in the financial district of Toronto and being driven in fancy black BMWs, I couldn't help but smile as I exited my front door at 6 a.m. to see Marko waiting, proudly, in his newly acquired bright orange 1968 Skoda. The car

177

resembled something out of a cartoon, and it rumbled and rattled so much, I feared waking my neighbors.

As he shifted gears and stepped on the accelerator, the intensified noise gave me new reasons for alarm. Cars, like people, communicate when something is not right. His car was undeniably making a statement. The squeals and groans were a cry for help, but Marko ignored them, hoping they would magically go away. And so he drove me down the charming avenues of Zagreb, through the upscale downtown core to my office. I preferred that he drop me off around the corner, but he insisted on front-door service, much to the amusement of my coworkers.

Wherever I went, Marko and his orange car loudly waited. I visited my grandmother every weekend, and on returning, I heard, then saw Marko waiting in front of the train station, ready to drive me home. Before he dropped me off, he insisted on taking me out for coffee in the most chic cafés. He seemed to have good taste in everything, except cars, haircuts, and clothes. Or perhaps more accurately, he had good taste in cafés.

We chatted easily, and though he wasn't good looking in the classic sense, nor was he the dark, handsome man I had dreamed of marrying, he had charm that I eventually succumbed to. So I stopped asking him to leave me alone and gave up my long-time dream of marrying an Italian. Yet as a tribute to my past, I faithfully wore my peach-colored swing coat when out with Marko.

He began English lessons twice a week, and when the teacher asked the students why they were learning English, he responded, "Because I love a pretty girl from Canada." After we dated a while, Marko took me to the countryside just outside Zagreb, to the nearby town of Samobor, established in the thirteenth century and noted for its quaint, narrow cobblestone streets and beautiful main square. He proposed in front of the old fortress ruins on a hill in Stari Grad. The ring was humble, but that didn't matter, and I accepted—

much to the delight of my father, because Marko was Croatian, and much to the fear of my mother, because Marko was Croatian. Though my father never interfered with our lives and was shy about discussing my love life, prior to my dating Marko, he had asked my mom whether I had any prospects or plans of getting married.

"She is looking for love. She doesn't want to marry just anyone, but wants to marry someone she can be friends with and be happy with," my mom said.

My dad reflected for a moment, then said, "Yes, but she's twenty-six."

Apparently, my time had run out to find true love, and I should take what I could get. After all, those bottles of *šlivovic* were just waiting to be opened at one of his children's weddings. My mother worried about the clash of cultures, because although I spoke Croatian I had been born and raised in Canada. Nonetheless, she was supportive and began making plans for the second reception that my friends would throw us when we arrived in Canada. Among that group was a man named David, a new neighbor who had become friends with my mother and sister. They enlisted his help with the preparations for our wedding reception in Canada, and he readily agreed.

VISIONS OF GRANDEUR

by Ivanka Di Felice

WITH ME GETTING MARRIED, MY father assumed my stay in Croatia would be permanent, more than a whim, and although he and my mother had been divorced for years, he decided to purchase a house in the village she'd grown up in, which he had spent months cruising past in his Ford Galaxy XL. Though things hadn't turned out as expected with my mother, perhaps memories of good times prompted his purchase.

I found a small house, set off from the main road, with two rooms: a kitchen and a bedroom, plus a bathroom. The lot was considerable, and the house came with a garage, which we hoped my father would not rent to a tenant. In any case, the house and the property should suffice for my father's stays during the summer. Yet my father had grand plans, with visions of all of his children returning to the homeland and laughter and squeals of delight from *our* children filling the air. None of us were even married yet, nor were my younger sisters dating, but it didn't take much for my father to dream.

He got busy making plans for additions to the house, sending shipping containers from Canada filled with building supplies, such as two-by-fours, drywall, and roofing shingles, which were unusual for Croatia. He purchased and shipped another big white car—of course, paling in comparison to the Galaxy. Yet regardless, once again, the "American" was the talk of the small town.

In all of my father's elaborate planning, he omitted only one small detail: who would do the work. He was almost sixty, and no one in this town had ever worked with the likes of these materials. Yet the containers had arrived, and my father's imagination knew no bounds. He always had a soft spot for the underdog, so he found three poor young unskilled laborers in the village.

My father's next vision, perhaps an even a grander one, involved transforming these three men, who had never so much as picked up a hammer, into masters of every building trade. Tata was very clever and a quick learner; thus, he assumed the same of everyone. Because in Croatia it's customary to feed the workers, my father quickly showed them how to put up the two-by-fours for the living room and left to go grocery shopping—and, more important, to get another case of beer. The grocery store had a bar attached, so my father treated several men from the village to beers, while he updated them on the progress of his house.

The workers were eager and, unfortunately, quick. By the time my father had returned, they had indeed put up several walls, not correctly, but, to their credit, these were still standing. Because my father had other pressing concerns, such as making gulaš, he once again hastily showed them what to do next, then went into the kitchen to prepare the stew he would serve for lunch.

As the banging continued, neighbors and other villagers dropped in to see what was happening and to help my father, with the beer.

181

For the most part, the men had caught on, and it seemed the additional room would stay standing, as long as these parts never had to endure Mother Nature's wrath or the big bad wolf, huffing and puffing.

Months went by, and Tata got into a routine. In the morning, he would pick up the boys, give them the world's quickest lesson on a valuable trade, and leave them to their own devices, as he scurried to buy fresh bread, groceries, and beer. Cooking for three hungry men was no easy task, something my father had taken for granted all of these years. But he took his duty seriously, and large pots always simmered on the stove, as he alternated between the two recipes he knew. The boys, coming from a poor family, ate more meat in those few months than they ever had in their lives. And each afternoon, several villagers dropped in, to help with the beer.

Every Sunday, Marko and I drove the one hour from Zagreb through the gentle rolling green hills, risking my life and eardrums in the loud orange car, to visit my grandma and my father. While Tata was glad to see us, he also enjoyed the break he got from cooking, because we ate at my grandma's or a local restaurant, Prc, in the hilly countryside of Koprivnica. I loved going there. The outside was rustic, with a hay roof, and the interior had the original wine presses and massive hand-made tables. The food was excellent. For what my father was spending on meat, he could have taken the three boys to eat there each day.

The house was slowly coming along, and I gave my father credit for his unrelenting vision. Few could have clung to the image of a grand villa after seeing this house. This week's speedy lesson involved the technical aspect of laying tiles. Unfortunately, my dad's preoccupation with his progress report at the local bar took precedence over an equally important phase—namely, the aesthetics behind laying multicolored tiles.

Mike had grasped the concept of laying tile and randomly opened boxes, then placed the tiles in the order that he pulled them out. Hence, he completed the floor with mostly white tiles, interspersed with random dark gray ones, giving the impression that the floor had been patched. When my father came home, his shocked expression showed that the floor tested even his vision.

The second-story addition didn't fare much better. My father miscalculated the height of the average person, for his workers stopped several cement blocks short of standard height. But since the room was sizeable, seven dwarves could sleep comfortably. On a brighter note, though it took him away from adequately supervising, the many hours he spent slaving over the stove rendered him a better cook. And thanks to all of the meat he purchased, the family-owned grocery shop was finally turning a profit. Aside from the laborers' weight gain, my father's beer, gulaš, and bread combo menu was a success.

My father continued to train his minions and introduced them to the marvels of the caulking gun and silicone. My father's love of these substances and his theory of "more is more" when it came to using them was evident everywhere. Caulking was a man's best friend when it came to filling gaps and covering up mistakes, especially in a *new* room, where nothing was square.

He put on his shorts, but because he couldn't find his belt, he grabbed a TV cable and weaved it through the belt loops, then attached both ends. Prada beware, someone might make a budget line called TATA, with virtually no overhead or anyone protesting the use of leather.

Then he left each of the boys armed with a caulking gun and went for his morning grocery run. On his return, several hours later, the students had outdone the teacher. Despite their admirable intentions, their skill level left much to be desired, proving that the only way to become proficient at caulking was by trial and error. They had perfected the error part. Either my father didn't realize caulking was a two-step process or, in his haste, forgot to mention the part where you wipe off the excess, smoothing it.

Eventually, the house was finished, much to everyone's chagrin. The three boys had no other work but had developed a craving for meat, while the poor village men had lost their source of free beer.

Next, my father purchased a vineyard with a small cottage located a few miles from his house, on a pretty hillside. Though the vines and the land would need a lot of work, this didn't deter him. He pictured robust grapes producing fine wine. The small white-stuccoed cottage with two rooms, one above and one below, without electricity or plumbing, also became a grand vacation spot in my father's imagination.

Marko and I often joined my father in the vineyard, and he roasted a lamb on a spit over a low fire, with the help of an automatic spinner he had ingeniously rigged up to a car battery.

After years of living abroad and donating thousands to causes that my dad felt would make his country great, he was happy to own property in Croatia.

He dreamed of me and Marko and our four little Croatian children playing in his fields. Maybe I took after my father, for I dreamed about that as well.

OH, TO BE YOUNG AGAIN

by Ivanka Di Felice

AT MY AGE (THIRTY-NINE, plus several, several months), I now feel that speeds above 30 miles hour should be prohibited on any motorway. As per the movie they showed us in driver's education, drivers must keep both hands on the wheel at all times in the 10/2 position. Changing CDs should be outlawed, and people found texting should be imprisoned for life. Before I venture onto any journey longer than an hour, I confirm my will is up-to-date, and if it's more than a mile away, I hook up the GPS.

I'd arrived in Croatia at the age of twenty-six, a couple of years after the nation had declared its independence. Although much of the fighting had ceased, conflict still continued in pockets of the country. I was aware of this when my director asked me whether I would deliver a package to Hungary. Being young, I was invincible, so I agreed.

I got into the standard-transmission blue Volkswagen Golf they provided me with and left Zagreb without anything more than a map and an address in Pecs, Hungary. I drove through the lush green fields of the Croatian countryside, stopping occasionally to ask if I was heading in the general direction of Hungary.

I entered villages with abandoned homes and buildings with gaping holes left by shrapnel, bullets, bombs, or artillery shells. Some were beyond repair. Among the rubble-choked streets, I saw the odd person and some mangy stray dogs roaming and heard weapons firing every so often.

I continued to drive fearlessly past the UNPROFOR (United Nations Protection Force), which was deployed throughout the region to maintain the ceasefire. They were recognizable by their blue hats, and I greeted them as I continued on my journey. Not for a second did it occur to me that I might be in danger. I merrily listened to Croatian music as I drove quickly, not out of fear, but out of a need for speed.

I reached Hungary, where it appeared as if the entire population had been frozen in ice for the last century. Not one person I encountered spoke English. I suddenly felt more alone than I had an hour earlier, driving through mostly abandoned villages, because at least the UNPROFOR spoke English. Thankfully, the majority of Hungarian people I stopped were friendly and were experts at deciphering body language and hand signals; thus, I somehow arrived at my destination.

I was ready to head back, when the Hungarian couple to whom I had delivered the package invited me to lunch. If only I could have declined the invitation, but they were persistent. They led me into the house, and, with more gesturing, we sat down at the table already set. I soon discovered that not one word in Hungarian was similar to any language I was familiar with: English, Croatian, or French. Yet since I was young and full of hope, I babbled away, convinced that they must understand some of what I said, albeit I could not comprehend a word of theirs.

I later discovered that Hungarian belongs to the Uralic language family, with its closest relatives being Mansi and

186

Khanty. It's one of the few languages of Europe that isn't part of the Indo-European family. All of that blabbering, and, to them, I must have sounded like the "whaa-whaa-whaa" trombone effect, similar to Charlie Brown's teacher. After a few hours with this sweet couple, I got enough arm exercises for a month, and they did likewise. I had a four-hour drive back to Zagreb and left while it was still light, so I could see people gesturing if I stopped for directions in Hungary.

I got out my map and followed the route home, chatted briefly with the UNPROFOR forces, and drove on. In Zagreb, I dropped the car at the office and called Marko, who immediately roared over to pick me up. Since he was younger than I was and even more invincible, he never gave it a second thought that I'd been sent through recently bombed areas that were now occupied by UNPROFOR forces.

I recounted my adventure and how I managed a three-hour lunch using only nonverbal language. We laughed over drinks in one of Zagreb's hip bars in the vibrant main square, with its antique street lamps shimmering beside stately pastel buildings. Oh, to be young again.

THE THIRSTY NEIGHBOR

by Anica Blažanin

IN 1994, I CAME FOR a one-month holiday to visit Ivanka, who early in life exhibited very similar personality traits to mine, but in reverse. Her dreams were about Europe. She was engaged to a Croatian guy, Marko. I knew better than to try to dissuade her; her mind was forged too much like mine.

Just before I planned to return to Canada, my mother was hit by a car, while walking on a sidewalk to visit her sister next door. Her hip was broken, and she suffered a concussion. As a result of the shock, pain, and unfamiliar surroundings, along with the fact that hospital visiting hours were restricted to one hour per day and enforced with military precision by nurses, she developed dementia.

Despite the surgery being successful, she was uncooperative with the physiotherapist, so she made no progress in regaining her ability to walk. Then she caught an intestinal bug that dehydrated her and left her dying at seventy-six years of age. The hospital informed me that the doctors could do nothing else and to expect the end—death—within days.

My father had died ten years previously from a stroke, so I stayed alone with my mother. I lived in her house without indoor plumbing, because my mother refused to have water installed in the kitchen, claiming she didn't want to drink water that smelled of metal pipes. Hence, she drew herself a bucket of well water for drinking. She also offered well water to people walking home in the summer from the train station or from the graveyard, which was a favorite hangout for older ladies in the village. They all praised her uncontaminated water and stopped by often. With the water, she served Turkish coffee and plum brandy, so it's hard to know what really drew her guests.

After her accident, I visited a home for the disabled in Koprivnica, which told me the waiting period was two years. So there we were, mother and daughter, who had never been close and who never saw eye to eye.

It's amazing how many things we think we could never do, yet we do them—and well—if the circumstances demand it. In my case, this included changing diapers, bathing someone, and cleaning up vomit. I reasoned that people go to school to become nurses, and part of their job involves those very tasks. So, how was I better than them? I rolled up my sleeves and was determined to do the job well.

I slept in the kitchen, where I kept the woodstove burning through the night, so in the morning I had hot water for Mom's bath and to cook breakfast. I tried home remedies for diarrhea, and, together with the medication from the hospital, I managed to stop it. Our family rallied, with my aunt cooking dinner, my cousin's wife doing the laundry because she had a washing machine, and my cousin helping with the outside work.

Many friends came to see her, thinking she would die soon, but I encouraged them to talk to her about the things they'd done together and people she knew. I provoked their memories, plying them with pure water, Turkish coffee, and brandy, then offering seconds. I talked to her a lot about my childhood, avoiding anything negative. I reminisced about her visit to Canada and babysitting her grandchildren. I also related, together with others, all of the gossip about people I knew.

Miraculously, it started to work. Most of the time she knew who I was and started to recognize others and very gradually participate in conversations. Then we had a breakthrough. Naturally, my reward for visitors attracted a few of the village alcoholics. One man, in particular, visited daily, but I was on to him when he came a second time in one day. I told him Mom was resting. Undeterred, he arrived the following morning, and I gave him his usual coffee and brandy, because from day one he had declined the pure water. He was slurring more than usual, which made me suspect he had already visited several other neighbors earlier.

As he babbled on to my mother, aware of his duty to engage her in conversation, my mother's face grew wrathful. Her eyes looked so stormy, I thought a new crisis was brewing.

Infuriated, she burst out loudly, "Why did you give him something to drink? Don't you see he is already very drunk? He doesn't come to visit me; he only comes for the brandy! Even though he'll ask for it, don't you dare give him a beer, too. Don't think I didn't see you giving him beer before!"

That was the longest, most coherent speech she had given since the accident. She was good and angry and that gave a kick-start to the neurosis in her brain, shocking it into scurrying through new pathways connecting her personality.

I told her that she owed her revived sanity to her thirsty neighbor.

Because his conversational skills were no longer required, now that my mother would choose the visitors, the neighbor had to find an excuse for making the village rounds.

He dropped in and said, "I just want to say what may be my last goodbye."

He then explained that he was going to enlist in the army to aid his country. He was certainly not the kind of help the military was looking for: he was way past the maximum enlistment age, his hands shook something fierce, and he couldn't see well enough to shoot his own foot, despite it being the size of a watermelon. Though I knew my mother didn't want him back, I was bemused by his resourcefulness, so I snuck him a drink or two on the porch, for, after all, it was "possibly his last goodbye."

It took a whole month before we heard that we had the right to have a nurse and a physiotherapist come twice a day to change and bathe my mother and help her start walking. The nurse praised me and our family for taking such good care of her. The room smelled fresh, and there was no sign of bedsores. Her color was good and her mood cheerful. When the nurse reported the condition of her patient to the doctor, on seeing my mother's name he was surprised. He'd thought she had only a few days to live and that was why the nurse was not sent out to help earlier.

I should have been resentful of this medical oversight, but I wasn't. That difficult month gave me the opportunity to learn to love my mother. I realized that I was just angry with her, as she was with me; some of it was justified, while some had been due to my attitude in my later teenage years. We tend to blame our parents for their wrong conduct, and in an ideal world, we would be partly right. My vivid imagination from early on had been misconstrued as lies.

I recall being about four years old, at a local fair, and I ate so many heart-shaped cookies dyed red that later I had an awful tummy ache. I groaned in the middle of the night, and my mom lit the oil lamp and came to see what was wrong. She lifted my pajama top to find my stomach covered in red, which in the glow of the lamp resembled blood. She screamed and asked what happened, so I quickly invented a tale: "I fell on sharp nails."

Thankfully, on closer examination, my mother recognized that my "bloody wound" consisted of smeared red heart cookies, and she didn't have to take me on foot the four miles to the nearest hospital.

But now, my memories of her calling me a "liar from the day you were born" were forgotten. Being the sole caregiver, I had the opportunity to see Mom's emotions and characteristics that I had forgotten she possessed. She was very grateful for everything I did: feeding her, changing her bed, even fluffing her pillow. I saw vulnerability, helplessness, and fear. They had always been there but were often smothered with anger. With the anger mostly gone, what a wonderful person remained! And as for the bit of anger that she expressed toward the thirsty neighbor, well, perhaps I should even be grateful for that, as should the neighbor's liver.

Since that time, she sometimes got upset with me and vice versa, but never bitterly. We both had a chance to get to know the other person's previously obscured endearing qualities. Yes, the Croatian saying *"Svako zlo za neko dobro"* ("From even bad things one can draw out something good") once again proved true.

AIR BLESSED

by Ivanka Di Felice

My GRANDMA RECOVERED QUITE WELL, and my mom went back to Canada. My grandma was invited to go, but she declined. She probably wanted to ensure that she drank only pure water and would be around to serve it, among other things, to thirsty neighbors.

I was working full time, eating dinners with Marko's family, spending weekends with my father, and helping my grandmother, plus planning the wedding. Both here and abroad, everyone was excited. The official ceremony would be in Zagreb, with a second reception to follow in Canada. Marko's deep love for me was confirmed when he grew his hair, and the crew cut was no more.

I had left Canada a couple of years previously, and I envisioned the happy reunion with our large group of friends, as we exited the airport doors. I could hardly wait.

My friend Shirin, who had sewn several suits for me when I used to spend my pay on designer fabric, offered to make my wedding dress. She was an excellent seamstress and a very good friend, her only flaw being that she didn't live by the same calendar I did. Sometimes she was off by weeks, which

193

was fine if I wore my gray business suit made of Venetian fabric to the office a month later than anticipated, but a wedding dress definitely had an expiration date.

Yet she so wanted to make the gown as a gift and promised it would be ready in plenty of time. Because the dress would be custom made and fitted, I had to ensure that I wouldn't gain an ounce in the next few months. I weighed myself, spent a day shopping for lace, and sent it off to Shirin, with my measurements and a calendar.

Despite Marko's protests and his deep affection for his worn beige loafers, I bought him and his brother new Italian shoes for the wedding. Getting my father outfitted would be my next undertaking.

My sister and a friend, Chantal, would soon be coming, and Marko and I would pick them up in Venice. We could do some more shopping there for the wedding and our home. Those were very happy times.

May 2, 1995, started like any other day, with Marko waiting outside my apartment building in his orange car at 6 a.m., ready to drive me to work.

While I sat at my desk mid-morning, pondering a bit of translation work and a lot of wedding plans, I heard what sounded like a car crash not far from our building. Soon thereafter, the air raid sirens went off. Everyone knew what to do, except me. They scurried us to the basement and opened the front doors, letting in neighbors and those on the street looking for a bomb shelter. Several rockets had been launched and had struck locations in Zagreb, including the main square, the shopping districts, a school, and the airport. Five people, all civilians, were killed and at least 160 others severely injured. The attack had been carried out as retaliation for the Croatian army's offensive in Operation Flash.

The rockets fired against Zagreb were armed with aviation cluster bomb warheads (called *cassette bombs*), each of which contained 288 "bomblets" (smaller ammunition). On impact, each bomblet exploded and released 420 small bombs filled with pellets, each with a lethal range of thirty feet. Each rocket released around 120,000 of these pellets, with the intention of killing or maiming many.

Hospitals soon filled with bleeding and lacerated citizens, frantic police rerouted traffic from downtown, and schools were ordered closed. The charred wreckage of several cars could be seen smoldering. Some windows had been smashed, rocket fragments littered the sidewalks, and sirens pierced the air as ambulances responded.

I huddled in fear in the basement, while my colleagues took this opportunity to stop work and play cards, which they had somehow remembered to bring down with them. They hadn't lost their sense of humor, as they teased me by drawing a picture of a jumbo jet with me in the window, clutching my Canadian passport and waving, "Goodbye!" to them in the airline carrier: Air Blessed.

We spent most of the day in the shelter, until the authorities deemed it safe to go home. My coworkers were deeply embroiled in their card game, thus in no hurry to leave, and only called it a day when one of them won the final hand. I still felt very nervous and begged Marko not to come get me, but he insisted. I was marrying a brave, if somewhat stubborn, man—in other words, young. But his love for me knew no bounds, and in no time I heard the sound of his car outside, which somewhat resembled the reverberations of the earlier bombing.

Aside from Marko's car, an eerie silence descended on the central streets, amid apparent incredulity that rockets could fall out of a clear blue sky on a European city of one million people. The streets were empty, and all one could hear on the radio was nationalistic Croatian music. "For home, brothers, for Freedom ... Croatia will never forget her warriors." Regardless, the blasts had left people in fear that the war would escalate, and it panicked and stunned a city that believed it lived in an oasis amid the conflict.

The U.S. Embassy evacuated dependents and advised its citizens to leave Croatia.

Marko took me to his mother's house for dinner, though I had no appetite. A few hours later, he drove me home, while I worried that Marko and I made an easy moving target, because the bright orange car could be seen—and heard—from a long distance away. Terror gripped me, and I slept little that night, with the slightest sound waking me. Overnight, my life in a stylish European city had lost its appeal, and I wanted to be back with my family in Canada, the safe land, the country whose national symbol was a beaver. I didn't want to leave Marko behind, but I knew he would never leave his family. It was my preview of the difficult realm of cross-cultural dating.

People tried to resume their activities. The next morning I nervously got into Marko's car, which I felt had a bull's-eye on it, and he drove me to the office.

I was in the middle of translating when, at midday, Zagreb was again shelled by rockets. These attacks claimed two lives and injured fifty-four people. A seat on Air Blessed began to sound appealing. The person who had fearlessly flown into Croatia two short years ago was fading away, replaced by a frightened woman I didn't know. My youth ended a little bit more with each passing day, and the feeling of being invincible disappeared.

Despite my new feelings, the city moved on, the radio went back to playing pop songs, and Zagreb once again felt safe. Marko and I continued planning our future together.

Months later, there would be a few more scares, with air raid sirens blasting and people scurrying to bomb shelters.

The war effectively ended on August 5, 1995. The country celebrated, while I began my own battles.

RUNAWAY GROOM

by Ivanka Di Felice

MARKO ALMOST LEFT ME AT the altar. If he'd had the courtesy to do that, I would at least have had a chance to wear the prohibitively expensive wedding dress, the only item my seamstress had ever made on time. Had he left me on our honeymoon, we would have used the airline tickets we had purchased to Canada; we would have made a grand entrance, received congratulations, and laughed with our friends. Then, when he consequently dumped me, at least I would be on home soil, so I could begin crying with people I knew. And they would have a face to put to the man who had done this to me.

Instead, he chose to leave me three weeks before the wedding. Six days after my dress was delivered, three days after I gave up my apartment and we leased one together, and one day after we booked our tickets to Toronto from Zagreb. But not before he crashed his beloved orange car and left me with whiplash as a "souvenir" of our time together for years to come. How the other party involved in the accident didn't see or hear us coming in that orange contraption is still beyond explanation. Once he broke up with me, the cartoon-like car ceased to be amusing.

Why did he leave me? I didn't know. But I exhausted all of my sources in asking that question: friends, acquaintances, workmates, and strangers. Unbeknownst to me at the time, I even begged my future husband to tell me why Marko had left me. I questioned anyone who would lend a listening ear, "Excuse me, do you know what time it is?" ... quickly followed by a teary-eyed "*Why* did he leave me?"

I finally gave up looking for the answer or, more accurately, ran out of unsuspecting souls to ask.

It no longer matters, and twenty years later, after years of absolutely no therapy, I can claim to be the same unstable person I was before this incident. Ask the one who didn't get away, my husband, David.

You see, once upon a time in a land far, far away, there was an Italian prince named David. He didn't want to end up like poor, pathetic Frank, who, despite his Mafioso hit man appearance, broke down bawling during his wedding speech when he told his mother how much he would miss her—all the while knowing that he and his new bride would be moving into his parents' basement. Hence, fearing this same fate, at the young age of twenty-four David proudly announced to his parents that he had bought a house.

They were impressed. "A rental property is a great idea!"

David paused, then mustered up the courage to say, "Well, actually, I thought I'd move into the house."

In shock, his sweet Italian mother was reduced to tears. Her sorrow was unrelenting for the next few days, as she wondered what she had done wrong.

And so Prince David moved into his castle or, more accurately, into a small duplex in the dodgy Keele and Eglinton neighborhood, not far from my mother and sister's house. They soon met and became friends. He had heard stories about this heroic woman Ivanka, who had moved to Croatia, and he had seen pictures.

Our prince, not unlike most, was confident and boasted, "If I had met her before she left, then she and I would be together, for sure."

Because I was far away, and we didn't have a chance to speak often, it was easy for my family to remember only my good qualities. Furthermore, I was selective about what I wrote, and to coincide with my perfection, pictures I mailed were only complimentary ones, in which I appeared taller, prettier, and, of course, bustier than I actually was. Hence, the more stories David heard and the more pictures he saw of our brave princess, the more he was convinced that he had missed out on true happiness by a few months. Had he only picked an earlier closing date.

David was, in fact, the type of guy I had long dreamed of marrying: a dark, handsome Italian. And he had just purchased a house, albeit not in my preferred neighborhood—but nonetheless.

He got to know, and was an instant hit among, the crowd of friends I had left behind. On rare occasions when I got to speak to my family, David was there, and the sound of laughter filled the background. Once I'd told him about my wedding plans and thanked him for helping out with the preparations.

My family had even foolishly proposed a skit where David would waltz in, well dressed and elegant, and they would say that was the man they'd always thought I would marry, but instead here was the man I was marrying, and an unequivocally goofy-looking friend would saunter in. Thankfully, David, if not my family, had the sense to refuse to have any part in a skit that could humiliate the groom. Despite never having met me or the groom, David was such an integral part of my family's and friends' lives that he received an invitation to my wedding. To boot, Italians were known to always give substantial cash gifts.

Yet as time went on, David dated other women and long forgot his earlier proclamation of devotion to Princess

199

Ivanka. Just as well, because the princess had already found her prince, and duels were no longer in fashion.

DAZED AND CONFUSED

by Ivanka Di Felice

SINCE I WAS ACCUSTOMED TO living in my own fantasy world—which made sense, given that the flight of my imagination often proved far more glamorous than my life—I couldn't accept what was happening. I couldn't rid myself of visions of waking up at the altar in my wedding dress, just at the moment when the groom is told he may kiss the bride.

We weren't like couples who divorced after fighting for years and who still felt pent-up frustration and bitterness. Weeks ago, Marko and I had been deliriously happy. Aside from the noisy orange car and the occasional bombing in the city where I lived, my life went from being a fairy tale to a nightmare, with nothing in between.

I sat in a daze, in tears, asking myself, "Why did he leave me?" then asking the same question of Vesna, my sister, who had fortuitously come the month prior. The only person who, I assume, knew the answer was Marko, but if he did, he wouldn't let me in on it, despite my pleading. My mind raced, going over every possible mistaken word, thought, accidental snort, joke about family or homeland, and so on. My brain got the exercise of a lifetime.

201

There was no point in my staying in Croatia. I sat there crying, watching my sister pack up virtually all of my worldly possessions and my dreams with them. I was forced to come to terms with what had happened when she took me to the travel agent to cancel Marko's ticket and re-book mine to fly home with her. The shock of the re-booking fee was in itself quite sobering.

Worse still, I had one more thing to do: bring back the hideous mustard yellow couch. Maybe my landlord's son would get married before me, after all. This thought sent me into another fit of crying.

***

Vesna drove me back to Koprivnica, as I stared out the window at the countryside that no longer appeared as pretty as in the past. I tried to compose myself and put on a happy expression for my father as I exited the car, but my swollen face and eyes gave away my true feelings. He stared at the ground awkwardly, not knowing what to say. The eerie silence was as if a death had just taken place in the family.

It broke my heart, because I wasn't the only one suffering. Every choice we made (or, in this case, that others made) affected someone, and those dear to me were also in pain. With my returning to Canada, my father's dream of a house filled with little Croatian children was shattered. All of that cooking, construction work, and drinking beer had been for naught.

Next, we drove in silence to the home where my grandma now lived. They'd found her a place, and she loved it there, not wanting to even come home on weekends, fearful they would give away her spot. She greeted me with a kiss and sympathetic eyes. At her age, with the many difficult times she had experienced, she knew that life didn't always deliver what we expected. Hence, she was pragmatic.

"You're young, you'll find someone else."

Her words confirmed that she didn't believe Marko would change his mind, and this sent me into another round of tears.

Poor Vesna had spent three precious weeks of vacation babysitting me, time that she would never get back.

As the plane took off, I knew it was over. The last-minute dash to the airport where Marko stopped the plane, boarded it, and carried me off wasn't going to happen. Instead, I would be exiting the automatic doors at the Canadian airport, where a few of my friends, with sad faces, would await, hoping to help pick up the pieces of what was left of me.

Though the pain was too fresh, and it seemed inconceivable at the moment, I would eventually have to get over it, and I hoped my father could, too.

In an effort to lift my mood, Vesna said, "There is always David. I think you will like him."

I closed my eyes and attempted to sleep, hoping the other passengers wouldn't notice my whimpering.

"MY NAME IS INIGO MONTOYA"

by Ivanka Di Felice

WE LANDED, AND EVEN CUSTOMS must have felt sorry for me, because they quickly whisked me through with virtually no questions—a first for me. I was returning to a city of six million inhabitants, with a roomful of good friends waiting, yet I felt utterly alone. My life mimicked the final scene of an opera.

My mom hugged me, teary eyed. I looked at her, in awe of how she had survived these last few tragic years: the death of my brother, Kathy's poor choice in living quarters, the near death of her mother. Now, Marko's leaving me paled in comparison to the other events. Had someone told her in advance what she would have to endure, she said she would have begged, "Just shoot me now, please."

Yet she discovered an inner strength greater than she'd ever imagined. She would have one more test, for they say a mother is only ever as happy as her unhappiest child.

David dropped in to visit a few days later. I had never been an elegant crier. My eyes didn't "sparkle with tears," and my nose and face swelled, turned bright red, and rendered me clogged, no longer able to breathe quietly, blubbering. Thus, the image David had in his mind bore no resemblance to the woman in front of him. The brave princess who'd written witty letters of her adventures abroad was no more. The smiling woman with the long, bouncy waves and fashionable European clothing was in hiding. The little he was able to see of me, prior to me running upstairs to my room to cry, was not very appealing. Getting dressed up or washing my hair was not on my list of priorities—or, really, on any list of mine. I could easily be a poster child for "thirty is the new sixty" and a disheveled, crazed sixty at that.

And although I wasn't the woman he expected, neither did he live up to my fantasies. At the time, David sought employment as a teacher, and, in hopes of appearing older, he had chosen to grow a mustache. This wasn't my favorite look. In my experience, only Burt Reynolds and certain elderly women sported mustaches.

The indisputable power a mustache had to transform a formerly handsome person into an eccentric, odd character was proved. He looked like Inigo Montoya from *The Princess Bride*, and our friends teased him, "My name is Inigo Montoya. You killed my father. Prepare to die."

I'm aligned with the Amish, who strictly forbid their members to grow mustaches. The dark, handsome Italian I had heard about was incognito.

Thus, our journey together began as a somber affair. Months passed, and I remained despondent. I returned to work at the brokerage firm, but the one-hour ride on public transit afforded me more time to ask, "Why did he leave me?" followed by light sobbing.

I slowly drove my family insane. They felt for me, but this had dragged on far too long. Although they had liked Marko, they didn't feel it was worth destroying my life over losing him. I had lost perspective and only regained it when Vesna, normally the sane one, started speeding like a demon on a main road in Toronto, stating, "Well, if you want to die, I might as well go with you."

It was time to do something—if not for my sake, for the sake of those around me.

I went to my doctor, a Chinese lady with an affinity for short skirts, wild hair, and lots of makeup. The only part of her attire that even hinted she might be a doctor was the white jacket she wore over her otherwise nightclub attire.

She listened patiently as I droned on. Having exhausted all of my friends and acquaintances, I took advantage of my latest victim and poured out my heart, much to the dismay of the other patients in the waiting room. After more than the requisite amount of time, she plainly said, "You keep scratching a wound, not letting it heal. You need help!"

She took out her prescription pad and scribbled something legible only to pharmacists'. "This is an antidepressant and will help you get up again."

That sent me into an even deeper depression. I wasn't the "type" of person who needed help via prescription drugs, but as I sat there, sobbing, dehydrating myself, and remembering the scene with my sister in the car, I realized it might be time to get help.

I got the prescription filled, and, as time went on, I began to see the light at the end of the tunnel. The vision got even clearer when I received an invitation to come and stay in Paris with my friend Leah. She probably hadn't intended for me to stay three months, but I did. Time spent in the "City of Lights," drinking fine wine, whipping up gourmet food, and strolling the streets of Paris, did wonders for me, as undoubtedly did the antidepressants.

It was time for me to go back to Toronto, and my ever-patient roommate must have felt the same. I unwittingly spent the last of my money on a chic French haircut, ready to face the world.

I eventually didn't need the medication but, ever since, have been an advocate of meds when all else fails. Plus, a little Paris, a French handbag, and a new haircut never hurt.

In my absence, Inigo Montoya had taken leave. In his place was a man whose eyes sparkled, and his previously hidden dimples now emerged when he smiled. With the mustache gone, he might just stand a chance.

"HAPPILY EVER AFTER"

by Ivanka Di Felice

DESPITE BEING ITALIAN, DAVID WAS private. My family was
anything but. Balkans were not known for keeping their
emotions or their opinions in check, as two world wars had
proved. My family was intrusive, while David was elusive.

"Would you like to come over tomorrow?" my mother
asked David.

"No, thank you, I have *plans*," David would respond. In
our family, that statement meant we had an open invitation to
follow up with the question "What kind of plans?"—so
Vesna would ask.

"Plans," was always David's final response, patently
unaware that this answer wouldn't satisfy us. Yet because my
mother had her own plans—namely, that David should marry
one of her daughters—she didn't give up.

As David had no "plans" one Friday night, he arranged
for a group of us to come over to watch the uplifting movie
Who's Afraid of Virginia Wolf?

It was a crisp winter night in Toronto. The snow fell
gently, slowly accumulating, turning everything a powdery
white. Even the small homes in this otherwise poorer

neighborhood in the city suddenly appeared pretty. The lights from their windows sparkled as brightly on the pristine snow as did the ones in the richer neighborhoods; the snow brought equality. Dinner plans did not bring the same equality, because they included purchasing Kentucky Fried Chicken.

Because my mother had her own "plans," she was glad to accompany David to walk in the pretty, snow-covered city, but mostly to take advantage of her time alone with him. I feared she had watched *Pride and Prejudice* one time too many.

As they climbed up the hill, they discussed the usual subjects that had helped bond their friendship: the latest books they had read and movies they had seen, with my mother providing most of the commentary on each one. Not wanting to appear overly zealous or ruin any chances to get the Kentucky Fried chicken, she waited until the return home to discuss with David the real reason she had so readily volunteered to accompany him.

Having secured the purchase of the chicken and being close enough to his house, in case any quick exits were required, she asked David, "So, what's wrong with one of my two daughters?"

David almost dropped the bucket of KFC. Instead, his jaw dropped. He would not be answering that question, and my mother thought it best to ask one more time, "in case he had not heard" her properly the first time. David knew better than to reply. To avoid further interrogation from my mother, he quickened his pace and in no time reached the front door.

"Where's my mom?" I asked.

"Oh, she should be arriving soon," said David. "She is walking slowly to enjoy the beauty of the night."

My mom made an appearance soon thereafter, and she kept her interrogation of David secret. Yet as time went on, she couldn't help bringing up other controversial topics with David, so they got into many heated discussions. In our family this was normal, but David would vow he didn't need this. He would disappear for several weeks, and we all missed him on those occasions.

There was something that made David special. Everyone loved him. Perhaps it was that mischievous glint in his eye or his charm and charisma or how he loved to tease others, irreverently telling my mother her fashion icon appeared to have been "Mrs. Roper from *Three's Company*," and letting her know her muumuus were not as fashionable as she assumed. We weren't sure why, but he must have missed something about us, too, because after a few weeks' absence he would be back, sometimes despite his better judgment.

And so it happened that I fell for this handsome man, who years ago had said that "she and I would be together, for sure," if I hadn't left for Croatia. I hoped he would prove to be a prophet.

Months went by, and David kept dropping in more frequently, thus I got my hopes up. I patiently waited for him to ask me out, while my mom not so patiently waited for him to ask me out. Every so often, she reminded him that she had "a perfectly good daughter, so why look elsewhere?"

To make matters worse, in 1996 the movie *Emma* was released. David bore not only a strong physical resemblance to the character Mr. Knightly in the period film, but my mother imagined that his character was similar as well and that while he was Mr. Knightly, I was Emma. My mother once again took on the role of a matchmaker. David then took on the role of Mr. Knightly more fully and disappeared for another long while. With all of her "help," David and I stood no chance of getting together.

Yet she wasn't the only one with a plan. My sister and I surprised our mom by renting her an apartment in downtown Paris. Because, after all, such a cultured woman who loved art and classic literature must see Paris, and she must see it before David disappeared again—perhaps for good. Then a friend, Chantal, a member of the Davey family, arranged for my mother to spend time in Switzerland with her elderly aunt. The combination should prove amusing: a bohemian Balkan and a woman who had lived her entire life according to the precision of a Swiss watch. Then off to Croatia to visit family. Surely, this would buy us enough time so that if David and I were ever going to get together, it would be now or never.

So I spent my summer days working and, evenings studying for the Canadian Securities course, which was required for my job at the brokerage firm. David spent his time working at a cabinetmaking shop, and then afterward he would drop in with snacks for me to enjoy, during what he called a "much-needed break" from my studying. As his drop-ins became more frequent and my breaks became longer, I feared not passing my exams but was rather helpless about saying no.

I let my heart believe that David must be interested. Someone who was "just a friend" wouldn't be that concerned with others' nutritional needs. Yet time went on, and David didn't ask me out. So, not wanting to invest my heart any further, even though it might mean I would have to procure snacks for myself, I set a deadline: he would have to ask me out by August 15, or else the frequent visits would have to stop. I couldn't risk another heartbreak—not only for my sake but for the sake of others as well.

It was early August, and my hopes and aspirations of wearing a wedding dress were once again dashed.

With my mom safely in Switzerland, touring according to the grueling schedule of the aged aunt, David had invited a few friends over for after-dinner drinks. We met him as he arrived home from a meeting. He was strikingly handsome in his Italian suit.

"Make yourselves comfortable while I change," he said.

We sat down on his L-shaped couch and waited for him in the stifling summer heat.

He came out of his bedroom, and he had definitely "changed" and made himself more than comfortable. Gone was the handsome Italian in his thousand-dollar tailored suit, it being replaced by something "priceless"—priceless, in the sense that it couldn't be worth a cent. His deep attachment to his baby blue pajama bottoms from the sixth grade was evident. Worse yet, not only were they made for someone twelve years old, they were pilled. They came below his knees and made him look like a ballerina. Completing this "look," he'd shed his crisp white shirt and was down to a wife beater undershirt, with the gold chain his mother had given him—which was usually, thankfully, hidden under his shirt—in clear view around his neck.

My heart plummeted. Anyone who would come out dressed like that obviously had no interest in me. Because I had already invested part of my heart in him, I would again be reduced to asking anyone who would listen, "Why doesn't he love me?"

I tried to make the best of the evening but returned home saddened, because I had suffered all evening, uncomfortably sweltering in a pretty dress for hours, while David sat happily in his ode to childhood.

"I'm certain that David isn't interested in me," I told Vesna. "If he had the slightest interest in me, would he have dressed like that tonight?"

Vesna, who usually told me I put too much emphasis on looks and that I imagined things, was quiet, then said, "You're right."

There would be no need for any deadlines.

I studied furiously for my Canadian Securities course. Because romance was not in my near future, at least I could pass the exam with flying colors and please my work-obsessed boss.

"Time is money," he would chant.

David still dropped in with snacks, but less often. My exam was on August 12, and I hoped those long hours of studying would pay off.

On August 13, David came over. He said he would like to speak with me, and I later learned that I reacted like a deer in the headlights. This threw him off somewhat, but he told me, "I really like you and your family."

I laughed, because a young Portuguese guy had once written me a poem, saying, "Every time I see your face, it makes me stick around, that means I like you and your face." This time it was me and my family.

August 13th. He'd beaten the deadline by two days, not even aware one existed or that I had recently removed it, convinced there was no need of it. He had waited until I finished my exams, not wanting to distract me. If only he had known how much those baby blue pajama bottoms had done so.

He admitted to "secretly dating me for months," to ensure we wouldn't court for a while, then break up. He had seen firsthand what that had done to me. If I were going to ask strangers what had happened to my love life, then it wouldn't be due to him.

His timing, though, was slightly off, because Vesna and I had arranged to have the bathroom and kitchen tiles replaced. As a result, David spent the first two weeks of our courtship renovating my mom's house. Still, he was somewhat pleased, because in two weeks of dating, all I had cost him was a few dollars in roses. Thankfully, his calculations didn't include the backbreaking labor he did each evening, or he might have determined I was too high-maintenance.

My mom returned from Europe full of stories, happy that we were dating. On seeing her bathroom and kitchen, she was even more ecstatic that I had found a man who could renovate. Taking a chance and buying David that Swiss watch had paid off.

My father, too, was thrilled that I was "finally" getting married at twenty-nine.

And just as Emma and Mr. Knightly got together and lived happily ever after, so did we.

Only then did I find out my mom had asked David, "What's wrong with one of my two daughters?" I was grateful that he never told her.

I also learned that although things may not always go the way you planned, sometimes things turn out even better.

My only regret is that my grandmother passed away three weeks before our wedding. Since she had always lived vicariously through us, I felt sad not to be able to share this day with her, mailing her pictures and showing her wedding dress number two. I was happy, however, that she knew I had found a wonderful man and that she assumed I would "live happily ever after."

And I was happy to hear that the family honored her wishes. Though it was an unusual request, they buried her without shoes. She hated wearing them, always complaining they were never comfortable, and had asked us to let her rest in peace, shoeless.

HOT STONE MASSAGE

by Ivanka Di Felice

ASIDE FROM LEAVING ME WITH a broken heart, which was fully healed, Marko had also left me with a sore neck from the accident we were in, just prior to breaking up. Although Marko was an ambulance chaser for work, not for a second did I imagine he'd caused this accident for the $150 reward the lawyer gave him for bringing in a new client. Yet even though he must have known he would be breaking up with me, there was no use leaving $150 on the table, so he referred me to the lawyer he worked for.

I thought the pain in my neck would eventually pass, as did the pain in my heart, but instead it lingered for years. When I woke up one morning, I couldn't lift my head. I placed both hands behind my head and, with David's aid, lifted myself out of bed. In desperation, David and I searched the yellow pages for a massage clinic, avoiding any with exotic-sounding Asian names or in dodgy parts of town.

We found one in the High Park area, a distinguished neighborhood, my old one, and made an appointment with a gentleman named Harold. Fortunately, he had an opening, so we drove right over.

We found the address on a residential tree-lined street and knocked. A very tall man with long white hair, resembling a mad scientist, opened the door. He invited us in, and a German shepherd greeted us. The historic home had large dark beams running across the ceiling, and the ancient oak floors of the house squeaked as we walked across them. The place was rather messy, and his living room doubled as the waiting area, strewn with articles of clothing and leftover food sitting on the coffee table, instead of the customary *Vogue* or other magazines.

Harold told me to follow him to a room in the back, while David waited in the living room with the dog.

He instructed me to undress down to my underwear and to make myself comfortable on the massage table. I took off my clothes and crawled under the sheets, which felt as if Harold had not discovered fabric softener. Or, by the smell of them, laundry detergent. But I was desperate, so I stayed and tried not to breathe.

Harold returned and began to massage my neck and back, while I cringed. He was very strong, and his motto was "No pain, no gain." On more than one occasion, I had to beg for mercy. I cursed Marko each time Harold worked on my neck.

The second half hour would involve a "relaxing hot stone massage." Harold got the stones ready with a lot of clanging and banging. The noise got the attention of the German shepherd, and the dog pushed open the door. I laughed to think we had chosen this address because it was in a good neighborhood. Thus, I anticipated soft music playing, the air scented with lavender. Instead, the clanging continued, as the German shepherd sniffed me, his cold wet nose touching my skin. I struggled to remain calm, as I pictured his teeth digging into pounds of my flesh. Harold paid the dog no mind, as he panted next to me, his smelly breath hot on my skin and his brown eyes staring at mine. Harold, having completed what he was doing with the stones, much to my relief, shooed the dog out.

As he laid the warm stones on my back, he caught me up on his life, which incidentally hadn't been easy these last few years. Harold finished up, while I felt sorry for him and grateful that my only real problems the previous year had to do with my neck.

He sat down next to a little machine and typed a receipt. He left while I got dressed.

David had booked an appointment for himself, so we waited together in the living room/waiting area while Harold, I hoped, changed the sheets.

"David, the room is ready," yelled Harold from the other end of the house. I took that as a good sign.

David left me and the German shepherd amid the mess. It was just as well there weren't any magazines, because I wasn't comfortable taking my eyes off the dog. German shepherds can be very vicious guard dogs. He stared at me and didn't appear menacing, but one never knew.

As I sat uneasily, it seemed as if David was getting a two-hour massage. Finally, the door opened and Harold came out, followed by David.

David paid Harold, and we both thanked him for the great, if rather strong, massage.

As soon as we were out of earshot, I said, "While you were having a long massage, I sat frightened in the living room with his guard dog."

"Guard dog? Are you crazy?" David asked. "That was his seeing eye dog! Don't tell me you didn't notice that Harold is blind?"

It took a moment to sink in, but it all made sense. Yet admitting I hadn't noticed would have been too embarrassing. I gave David an all-knowing smile but didn't fool him, not even for a second.

TABLE FOR FIVE, DINNER FOR ONE

by Ivanka Di Felice

I LEARNED TO COOK FROM Alice, or, rather, I learned to choose and follow gourmet recipes from Alice. She loved making fancy dinners and often spent three days and hundreds of dollars preparing a feast for family and friends. The tablecloth was ironed, the table set with china and crystal, and candles were lit. It was always a special occasion going to Alice's for dinner. It provided many who could otherwise not afford it with an evening out, comparable to dining in a fine restaurant.

My family often called Alice to ask for a recipe, and she always kindly gave us a copy. Weeks later, we'd call again, asking for the same one. It was easier to keep getting them from her than it was to organize them somewhere in our house.

After all of these years, Alice thought she could reform the gypsy family down the street. She painstakingly copied all of her popular recipes and put them in a book for us. We were thrilled and profusely thanked her for this wonderful gift, which we used for months, until we lost it.

And after all of these years, it was still easier to call Ed and ask for a phone number than to keep the pencil sharp and a piece of paper handy.

Vesna never did learn to cook from Alice or from my mom, who was known for making wonderful Croatian food and sharing it with others. Our dinners never had fancy tablecloths or china or crystal glasses, but, nonetheless, people enjoyed dining at our not-so-fine establishment.

However, Vesna did learn hospitality from both our mother and Alice, thus invited her boss over for dinner. She also phoned to invite David and me.

"What can I bring?" I asked.

Vesna unhesitatingly replied, "I will be serving spaghetti with meat sauce, garlic bread, and a salad. So, can you bring the meat sauce, the garlic bread, and the salad?"

My jaw dropped, but she assured me, "I will take care of the pasta."

I had a good laugh and agreed to help her out.

On the evening of the dinner, needless to say, we arrived early, because I was bringing most of it. Vesna hovered over the stove with a wooden spoon in her hand. She waved us in and said, "Everything is under control."

I began to feel a sense of doom.

I opened the lid of the pot that was boiling away, and, indeed, Vesna had prepared the boiling water.

I handed her the garlic bread, and she put it in the oven to keep it warm.

Kelly would be coming soon, so I had to hurry to put everything I had brought on the stove.

Soon we noticed black smoke escaping from the oven. Vesna had inadvertently turned on the broiler and burned the garlic bread. To compensate, she scrounged through the fridge and found a scrap of cheese, which she cut up and put on a small plate with some crackers. They were most likely stale, but I couldn't be certain, because there weren't enough for us to have any.

219

Vesna suddenly remembered she had forgotten to buy dessert, so she emptied the contents of her freezer, searching for two frozen chocolate crepes that Alice had sent home with us months ago. Because Vesna didn't believe items in the freezer had an expiration date, she would serve them to Kelly. Since there also wouldn't be enough dessert, Vesna devised a plan. Not wanting to appear ridiculous serving the crepes only to Kelly, she would offer them to all of us; however, we would politely decline. Dessert would be easy, because we could feign being too full, while Vesna's lactose intolerance would finally come in handy.

We discovered the same was true of pre-dinner drinks. Kelly was on time, and Vesna immediately offered her a rye and ginger ale. She gladly accepted, and Vesna took out a miniature bottle of rye she had saved from a plane trip and opened the one can of ginger ale in the fridge.

She whisked Kelly into the living room and soon emerged with the pre-dinner drink for Kelly and placed the miniature plate of cheese and crackers on the coffee table. Kelly sat back and politely waited for the rest of us to be served before she began drinking.

Vesna sat down, and Kelly asked, "Is no one else having a drink?"

Though I longed for a drink, I replied, "Oh, no, thank you, I really couldn't."

Although David certainly could, he also "couldn't."

We eyed the cheese and crackers but also "couldn't." Kelly must have admired our self-control as our stomachs growled, yet we still didn't permit ourselves even a small piece of cheese. My mom, too, displayed willpower as she limited her intake of cheese to none.

Thankfully, we could break from acting for a short time, because we all had a heaping plate of pasta with meat sauce and salad.

The Oscar–worthy performance resumed when dessert was served—for one, along with an after-dinner drink, for Kelly.

Vesna forfeited the Best Supporting Actress role when she even forgot to feign offering us dessert.

"No wonder you stay so slim," Kelly said.

We only watch our diet when we come here and Vesna has "everything under control," I wanted to say but instead just grinned.

Kelly had a great time and left full and happy and none the wiser. We left, though amused, much wiser.

Yet our family and home created a favorable impression with Kelly, for soon thereafter she moved into the basement, supplementing her role as Vesna's boss with one as my mom's tenant.

I wondered how long it would be before Vesna told Kelly what had really happened on the night of Table for Five, Dinner for One. I wished I could be there to see Kelly's undoubtedly astounded face.

***

The following day, in the spring of 2000, the movie *Lumumba* was released. On seeing the advertisement, my mom immediately remembered the demonstration. Forty years had passed, and she would finally learn who Patrice Lumumba was. They say that strong emotion can strengthen memory for positive events. Because my mom had left the protest invigorated, despite not knowing who Lumumba was or what happened to him, she was convinced that she played a large part in the destiny of Mr. Lumumba.

Hence, she vividly described to us the event that had taken place decades ago in her hometown.

Vesna took our mother to see the movie about the man she had lost her voice for.

"What did you think?" Vesna asked afterward.

My mother, unchanged from her youth, replied, "Had I known, I would have shouted even louder, if that was possible. To protest the inhuman treatment of him and against inhumanity of people in general. The movie broke my heart. I cried for him not as a politician but as a man who tried to help his people, but now I know that shouting does not help. The forces ruling the earth are impervious to human suffering and shouting."

Patrice Émery Lumumba, born on July 2, 1925, was a Congolese independence leader and the first democratically elected leader of the Congo. He played an important role in campaigning for independence from Belgium. Within twelve weeks of Congolese independence in 1960, Lumumba's government was deposed in a coup, and he was subsequently imprisoned by state authorities and executed by firing squad on January 17, 1961. He was thirty-five years old. After the announcement of Lumumba's death, street protests were organized in several European countries; in Belgrade, the capital of Yugoslavia, protesters sacked the Belgian embassy and confronted the police. Not remembering the exact date of the demonstration, my mother might even have been protesting his death, not what he stood for in his life.

At least, forty years later, she now knew who he was.

"RENT TO OWN"

by Ivanka Di Felice

DAVID AND I DROVE DOWN our street past small homes surrounded by few trees, a testament to the one-time prominence of Italians in the area. Tall trees, known enemies of tomato plants, had been hacked down, enabling sunlight to reach the vegetable gardens, while denuding the streetscape. Then Jamaicans slowly took over the neighborhood, as the majority of Italians moved north to the newly formed, and fortuitously treeless, suburbs.

We arrived in my father's neighborhood with its tree-lined streets and grand homes. For years, I'd dreamed that David and I would be able to buy a home here, but with real estate prices through the roof in Toronto, we would never be able to afford it, not without tenants. Roncesvalles Avenue was alive with hip restaurants, cafés full of fashionable people, and shops selling fruit and colorful flowers.

I laughed, as we pulled up to my dad's house full of more varied types of individuals. My father, on the porch, waved when he saw us and looked at his watch. I'd said we would be here *sometime after* 2, and it was now 2:15. He had most likely

223

been waiting on the porch for the last fifteen minutes, wondering where on earth we were for fourteen of them.

A tenant marched past us in a huff, not returning my greeting. My father gestured the cuckoo sign.

We exchanged double kisses with my father and followed him through the kitchen to his large, shady backyard. Mirko was outside, wearing, as always, an unflattering black leather cap. Poor Mirko, I suspected that he covered his head to avoid hearing the Croatians quote, *"Pametna kosa ostavlja blesavu glavu"* ("Smart hair leaves a stupid head"). He'd finished lunch and was spreading the remaining polenta on a wooden board, one of many contraptions used to feed the birds. He added fried sausage and completed this culinary masterpiece by sprinkling the fat drippings on top. As if having studied the feeding habits of birds at length, he launched into a long sermon on how birds preferred his cuisine to birdseed. I expected to see plenty of fat sparrows, barely flying around. A jug of red wine sat on the table, half empty, alerting me to what type of afternoon this would be.

My father, meanwhile, was engaged in his favorite pastime: painting. A can of bright red paint sat open on the ground, the brush hanging off the edge, dripping paint. This time my dad was painting a birdhouse, along with his pants, his new jacket, his Chinese flip-flops, and the cement patio below. My mom had nicknamed my dad "Picasso," and today he lived up to the name.

"What's with that guy?" I asked my dad, referring to the tenant who had snubbed us. The second I asked, I was sorry I had, as my dad explained that he had been given his eviction notice.

"That idiot decided to stop paying rent," my father said.

Mirko, as always, excitedly interrupted, also calling the tenant "Idiot," as if that were his name. He marched back and forth, shouting, and completely worked himself into a rage, as if the tenant owed *him* large sums of rent.

My father waved his hand, shushing Mirko and demanding that he calm down.

"What do you mean, he decided to stop paying rent?" I asked. "Did he lose his job?"

My father laughed sinisterly, at the mere thought of this guy ever having worked. "No, he said he's done paying rent. He has paid me rent for many years and that's enough. So your sister told him that 'This is not rent to own,' and his response was 'Your dad has way more money than I do, so I'm not paying him any more rent!'"

My father shook his head at the ludicrous situation, but I sighed, picturing a possible court battle, which my sister Kathy would contend with. My father never dealt with the legality of being a landlord, so he assumed these tenants, of their own volition, would just move on.

Mirko took another swig of wine and, having found courage in the bottom of his glass, enthusiastically offered his own method for getting rid of this troublesome tenant. My father preferred Mirko's plan of intimidation as a quicker and easier solution, so I got involved in the debate. In Mirko's haste to blurt out words, he couldn't decide which language to speak, so he mixed Croatian and English and threw in a bit of Italian, he said for David, even though David had been born in Canada. Mirko was one of the few people trying to keep the language "Esperanto" alive.

Mirko insisted we have some wine and, despite our protests, grabbed two dirty glasses from the shed. He "rinsed" them by pouring in some wine, swirling it vigorously, and chucking it into the shrubs. David gave me his "Now I've seen it all" look and fearfully eyed the murky glass of wine Mirko placed directly in front of him, as if it were about to attack.

Although David viewed expiration dates as mere suggestions and wasn't finicky, his face showed his aversion to drinking out of receptacles that were stored in sheds.

"Cheers!" yelled Mirko and downed half of his glass, thankfully without waiting for anyone to join in.

David and I, meanwhile, suddenly developed a deep interest in the type of paint my father was using and put our glasses down to examine the can.

Mirko took another big swig and then peered curiously at the bottom of his empty glass, as if the wine had evaporated. Tata showed us how this birdhouse had an additional feature that would prevent the greedy squirrels from climbing up and snatching the food. He always strove to outsmart the squirrels, a battle he usually lost. All aesthetics had been thrown to the wind, as jagged spikes of metal jutted out from the bottom.

Mirko insisted I come into the house so he could show me his latest purchases. Mirko lived in a tiny room with nothing more than a bed and a dresser, but he was obsessed with owning expensive watches and silver and gold coins and repeatedly bought more of them.

"No, I'll wait here," I said.

Mirko jumped up and ran into the house. David, grateful, took this as his cue to dump our wine.

Mirko reappeared in a flash with a gold watch in his hand and a glass serving tray etched with flowers he had purchased at a garage sale. He handed me the tray to give to my mother and then explained the workings of the watch and how much it was valued at, how much he'd paid for it, and so on.

Mirko had his quirks, but I admired his generosity, and it was ever present as he noticed our empty glasses and immediately refilled them. David looked at me, startled into temporary paralysis. Meanwhile, Andy, a tenant from downstairs, who had radar for free liquor, stumbled into the yard.

"Steve, I wanted to tell you that I rinsed the garbage bins. All of them."

As usual, Andy announced some unsolicited work he'd done, in hopes of getting a reward. Mirko rolled his eyes for the benefit of my father and mumbled something in Croatian. Though Mirko shared a bathroom with some other tenants, he shared a kitchen with my father, which made him feel superior, almost as if he were the co-owner or, at a minimum, a VIP tenant. He delighted in pointing out other tenants' personality flaws, and if that failed to catch my father's attention, he invented scintillating gossip about them in the hopes that he would be my dad's favorite. When a potential tenant showed up, Mirko was always quick to determine that "something doesn't look right about him." In these situations, Mirko controlled his customary habit of shouting and instead whispered and winked at my dad, implying that the prospective tenant had placed spies everywhere.

My father shrugged and smiled, handing Andy some money. Andy also smiled, while Mirko shook his head. Andy longingly gazed at the jug of wine on the table. Mirko, though not a fan of Andy's, nonetheless grabbed another spotty glass from the shed and, without "rinsing" it, poured Andy a glass of wine.

Mirko downed another glass, then looked at the bottom of it as if its contents had again miraculously disappeared.

Mirko's noisy ranting, combined with Andy's, got on my father's nerves, so he headed inside. David and I took this opportunity to follow Tata in, "forgetting" our glasses still full of wine outside.

My father blared the TV, and we watched some episodes of reality shows starring gold diggers, fishermen, and planes going down. I was enjoying the "relative peace and quiet" when Mirko showed up—carrying our two "forgotten" glasses of wine.

I laughed. "David, we can run, but we can't hide."

CROATIAN CULTURE SHOCK

by Ivanka Di Felice

MY LAST EXPERIENCE IN CROATIA had introduced me to bomb shelters, and, for an encore, my fiancé had left me three weeks before the wedding, with two newly printed plane tickets for our honeymoon. Despite these memories, I wanted to introduce David to my family and Croatian culture. My father felt proud to have another male in the family and viewed David as a son. In Canada, David was a cabinetmaker, but in the Croatian community, he was purported to be an engineer. Ironically, Tata loved the fact that David worked with his hands and had chosen a job that he loved, but he understood the Croatian mentality and thus elevated David to engineer.

Sadly, I couldn't introduce David to my grandma. Yet her two sisters were still alive, and we had always been close, so we went to greet *Baka* (Grandma) Katica, who lived next door to my grandma's old house, along with my mother's cousin Ivo and his wife. My dad accompanied us.

Though it was only nine in the morning, David was handed a large glass half filled with *šlivovic* (Croatian plum brandy), then a Turkish coffee.

David stared at the glass, certain that if he drank even a small portion of it, he would hit the ground and be out like a light—for days possibly. So he shook his head in what he assumed was a universally understood gesture. For extra emphasis, he said, "No, thank you."

He hadn't been married to me long enough yet to conclude that all Croatian people had a hearing problem or that they didn't have the word *No* in their vocabulary. Although he had said, "No," the drink still mysteriously sat in front of him.

The same thing happened with the strudel. He gladly ate two pieces, but when he said, "No, thank you," repeatedly, he was amazed at how fast another portion appeared on his plate. To appease everyone, he kept eating the strudel but couldn't force more than a few sips of the strong liquor. And although, yes, it was 5 p.m. somewhere in the world, this wasn't David's philosophy when it came to drinking.

Yet rather than conclude that I had landed a gem, Ivo asked, "What do you mean, he doesn't want a drink? Why not?" He supposed that something catastrophic must have taken place or David must be on strong medication.

I explained that it was neither, which satisfied Ivo, because he could resume pestering David to drink. "Tell him it's good for him."

Eighty-year-old *Baka* Katica confirmed her son's statement: "It's better to be a little drunk than a little sick."

Apparently in Croatia, it wasn't an apple a day that kept the doctor away but, rather, a hefty shot of *šlivovic*. David took another sip, burning his throat, and left the glass barely touched, to the disappointment of my family. Other than that, he seemed like a really nice guy to them. David was learning the Croatian culture. His brother, Carlo, had taken an overnight boat cruise from Italy to Croatia, with breakfast included. Early in the morning, Carlo had been offered a ham and cheese sandwich, as well as a generous shot of *šlivovic*. He ordered a coffee but was told it cost one euro.

"But I thought breakfast was included," Carlo said.

"It is. But that doesn't include coffee," the waiter said.

Only now could David fully believe the accuracy of Carlo's story.

Next, I took David to visit *Baka* Štefa, my grandmother's other sister, being cared for in a home in a village a few miles away. My dad was in a hurry to get the visiting of friends and family out of the way, so we could have free time to do what he thought we really came here for: to watch soccer. Hence, we arrived in record time.

We entered the second floor of the stuccoed house and were taken to her room. It was sad, furnished with just the basics: a dark brown metal frame bed, a dresser, and one picture hung crookedly on the wall.

Everyone agreed that *Baka* Štefa used to be very beautiful, but her face showed the ravages of time, along with her affinity for alcohol. Once, she had drunk too much and couldn't walk home from a vineyard, so her nephew took her home in a wheelbarrow. She sat back, legs flailing over the edge, as he tried to avoid the eyes of astounded drivers while wheeling her several miles along the main street.

I could see that at one time she must have been stunning. Her face, though wrinkled, had a lovely shape, she had a perfect nose, and her eyes were still large, round, and deep blue.

If my self-confidence had been low when I left Croatia several years ago, then she would ensure it remained that way. When she saw us, she immediately started crying. This, in itself, was not unusual, because Štefa had taken to weeping uncontrollably for years. Her son, Đuka, my mom's younger cousin, who as a youngster had run after the Galaxy and then accompanied her to the airport, had hung himself years ago, at the age of twenty-six. My grandma had sent a letter describing how they'd found him, and this proved to be one of the most devastating events my mother had endured up until then.

Štefa had never been the same afterward. Her son's death shattered all of us. The last time we'd seen him was when my mother and I had visited, the time I stopped a jumbo jet to retrieve my hat. He wore a white sailor's outfit, as we stood around in my grandma's yard, roasting corn on a fire, the adults catching up and laughing. Not long after this, my mom got that shocking letter.

I handed Štefa the gifts my mother had sent and the ones we'd brought, but she barely glanced at them or at me. She was too fascinated by David and stared at him for a long while. She looked back at me, then at David, and burst into violent tears, shouting, "He is going to leave you!"

In case I'd misheard, she repeated, "He is going to leave you!"

She didn't smell of alcohol. Could they have given her a "healthy" dose of it before we arrived?

David asked me to translate, and I foolishly did. This was not the Croatia I wanted David to experience, but what could I do? I consoled her that *this one* wasn't going to leave me, but she kept gazing at David, repeating how handsome he was, and she wasn't convinced. Thankfully, I had developed a thick skin and was only remotely offended.

David, though a bit shocked, laughed it off, saying, "I should thank her for the tip. I didn't even consider that an option."

She finally opened the presents that "Joseph" had sent (she always called my mother *Joseph*, in that she was like Joseph from the Bible, who was sold into slavery, only to help his family later). She started bawling again, touched by my mother's kindness. Indeed, during all of the years my mom has lived in Canada, she has regularly sent Štefa and her husband gifts from abroad, money when they needed it, and clothes or a pretty scarf placed in an envelope to brighten Štefa's day.

On many a trip, my mother tormented us with finding postcards, then had us painfully write messages on them in

Croatian. We followed this with a mad search for a local post office, because the cards always had to bear the postmark of the city where they were purchased. We would get lost, but my mother's dogged determination forced us to find a post office, all to bring glimmers of joy to her relatives and friends left behind. Their eyes lit up when the postman stopped, waving the postcards. Their status in the village remained elevated, due to this, and they were as excited as if they had traveled to the exotic places themselves. Years later, the cards were still proudly displayed. Half a century had passed since my mother had left Croatia as a young lady of seventeen, but she still faithfully mailed cards to her family and friends, bringing delight to them, while torturing us.

My father also looked out for them over the years, even after my parents' divorce. He took Štefa's hand and placed some money in it. She thanked him, and because my dad had heard enough sobbing for the day, he told her we had to get going. So many relatives to visit, so little time. I leaned over and kissed her goodbye, while she looked at me one last time, then at David. Her eyes filled with tears, as she shook her head in pity, certain of my destiny with David. My father rolled his eyes, while David and I smiled.

Next, my dad took us to the restaurant Prc in the hilly green countryside of Koprivnica, where David enjoyed a "typical" Croatian meal. After lunch, David ordered a modest-sized *šlivovic* and said, "Croatians do two things well: they have beautiful women and make good plum brandy."

Maybe he wasn't going to leave me, after all.

"JUST TOBACCO"

by Ivanka Di Felice

WE WERE ON OUR WAY to my boss's cottage in Ellicottville, in western New York, and were just miles away from the state line when I told David "the border story."

If one went by outward appearances, then Gino Russo could have been perfectly cast as a hit man for the Mafia. In reality, he had a mild manner and wouldn't hurt a flea. One day Gino drove his ancient, rambling van down the Q.E.W. highway from Toronto toward the border of the United States. He pulled up to the window, and the customs officer asked him the routine question: "Anything to declare?"

"No." The first answer went smoothly.

"Where are you heading?" was the second question, which proved to be his undoing.

"*We* are going to Florida," said Gino.

"We? Who else is in the van with you?" asked the now very serious officer, peering into the vehicle.

"I mean I—it's just me," said Gino, but too late.

"Please step out of the van, sir."

Gino was about to find out that customs officers took words such as "I" and "we" seriously and expected the average citizen to be familiar with pronouns.

He had Gino open the back doors of the van, and Gino feebly smiled as the agent discovered several barrels of his uncle's homemade wine, which moments ago had been destined for his cousin's wedding.

Gino had been alone in the van, but perhaps he felt a real kinship with those barrels of wine when he foolishly answered "we." He should have paid more attention to pronoun lessons during English class.

The barrels were confiscated, and Gino was turned back, denied permission to cross the border. The bride and the groom, no doubt devastated, were now forced to spend money for the guests' wine.

As I told David this story, he laughed at Gino's awkwardness and his subsequent return to Toronto—though David did feel his pain at having all of that wine confiscated.

"Why did he get all nervous? You just have to answer their questions," David said with confidence, as we approached the border.

David pulled up to the window, and the customs officer asked, "Citizenship?"

"Toronto," answered David.

The officer rolled his eyes and repeated the question. David suddenly realized that Toronto was a city and not a citizenship and managed, "Canadian," feeling as if he had answered a difficult question on *Jeopardy* and would be going home with the prize money.

"Where are you going?"

David, like a deer in the headlights, paused for a long while, then meekly looked over and asked, "Where are we going?"

If I had been a customs officer, I would have concluded that someone had a gun pointed at the back of David's head, causing him undue duress.

I reminded David, "Ellicottville," and he repeated my answer to the customs agent.

"Any alcohol, weapons, or tobacco?"

"Just tobacco," David answered confidently, though he had never smoked a day in his life. Neither did any of us in the car smoke or have possession of any tobacco.

Though I got my lemons confiscated, fortunately the customs officer realized that David was not nearly sophisticated enough to pull off any major crimes in the United States and let us enter the country.

As we drove away from the border, we broke out in laughter. Everyone except David, that is.

We arrived at Greg's lovely chalet, which from the outside resembled a Pizza Hut. Inside, it had been decorated by an interior designer and by my mother, who was *not* an interior designer but had taken to "thanking" Greg for letting us use his place by repeatedly purchasing knickknacks and placing them around the cottage. The decorator had put a brightly colored wooden rooster on a shelf, which proved to be a great inspiration for my mom. Hence, the original rooster was joined by his parents, siblings, cousins, and many offspring, adorning each room. The rooster continued to proliferate in the form of blankets, china plates, and mugs. With all of my mom's gifts decorating the place, I wondered how much longer Greg would allow us to use his cottage.

I took out the latest present my mother had sent along with us and found a home for it.

We lit the fire, picked up our books, and enjoyed the few lazy days we would have until my father arrived. He would be there in a couple of days, and, despite his age, he was a man of action who couldn't stay put, so we'd have to plan several outings. We'd have to be up at dawn, to ensure that we got an early start on each day of our "vacation."

Tata arrived for the weekend carrying a vintage, hard plastic, moss green suitcase. *How quaint, he has packed this little suitcase.* David offered to carry it to his bedroom, but Tata, puzzled, instead brought it into the kitchen and placed it on the counter.

He opened it, and I discovered a new meaning for the phrase "essentials for a weekend away." Inside the satin-lined suitcase, decorated with brightly colored flowers, one pair of underwear made an appearance among six king cans of Foster's beer and two cartons of Tropicana orange juice.

"To make beer cocktails with," my dad quickly informed me.

I consoled myself that at least there was one pair of underwear and that no rooster-themed trinkets had traveled along with my dad, awaiting their release to Greg's shelves. Despite the several cans of beer he'd brought into the United States, my father had experienced no problems at the border. He knew his citizenship and where he was going, and when asked, "Any weapons, alcohol, or tobacco?" his answer was simply, "None."

"Italia"

by Ivanka Di Felice

I WAS NO LESS OF a dreamer than my mother or my father. I agreed with the shepherd in *The Alchemist* when he said, "It's the possibility of having a dream come true that makes life interesting."

Ever since I married an Italian, I assumed my days would suddenly become leisurely and carefree, my hair would grow long and thick, and my bust size would miraculously increase. I would take to wearing frilly white linen skirts, designed by Dolce and Gabbana. At last, I could sport ridiculously large black sunglasses without anyone assuming I was hiding from the law, and my lips would take on a permanent *Italian Vogue* pout.

For ages, I'd envisioned strolling down quaint alleys, sipping fine Tuscan wine in a piazza, and visiting a vast array of art galleries. In my dreams, passionate opera music always played in the background. My husband, meanwhile, dreamed of fast cars racing down Italian motorways.

And so, after our years of fantasizing, my prince agreed to take his *principessa* to the land his forefathers had built. But not without some "help."

One day in 2006, while working at the brokerage firm, I received notice that due to restructuring, I was about to be laid off. (Code for: after more than twenty years of loyal service, I was being kicked out. I blamed it on the never-ending flow of roosters.) After my initial feelings of shock and disappointment, I realized this might be my ticket to finally get to Italy.

I did have to fight hard against my North American mentality, urging me to find another job and feverishly save for a retirement that might never come. My years of seeing retirement charts at work had unwittingly taken their toll.

David, too, unexpectedly received the most unlikely news: the furniture-making shop that employed him was moving to a new location an hour and a half away. Not having the inner demons of retirement charts to contend with, he agreed to take a year off and go to Italy. We embarked on the colossal task of getting the necessary documents in order, so that this dream could come to fruition.

We answered Italy's call and moved.

We crossed the Atlantic Ocean, as both of our parents had earlier, only it was in the opposite direction, and we aspired to different dreams. Having immigrated to Italy, *we* were now the foreigners, albeit the "right type," according to the locals, in a weird and wonderful land.

We had family on both sides of the ocean, we would travel back and forth regularly, and they would also visit us.

As if my father and his tenants hadn't provided enough amusement for me, David's family took over with their hilarious antics. It wasn't long before my own expectations were shattered when I embarked on *la dolce vita*. I envisioned drinking unforgettable Brunello by candlelight and discussing art and history with elegant dinner guests. Instead, dinner discussions revolved around how to avoid a "bad wind," whether the Mafia ran IKEA, and bizarre theories on why the Chinese in Italy never had funerals. Now I drank David's uncle's own "unforgettable," almost undrinkable wine, while he paid long-winded tributes to the vile liquid as if it were an elixir of the gods. Rejoice with me—for mere mortals, or their livers, could not have lived to tell the tale.

AN UNLIKELY ENTOURAGE

by Ivanka Di Felice

IN ITALY, I'D GIVEN UP the dream of ever affording a home in High Park, because the regal homes in my dad's neighborhood were voraciously being snatched up by yuppies with money. And so, while the yuppies improved their homes, increasing the value with each thousand dollars spent, my father had a special renovation formula that we referred to as the "one over five." For each thousand that Tata spent, he brought the value of the house down by five, no easy feat. Outside of elderly Polish or Ukrainian men, few people could duplicate it. His front porch and picket fence paid loud tribute to the reason paint colors should be chosen by an elegant man named Giorgio.

While fancy German-engineered cars parked in the other driveways, my dad also honored the Germans, in his own way. He proved that his sixteen-year-old VW could be repaired by anyone, and that no skill, and certainly no aesthetics, need be adhered to. A loose steering wheel was nothing that copious amounts of duct tape couldn't fix; auto body mechanics were just a scam, easily avoided by applying large globs of gray putty. Glove compartments that didn't stay closed required just a simple four-inch screw bolted through them, and for automatic windows that wouldn't stay shut, a wooden wedge was the industry secret that most of us were unaware of. German engineers would have been horrified.

Yet alas, there was a price to pay to live in this high-end neighborhood, with its acres of park land. Humans were not the only ones who wanted to inhabit this prime real estate; raccoons, too, abounded.

And so, as the well-to-do slept, they could never have imagined—or suspected—what their neighbor Tata was up to. After years of battling with the raccoons and losing, he had devised an ingenious plan of "catch and release."

Thus, while most raccoons in this neighborhood scavenged through garbage bins that they pried open with their little paws, the raccoons at Chez Tata's feasted on home-cooked delicacies. Sauerkraut with sausages, polenta with meat sauce, and beef gulaš (goulash), to name but a few dishes, as each evening boasted a fresh menu for the critters.

Tata, now nearing eighty, couldn't do the job alone. Therefore, he'd enlisted the help of Andy, a diminutive Jamaican man with a big head of thick dreadlocks, who had a real affinity for large quantities of beer and a dogged determination to sustain profits at the Beer Store.

The sun slowly rose. Andy, affectionately known as "the handler," took his job seriously and had been waiting anxiously to count the catch for the day. Five dollars a raccoon were to be had, enough for a king can of Foster's beer. On good nights, there were enough frightened raccoons in the trap to warrant several beers or other mind-altering substances.

Finally, the sun had risen, and Andy did the tally. Three raccoons had feasted on beef gulaš that Tata boasted was "so good, angels would eat it." The poor raccoons never stood a chance.

Andy woke elderly Tata from his sound sleep. "Just to let you know that whenever you are ready, I am able to go."

Curiously, Andy's willingness to help always coincided with the opening hours of the liquor store.

"I'll be there soon," said Tata, half asleep, as he shuffled across the bedroom. He walked into his "timeless" kitchen and made breakfast. He hovered over the stove, stirring the oatmeal with a large wooden spoon. When it was done, he placed the pot directly on the table, eliminating the need for cutlery by eating straight out of the pot with the wooden spoon.

Tata swore, "It tastes much better that way."

Perhaps this was a secret Jamie Oliver wasn't aware of or was simply not willing to share with the masses.

Andy waited patiently by the trap, while three sets of masked eyes looked up at him in bewilderment. He promoted his services by declaring in his Jamaican patois, "If we don't get all the raccoons, the place will be *invested* soon."

Tata finished his last wooden spoonful of oatmeal and was ready to embark on phase two.

With great effort, Andy lugged the trap to the car and placed the frantic raccoons in the trunk. Neighborhood mothers decked out in designer clothes and pushing fancy baby strollers did a double take.

And so Tata and his unlikely entourage—a Jamaican sidekick and a trunk full of raccoons—headed north to the Home Depot parking lot. Releasing them into the vast acres of nearby High Park wouldn't do, for Tata was convinced that in no time they would all be back at his house, gobbling up his fine home cooking. Tata had spray-painted an X on the trapped critters, to track them. One raccoon returned, its bright orange X proving it loved Tata's gulaš and was willing to risk its life for seconds.

Hence, to ensure that they resided at a new postal code, he drove the few extra miles.

Tata had the driving finesse of someone fleeing the scene of a crime. To make matters worse, he encountered a pesky red light en route and bemoaned, "How could this happen to us?"

No doubt after this driving experience, the raccoons wondered the same thing.

His motto was clear—"Time is of the essence"—but perhaps at nearly eighty, it really was.

They arrived at the Home Depot, and Tata slammed on the brakes, bringing the car, Andy, and the raccoon trap to an abrupt stop. As Andy's head pitched forward into the windshield, the usefulness of his dreadlocks and oversized red, green, and gold Rasta hat was finally revealed.

The sight of Tata and Andy exiting the black VW speckled with Tata's nifty fiberglass mix was in itself enough to bewilder consumers in the Home Depot parking lot. The amazement on their faces turned to shock when Tata slowly opened the trunk, tapped twice with his cane, and out jumped three startled raccoons.

Innocent bystanders looked on in disbelief, while Tata smiled weirdly as the raccoons, slightly disoriented, scurried away to the relative freedom of the parking lot. I was quite certain they would never be tempted by beef gulaš again.

Tata felt gratified. They had caught twenty-three critters in the last two months alone; fifty-six in total for the season. Andy, too, was delighted, as the owner of the Beer Store must have been. Meanwhile, Home Depot employees wondered where this scourge of raccoons in broad daylight kept coming from.

Tata and Andy headed home with the same speed and determination, with Tata cursing all interferences, because, after all, "time is of the essence."

OCCUPY TATA'S

by Ivanka Di Felice

As was his custom every morning after checking the raccoon count, Tata went to the donut shop for his coffee. There he met several acquaintances from the old country, none of whom really liked or trusted one another, and they each nursed one coffee, avidly discussing politics for hours. When they exhausted solutions for the rule of Croatia, they caught up on community gossip. If Mirko had joined them, he would invent something outrageous, like the time my mom brought her cousin Ivanka from Croatia and she met Mirko. After chatting with her a bit, surprised, he said, "Oh, you are an educated woman. Steve and Anica told me you are a simple, uneducated peasant." Fortunately, my mom's cousin saw right through him.

Or he might describe how he caught so and so's ancient wife eyeing another man or might accuse someone of secretly harboring communist views. This incited lively debate, and I was convinced the likes of these guys inspired donut shops to set maximum time limits for customers.

As Tata walked out his front door, a somewhat disheveled person walked past him. Tata wondered who this person was but figured he was visiting a tenant. Tata got into his speckled VW Jetta and drove off, not giving it a second thought.

After several hours, Tata returned home. As he entered his apartment, someone marched down the stairs and casually greeted him.

"Hi! Have a good day," the unknown man cheerfully told Tata and walked out. While it was unusual to see two strangers moseying around the house unaccompanied by a tenant, Tata again didn't put much thought into it, because he had more pressing issues to take care of: namely, cooking his oatmeal.

Tata had breakfast, watched some TV, and fell asleep. He woke up and headed out for his afternoon stroll, at the Walmart in Dufferin Mall. As he left the house, another mysterious person stood on the porch, greeting him and causing Tata to do a double take.

He arrived at Walmart, grabbed a cart, and leaned his upper body into it, as he walked the aisles, checking out the sales, while simultaneously exercising. He pushed the cart back and forth, memorizing prices and cursing the cheap garbage they tried to pass off as shoes.

He had his second cup of coffee for the day at the McDonald's inside the store and looked for one of the Filipinos who worked at Walmart, to whom he gave his sticker, bringing her one step closer to a free coffee. He headed home along Bloor Street, where his patience was tested by someone ahead of him who'd had the audacity to make a left turn.

He entered his house to the sound of much fanfare upstairs, but since he had walked quite a bit, he decided to first check out his couch, then the situation above.

Tata loved chess and was a champion, so, after his nap, he set up his board and pulled out his chess book, his genius manifest whenever he played. Yet today he lost his concentration, because he heard loud noises. He slowly climbed the grand staircase to find a tall, lanky kid with long hair coming out of the shower.

"Hey," he greeted Tata as if he knew him.

Tata stared at the barefoot kid drying his hair with a towel and asked, "Who are you?"

The kid casually answered, "I'm a friend of James's." As if Tata should have known that.

And so it would be. For the next few days, Tata found unfamiliar people marching past him, as if a mission awaited them on the second floor. James apparently had many friends.

Meanwhile, in the city of Toronto, protests and demonstrations were being held downtown in the financial district. The movement was part of an international one speaking out against economic inequality and corporate greed, called Occupy Toronto. Some would say it was just a party in tents in a public park, with the protestors looking kind of thoughtful and angry. They did some first-class sitting and on a few occasions were motivated enough to go down to Bay Street and shout slogans at the office towers. But mostly they sat around and slept in tents. That is—unless they were showering at my dad's house. Occupy Toronto had turned into Occupy Tata's.

James, a tenant on the second floor, who had no job, thus plenty of free time, had joined the movement, turning his back on capitalism, except when he offered hot showers and a comfy warm bed to those wanting a break from being dirty and cold and sleeping in tents. James was very generous in offering my father's electricity and water, though he probably begrudged having to personally lay out capital to get several keys cut to give to other protestors, along with my dad's address.

When my father and my sister figured it out, they approached him, but James failed to see how he was breaking any laws and refused to comply.

"If you want to live in tents, then go live in tents, but stop occupying my house," my father said.

James "threatened" to move out and join the movement full time if my father wasn't more reasonable, and if Tata would give him several hundred dollars to do so. My father declined to fund this, and, as further protest against those with more, James stopped paying rent. At the best of times, James's payment of rent was spotty, and my father charged so little that after he paid for utilities, he was practically running a charity.

Mirko, the champion of my father's causes, had his own solution for how to stop the masses from showering and partying at Tata's house. Although Tata was tempted to take Mirko up on his offer, he knew better.

Thankfully, soon thereafter the Occupy Toronto movement fizzled out, and so did the number of people taking showers, hanging around, and sleeping in James's room. Occupy Tata was officially shut down when Tata handed James a notice for non-payment of rent.

Thanks to the Occupy Toronto Movement, James was in the habit of protesting. Thus, he wrote a lengthy letter to my father, asking him to reconsider "kicking him out." He highlighted that other than this incident and some other problems he had created, which had resulted in several thousand dollars' worth of damages, he has been a "model tenant" and that my father should "consider carefully the practical benefit of my monthly rent." He concluded by saying that the likelihood of my father finding another tenant like him would be slim. The last sentence we could agree with.

Though my father was almost eighty, his short-term memory, along with the latest electric bill, served him well. He wished James the best of luck, but elsewhere. My dad's theory on references being a scam proved true, because if James had needed one to move to his next place, my father would have provided a stellar report on this "model tenant."

Many people say the Occupy Movement didn't accomplish much, but my father disagreed. As James packed his bags and left, Tata felt that something good came out of the Occupy Movement, after all.

A BARREL, NOT OF LAUGHS

by Ivanka Di Felice

IT HAD BEEN A WHILE since Tata had made some "repairs" on the house. Yet Kathy had gone to work, and unbeknownst to her, he would take advantage of her absence and insulate her apartment on the third floor. Why call in professionals and pay, when he could take on this labor-intensive job himself?

He and his assistant Andy lugged up his tools, a drill to make the holes, and several cans of spray insulation foam. Drop sheets to protect the furniture, the bed, and the floor were deemed optional, so he forfeited using them.

Tata ordered Andy around, demanding tools, similar to a surgeon during a procedure. Tata made several random holes along the outside bedroom walls, the drywall dust depositing itself on the bed, the dresser, the windows, and any clothing in the near vicinity. After several hours of drilling and several beer breaks for Andy, the wall was done and, amid a cloud of dust, looked as if a violent shootout had taken place. Tata stepped back to admire his handiwork.

Andy insisted that Tata not overdo it and encouraged him to take a break. He quickly offered Tata one of Tata's beers, and the two made themselves at home in Kathy's living room.

After a few beers and a little rest, Tata resumed his activity. He took the can of insulation foam and sprayed it into each hole he had made. The foam expanded, and soon the walls no longer resembled the scene of a shootout but instead appeared as if they had an infectious fungus oozing out of them. As a finishing touch, Tata ripped off the pieces of foam sticking out several inches from the wall but neglected to remove the rest. Andy's skills as a cleaner left much to be desired, as he swept the larger pieces that fell to the ground into a corner but ignored the smaller ones, along with most of the drywall dust.

After another break, they turned to their next project on the agenda. Tata would have to do some repair work on the roof. Andy went downstairs to lug up the can of tar Tata had purchased, while Tata tried to pry open the screen. Not possessing the patience of Job, with time always being of the essence, he took his handy Exacto knife and cut the window screen, giving him access to the roof. Andy returned with the dark black tar and was instructed on how to apply it on the roof. Ropes to save Andy and drop cloths to save the floor were both considered unnecessary, and splatters of black tar joined the dust and the bits of spray foam left on Kathy's floor. The jobs done, Tata was happy, and they returned to the main floor, tracking tar on the steps on their way down.

Tata was left with just enough time for a quick nap before Vesna came over after work. Tata had been on a shopping spree lately and would be shipping several containers to Croatia for friends in the village there. He had a soft spot and cared about people of lesser means, especially those in his home country. He had purchased several winter jackets, shoes in assorted sizes, and baby clothes in various sizes, not taking into account each baby's age during a particular season, despite my mother having encouraged him to do so.

Mirko would take advantage of the trip to the warehouse and had several barrels to be shipped, because he owned a house in Croatia that he had slowly been finishing during the last few decades. His shipment mostly contained knickknacks he'd purchased from garage sales. The moment my mother and my sister came to visit my dad, Mirko popped out of his room and tried to pawn these "gifts" on them. Whatever they politely declined ended up in a barrel, awaiting shipment to Croatia. A plaster Virgin Mary lay on top of a carved wooden jewelry box, joined by picture frames and knives. Finishing the house before sending the ornaments didn't concern Mirko. Tata asked Andy to come along, as the muscle behind this operation.

Vesna arrived to find the three men drinking wine in the kitchen. She braced herself for what might be one of the longest journeys of her life, even though the warehouse was only twenty minutes away.

Vesna opened the back gate of her Dodge Grand Caravan, while Mirko and Andy picked up a barrel and shoved it into the van before Vesna had cleared out a space.

"Stop it, wait for her to remove her stuff," my father barked at them. But Mirko, anxious to go, and Andy, anxious to return to the wine, paid no attention and kept pushing. She couldn't help them, because her scoliosis had gotten worse in the last few years, as had her pain. She barely managed to retrieve her purse and her hand before the barrel landed with brute force in the back of the van. They kept loading more barrels until Vesna feared for her shocks and, worse, feared she would have to drive slowly, thus prolonging the pain of this mission.

With the van loaded—and Mirko and Andy, too—Vesna realized that having a van wasn't all it was cracked up to be. Perhaps she would have been better off with a small two-seater vehicle.

She drove as fast as she could, keeping in mind her shocks with all of the weight. My father sat in the front, constantly turning around and yelling at Mirko to keep his voice down. Confusion prevailed, as Mirko suggested a better route, speaking half Croatian and half English, while my father simultaneously instructed Vesna, who knew where to go, with a different set of directions.

Andy tried to make conversation, supposedly in English, amid Mirko's intermittent shouting of directions. Vesna hurried up, because ruining her shocks was better than ruining her nerves. After what felt like hours, though in reality it had been only twenty minutes, they arrived at the warehouse.

The madness continued during the unloading, with my father's repeated demands for calm adding to the chaos. Mirko had not put addresses on any of his barrels, thus slowly labeled them, saying each letter out loud, while Vesna waited each painful minute. Her next car *would* be a two-seater, one with no trunk space.

They returned home, with Vesna frazzled. My father headed straight for his living room, while Andy hung around the kitchen, hoping to be offered some wine. Mirko insisted on giving Vesna gas money, and as he entered his room to get it, Vesna noticed a peculiar odor.

She asked him, "What is that smell coming from your room?"

He immediately slammed the door shut, blocking entrance to it. Vesna was exhausted, so she left it. She went into the living room and watched *Jeopardy* with my dad, then gave him a double kiss and headed home.

Several hours later, Kathy came home and noticed a smell permeating throughout the main floor, almost as if a jug of wine had been spilled on the carpet. It appeared to be coming from Mirko's room, so she knocked on the door. Mirko was inside but remained quiet. Kathy banged harder several times, and, perhaps fearing she might kick in the door, SWAT style, he reluctantly opened it a crack. Henry exited his room to see what the commotion was. Kathy pushed Mirko aside and entered the room to find three barrels of fermenting grapes in the small space, perhaps as an ode to his days of living in the shed, once again proving he was resistant.

It was obvious Mirko had been partaking of the "fruit of the vine," and Kathy, annoyed, forced him to take the barrels to the backyard. Despite fearing their fate outside, Mirko was more afraid of Kathy and his fate inside, so he obeyed. Though she had great affection for all of the tenants and even generously hosted an annual dinner for them, she had recently threatened to evict Mirko if she found him drunk again. Meanwhile, Henry stood in the hallway, smirking, because he and Mirko had had a rivalry for years, and he rejoiced to see Mirko "in trouble."

Mirko and Andy, aware of Kathy's fury, quickly lugged the barrels outside, spilling wine on the hallway runner as they did. The red splotches blended with the black tar from earlier that day.

Kathy shook her head in disbelief as she climbed the stairs to her apartment. When she entered it, her disbelief turned to shock.

TATA'S TRAVELS

by Ivanka Di Felice

TATA WOULD BE EIGHTY IN December. Every year, my
sisters each took him on a trip, and some years he visited us
in Italy during the summer. While at a resort he sometimes
grumbled about the accommodations, the weather, and the
food. My sisters just laughed, because on occasion he was
right.

"Do you like the chicken, sir?" asked the waiter.

"This is chicken? Oh, I thought I was eating a coconut!"
replied my dad.

"Do you like the chicken, sir?" asked the waiter at another
resort.

"I think this chicken died of natural causes," my father
said with a wry smile, leaving the waiter speechless but the
other guests at the table in stitches.

Yet despite his complaints, once home he was always
eager to plan his next journey, talking about what a great time
he had—after the fact.

His many trips with my sisters and me afforded him the
opportunity to invent lavish tales of who he was, what he did,
and where he lived. His fellow vacationers at the bar in the

Dominican Republic were under the impression that Tata had made his vast fortune from the misfortune of others, because he owned funeral homes all across Florida. He would enlighten them on how Florida was the state where everyone in America went to die.

Then, with a broad smile, he added, "It is a booming business. Everyone is dying to get in."

He would pick up his mug of beer, take a long sip, and nod in confirmation. After he'd had several beers, he probably convinced himself of his vast funeral empire.

He took pride in traveling with his children, returning with a tan, and telling tales of shark adventures and what not, to Wrinkly, Two by Four, and other cronies of the donut shop crowd.

My sister Vesna wanted to help my father realize another dream of his, this one attainable: to travel via ferry from Italy to Croatia. First, they would stay with David and me in Tuscany.

After a week's visit, the four of us departed for Abruzzo, three hours south, so that my father could see where David's parents live. David sped along the highway, also living as if "time is of the essence," while I sat in the backseat fearing I might soon need one of those funeral homes my dad "owned."

We thankfully arrived at my in-laws' house, and after a wonderful meal of homemade gnocchi, followed by roasted sheep meat and fresh tomatoes from their garden, we took my father to the picturesque town of Ascoli Piceno. We sat at a table with stunning views in the renowned Piazza del Popolo.

"Isn't this beautiful?" I asked.

"Sitting here or sitting in my backyard is the same thing to me," said my dad. I grinned, knowing that he was teasing me and would go home and tell everyone about the magnificent places he had visited.

After a few days, David would stay with his parents, while Vesna, my father, and I would take the ferry from Ancona, Italy, to Zadar, Croatia.

We boarded the train to Ancona and arrived at the car rental office, where we were told that we couldn't take the car via ferry to Croatia.

"But it's part of the European Union, and I phoned to ensure there would be no problem taking it to Croatia via ferry. Can we drive it to Croatia instead?" Vesna asked.

The inexplicable Italian mind at work, the lady responded, "You need the original owner's documents to take it across the border, and we never provide the originals."

"But then how can you say we can take it to Croatia?" asked Vesna.

The woman behind the counter, somewhat frustrated—at whom, we weren't sure—shrugged her shoulders.

The prospect of dragging my eighty-year-old father onto a train and forfeiting the several hundred dollars he'd spent to sleep in a bed on a ferry motivated me. "Please get me a taxi. I will go and speak to customs myself to see if they will let us enter the ferry with the documents you give us."

The three of us hauled all of our luggage into a taxi and headed for the port. The taxi pulled out, and my dad, who had remained calm and silent at the rental agency, was suddenly mad as a hatter, and justifiably so.

"Darn, I can't believe this is happening," he said.

"Don't worry, we'll sort this out," I said, equally upset.

He looked at me, confused. "No, I'm talking about the traffic light that just turned red!"

Vesna and I burst out laughing. Perhaps he felt we had some control over the ferry issue, but the red light we couldn't do anything about.

I explained the situation to the customs official, who empathetically said, "Of course, the car can go on the ferry. The car rental people regularly put everyone in a panic. Don't worry about it."

Vesna and I were thrilled, and so was my father, for on the way back the taxi driver caught all of the green lights.

We boarded the ferry without a hitch, eager to embark on our next adventure.

Much to my relief, the ferry pulled out into the dark waters on schedule. My father checked the time and nodded in approval. We found our cabins, and my father found his beer. He grabbed his cane, removed the rubber bottom, and wriggled the cap to open the beer.

Happy at last, I laughed and tried to take a picture of my dad, but after several attempts I settled on one in which the expression on his face didn't convey extreme torture but merely looked as if someone was pinching him hard. Perhaps the only way to have him smile in a photo was to turn it upside down. We chatted, then kissed him goodnight and headed to our cabin.

As I closed the door to my and Vesna's cabin, claustrophobia set in. I longingly remembered the beer we'd left in my dad's cabin.

Early in the morning, the crew knocked loudly on the cabin doors, waking up passengers and alerting us that it was time to have breakfast before we docked. While Vesna and I groggily got out of bed, my father was ecstatic that we'd be forced to get an early start.

We docked in Zadar, a beautiful city on Croatia's Dalmatian coast, known for the Roman and Venetian ruins of its peninsular old town, including several Venetian gates in the city walls. A tourist site boasted, "Zadar's churches are worth visiting, and don't forget to take a stroll along the streets of the old quarter, where the spirit of the three-thousand-year-old Mediterranean city lives on." According to Alfred Hitchcock, "Zadar has the most beautiful sunsets in the world."

But my father wasn't about to find out. There was no time to explore, because he'd planned a full day, and we were on a tight schedule. We had a few days before we needed to arrive for a festival now held yearly, in the area where my father had been born but, unfortunately, had been forced out of. But the land had been reclaimed, and my father was eager to attend the festival.

First, we headed down the coast to visit Mara, a lady we had been friends with for years. Decades ago, as tourists in Pakoštane, one night Steven and I had stumbled into her sons' *Konoba*, an ancient stone tavern that served local wine and smoked Dalmatian prosciutto and cheese. We'd hit it off with her three boys, and from then on, despite the limited menu that offered only wine, cheese, and prosciutto, we ate there every evening and eventually rented a room in their house. We kept in touch through letters, and like mother, like daughter, I sent many postcards from our travels.

I had a picture of the five of us: her three sons and me and Steven, outside their *Konoba*. The three boys, along with Steven, were all terribly handsome: tall, dark, with large beaming eyes and charm that even oozed out of the picture. I'd felt proud to stand next to them.

Now only two of us remained. Steven had died in a motorcycle accident, and two of her sons had lost their lives during Croatia's declaration of independence in the early nineties. All three of our loved ones had died in their twenties. Even with the passing of years, it was hard for us to see her, for while our memories were pleasant, our reality was not. After more than twenty years since Steven's death, my family still desperately missed him.

We arrived in Pakoštane and drove through the ancient town, with its restaurants roasting lamb or pig on a spit outside, the fat from the meat dripping into a pan of roast potatoes beneath it. We reached Mara's house. We hadn't visited in several years, and the house had tripled in size, with a sign indicating tourist rentals. We knocked, but no one answered. We walked around the back of the house but still didn't find anyone.

To prove the effectiveness of the Pakoštane neighborhood watch program, a lady looked over the fence and suspiciously asked, "Who are you looking for?"

"Mara," my father said.

"You're too late. She died three months ago," the lady blurted out in a matter-of-fact voice.

We remained silent for a moment. We had taken for granted she would be at home, almost as if waiting for us, as she always had in the past. We'd never called during our years away; we just dropped in. We felt deeply saddened, and my dad showed his sorrow by remaining silent.

Though the town thrived, and many restaurants along the seaside were filled with tourists, laughing and enjoying life as they drank Croatian beer and looked out onto the clear blue waters, an overwhelming feeling of loneliness prevailed. My father stared at the ground, contemplating how hard life could be.

We strolled around town, trying to find her youngest son. We walked the narrow gray cobblestone street to the *Konoba* and noticed that the ancient carved wooden sign had been replaced by a modern neon one, and the *Konoba* was now a nightclub. Nothing was the same, and although, at my age, I should have been gradually getting used to it, nevertheless, this, too, broke my heart.

We found Karlo, who was pleasantly surprised to see us, and we reminisced for a while about old times and those no longer with us. His mom had been eighty-three and in good health but got cancer and died quickly.

We snapped pictures of the four of us, and Karlo took us to one of the rental apartments in his mother's house. We stayed the night, and the following day he didn't want to take any money, but my father insisted, and eventually he accepted.

While I would have loved to nurse a cappuccino and enjoy my last views of the sea—and, most likely, my last views of this village—my father reminded us that we needed to rush to reach the festival by noon. Because it was very popular, if we arrived too late, there would be no parking.

We climbed into the car, and Vesna sped off. My father struggled to put his seatbelt on, as the alarm bell beeped impatiently, and my father cursed the inventor, the manufacturer, and Renault itself.

Although I didn't have time for a cappuccino by the sea, en route my father spotted a sign for Karlovačko, a Croatian brand of beer, and we miraculously had time to stop. We entered the bar, and an encounter with a bear in the woods might have been a friendlier experience. The waitress indifferently took our order, sauntered back with it, and, without so much as a smile, placed a bill on the table. At least, this time my father was justified in wanting to leave quickly, as soon as he'd finished his beer.

As we walked to the car, Vesna devised a plan to prevent the seatbelt alarm from sending my father into a fit. Before she turned on the ignition, she waited for him to buckle up. My father noticed her hesitancy and indeed no longer cursed the seatbelt alarm. Instead he said, "Get moving! Why aren't you driving?"

Though his seatbelt wasn't yet buckled, she drove off, the alarm beeping, not sure which was the lesser of two evils. Vesna and I couldn't help but laugh.

My dad looked at Vesna driving confidently and was suddenly reflective.

"Do you remember the first time you drove?" he asked her with a weak smile, recognizing the insanity of it.

"Yes, I was twelve years old," she said.

After a night of drinking at a bar, in a place named Čingi Lingi, in Croatia, my dad and his friend miraculously realized it was best they didn't drive. The only person "able" to was Vesna, who, at twelve, must have been the world's youngest designated driver. She hopped into the driver's seat. Because she had always been small for her age, her feet barely reached the pedals. With no prior knowledge of driving, she took on the role of chauffeur. She did her best, but Tata wasn't satisfied, thus provided guidance.

Finally, his companion, sobering up from this experience, told my dad, "Leave the kid alone. Stop nagging her. The child knows how to drive!"

My father sighed deeply and shook his head in regret at the thought of little Vesna driving them through the dark country roads of Croatia.

They had kept this escapade a secret from me. This was the first I'd heard about it. Still in shock, I said, "You're lucky she got home safely, because I bet there's something in the fine print in the insurance contract that prohibits twelve-year-olds from driving."

"Yes, we were lucky that night," he said.

When we arrived at the spot where the festival was being held, oddly, not a soul could be found. It was as if we'd entered a ghost town.

We drove through the barren village and spotted an elderly gentleman tending his front yard.

My father rolled down his window, scaring the man half to death as he yelled out, "Hey, we're looking for the festival. Where is it?"

The startled man reflected for a minute, while my father waited anxiously for directions so we could head out to get a parking spot.

"It was held two weeks ago. Everyone's gone. Just us old timers left here now."

I gasped. This entire trip had revolved around the festival, the mad rush this morning . . .

I had assumed my father *knew for a fact* when the event was being held. Evidently not.

We found ample parking and slowly walked through the vacant town to a church overlooking a valley. Despite missing the festival, my father was pleased to see a Croatian church had been built. It was dedicated to the memory of all Croatian martyrs who'd died for their homeland. My dad, though a fervent Croatian, wasn't religious. He was skeptical but thought it brilliant that the people of Međugorje had found six gifted actors and invented the apparitions of the Virgin Mary.

The name Međugorje literally meant "between mountains," and my dad said, "There was no other way on earth they ever could have gotten people to visit." He didn't view it as fraudulent but rather as an innovative way for poor folk stuck in between two rocks to make money.

Two people exited the church, and my father asked them about an old friend of his, Petar. They directed us to his house, and we found him at home. He was close to eighty, and he, too, had left at the same time my dad did, but many years ago he'd returned to his family's land. He had a small, modest house and invited us in. My father gifted him with a bottle of Courvoisier, and the man offered my father a beer. I asked them to pose, and my father finally smiled, a large, broad smile, and it had nothing to do with the beer. I captured the moment and would print a copy to include in the album we made with my dad after each trip.

Petar filled my father in on how packed and what a success the festival was. One couldn't even find a parking space. Though we'd missed it by two weeks, my father was nonetheless satisfied. And since he was, so were we. Sometimes, things didn't turn out as expected, but at least we'd found parking. And for the first time in a long while, my father wasn't in a hurry to get to his next destination.

DIVORCE DUST

by Ivanka Di Felice

THE "GANG" FROM OUR NEIGHBORHOOD in Toronto was slowly dispersing. My mother and my sister could no longer manage the many stairs leading up to their house and were too old for tenants, so they purchased a condo across town. David and I came back to help them move and to renovate their condo. My mother and Vesna offered to pay David several times, but he refused, saying, "You can't afford me."

Unbeknownst to them, they would "pay" in other ways.

David and I had returned to sell our duplex and purchase a triplex from our good friends the Davey family, who had also opted out of the landlord business. As Vesna's bedroom was taken over by our things strewn everywhere, and she was reduced to sleeping on the couch, clearly it would have been much less painful to pay David in cash, even large sums.

Meanwhile, a For Sale sign sat on our old friends Ed and Alice's front lawn, as they eagerly awaited the sale of their home, ready to embark on a new adventure in Mexico, as they approached eighty.

To facilitate a quick sale, we decided to make a few improvements to our duplex. It was early morning, and I

263

could already feel the hot sun beating down on my head. I stared at what appeared to be an endless supply of packages of insulation being unloaded from the delivery truck.

Be warned that the pros and cons of doing it yourself listed on websites never mentioned one of the cons being "probable divorce."

David was up in the attic, blowing in the insulation and directing its flow through a long hose, while I opened the packages and put the bats into the machine designed to break the insulation down into tiny pieces.

The bats were heavy, I had trouble carrying and opening them, and I kept jamming the machine. David was hunched up in the sweltering attic, which was only four feet high. When only air came out of the hose, and his shouting didn't miraculously produce a flow of insulation, he ran down to help. He was hot and sweaty, his black hair now completely gray.

My father pulled into our driveway and exited the car carrying his favorite lunch, assuming it was also ours: Kentucky Fried Chicken with french fries. Because it was important to eat our vegetables, he had bought fluorescent green coleslaw. I found an old cloth, wiped away several inches of insulation dust from the patio table, and called David down to take a well-deserved break.

On catching sight of David, my father gasped. David had aged about twenty-five years since my dad had seen him two days ago. Even my father, a do-it yourself advocate, wondered whether we should have paid someone to do this.

My father had a soft spot for David and considered him like a son. I recently found out that he'd told my mother, "My heart would break if anything ever happened between David and Ivanka."

Hence, my dad offered to get us help. Perhaps fearing that my father might bring back Mirko or Andy, David declined, but this would be the last time we did this job ourselves.

We survived a day of this dirty, grimy work, with the good news that we had saved a thousand dollars by doing it ourselves. The bad news was a divorce lawyer cost triple that. Just kidding, there would be no divorcing. We would hate to break my father's heart.

Next, we risked our marriage by taking on the role of landscapers. The house we would purchase overflowed with flowers and shrubs; hence, we dug up half of the garden and transferred the plants to our current home, so that we could advertise "perennial garden." Not a word of this was a lie—it was someone's perennial garden.

My father lent us his VW Jetta, and we made several trips, each time loading a veritable nursery into the trunk and the backseat of the car. We carried the plants to the yard, leaving dirt from the crumbling root balls in the Jetta. Soon, a foot of soil covered the trunk and the backseat.

Our work was finished on the house that would be put up for sale. Because it was vacant, we left the final touches to the home stager, while we embarked on renovations at the triplex.

After only a week of working together, I could have written a manual on why a husband and a wife should *not* work together. Deceptively, there were different bits for drills, not every tool could be used as a can opener, and when David barked for "a Robertson," I was supposed to know what that was and furthermore what type of screwdriver it was and hand it to him at record speed while he still needed it.

However, in some respects David still felt that I was a capable wife. Instead of paying some kid minimum wage, David found me capable of lugging down thousands of pounds of construction garbage, loading it into Vesna's van, and taking it to the city dump.

As I hurled the dated ceramic tiles and old strip flooring into the construction bin, I smiled. Because we were saving all of this money, I would be spared from teaching children

English back in Italy, a country with one of the lowest birthrates in the world. That was priceless and worth a broken back.

We toiled fourteen-hour days renovating.

We ordered a quartz countertop from a Chinese company, and, thankfully, David's astonishment at a lack of knowledge was now directed toward them.

Four men carried in the countertop, all the while yelling in Chinese. The four of them combined still couldn't come up with one sentence in English.

They had to have been getting paid not by the hour, but by the job, because they were eager to finish. When David pointed out that at the seam, one counter was higher than the other, they called their boss, who told me, "You are too fussy."

Since they had just moments earlier put a few dabs of silicone under the counter, David recommended simply lifting it up and adding another dab. They deliberated in Chinese for a long while and insisted on sanding it down. David protested, fearing it would ruin the finish. They assured us it wouldn't, but it did. David wasn't pleased, so the four men lugged the counter back to the truck and promised to return with a new one.

They kept their promise and came back in three weeks. The part of the promise they didn't keep was bringing a new counter. They reinstalled the same one they had damaged, hoping we wouldn't notice.

With the counter in and the four men out, David locked the door and called their boss on the phone.

After much debate, the boss gave it to us for half price, but he wasn't pleased, and I doubted *he* would ever do business with *us* again.

My father dropped in with lunch: Kentucky Fried Chicken and french fries. I smiled and shrugged at David. With his steady diet of KFC, a wife who thought Robertson was a friend of ours, and stress from the Chinese counter incident, I would have to check David's blood pressure—sooner, rather than later.

I drove over to the house we would sell to check the progress of the home stager. I could see that she had begun, because several pieces of furniture had been hauled into the house. An ugly old desk was pushed up against the window in the den, and a beat-up brown armchair sat in the living room. Black accent pillows decorated with gold cows sat on the chair, and numerous other pieces of furniture appeared to have been picked up at the curb.

I called our agent to see what was going on. He assured me that I had to wait to see the final outcome. I feared it would be a house that looked like Grandpa's estate sale, but I patiently waited another few days.

I checked back, and indeed my suspicions were confirmed. She had placed a worn, rainbow-colored, braided oval rug on the floor, along with other items surely purchased at yard sales. I was aware of mix and match, but this wasn't that. This was just junk. Even worse, the house had taken on the smell from this old furniture. The woman either needed to enroll in a refresher course on staging or perhaps use her furniture to become a set designer for movies from the seventies.

I searched for Home Stager on the Web and came across a site depicting rooms decorated in cool grays, icy blues, and beige accents. I called, and incredibly the stager had an opening, which she said was very rare. She was usually booked months in advance. I told her my story, and she felt our partnership was meant to be.

She arrived one day before we went back to Italy and transformed the house with modern, hip furniture.

We left the following day, with me all the wiser from having learned a few things: leave the granite and quartz to the Italians, not everyone claiming to be a home stager had good taste or access to furniture from this century, Kentucky Fried Chicken never killed anyone, and, most important, Mr. Robertson was a screwdriver.

I also knew why they called it "divorce dust," but, thankfully, we survived. I smiled and put my arm through David's, as we boarded the plane, ready to go back to our tranquil life.

TATA DRIVING MISS ANNA

by Ivanka Di Felice

MY MOM IS THE ONLY person I know who can comprehend black holes and quantum mechanics (as much as they can be understood), subscribes to several science magazines, and from a tender age has read and understood Russian classics, but can't spell my married name. She kindly sent us postcards from all of her travels but wrote our last name differently each time. Admittedly, though, with all of those variations, once she spelled it correctly. And ever since the invention of the remote control, she could no longer turn on a television. Throw a VCR into the equation, and she'd want to kill herself.

For years, she was against getting a dishwasher, but we insisted. Then she couldn't get enough of it—she wandered around the kitchen looking for things to put in it. When we stayed with her, David and I had to keep a vigilant eye on our toothbrushes, because they often went missing, only to be found in the basket of the dishwasher. She was obsessed with "sanitizing them," while I found bits of old food, likely other people's, in the crevices of the bristles.

269

Watching her load the dishwasher (David always had to leave the room) made me presume she'd been deprived of puzzles as a child. The grooves of the dish rack were mere suggestions, because my mom's creative mind theorized new angles in which to deposit the plates. Glasses, too, escaped the humdrum routine of being on the top shelf. Knickknacks from the living room also joined in, and porcelain dolls lay across plates for a time, then danced amid pots during the rinse cycle.

My father had his own quirks, for though he could find any obscure city on a world map and was a chess champion who could beat even computers, he couldn't grasp the concept of time and realize that because he had nowhere to go, he didn't need to be in a hurry.

Despite all they had been through together, my parents had an interesting relationship that no one quite understood, including them. For years on Sunday mornings, my dad dropped in for coffee with my sister. They would amicably chat until my mother woke up; then she and my dad inevitably got into a heated discussion.

My mother had a bus stop right outside her door, so why she sacrificed her sanity to have my father drive her a few miles even she couldn't explain. Why my father agreed to chauffeur her was another mystery, because from the minute she stepped into his car, he was agitated. Perhaps this mystery was even more complex than black holes and quantum mechanics, for, after all, my mother understood those.

Yet for inexplicable reasons, this was their relationship, if it could be called one, and though it didn't work, it continued.

My father had recently been relieved of driving my sister Kathy to work and home each day. Even though she'd had foot surgery and needed crutches, she decided that hobbling through a crowded streetcar was easier than riding with our father. One day, as usual, he had shown up early and waited on a main street, blocking rush-hour traffic. As she limped toward his car, she noticed a raccoon on the sidewalk, disoriented and scurrying in the middle of the financial district of downtown Toronto.

"Look at that poor raccoon," she said. "How on earth did it get here?"

My father remained silent, then with a smile, admitted, "I forgot he was in the trunk, so I let him out."

At that point she resolved to have mercy on traffic and raccoons and to take public transit home.

Thus, he now had a lot more time to drive my mother to go shopping.

The following morning, as usual, she was ready ten minutes early, but, as usual, he was twenty minutes early.

My sister Vesna was still home, so she made him a coffee and offered to measure his blood sugar. He was reluctant to let her do so, because the previous night he and Mirko had celebrated the arrival of nice weather in the backyard with several king cans of Foster's beer. Vesna worried about his health, and he knew she would disapprove.

She measured his blood sugar, which had a normal reading. He felt relieved to have escaped a lecture. My mother, not a diabetic and who hadn't had a drink in decades, wanted hers measured as well. Vesna obliged, and the reading was far higher than my father's.

He laughed and told my mom, "You should take up drinking."

Vesna rushed off to work and left the two of them.

"Hurry up!" my father said, grabbing his jacket and rushing out the door.

My mom, for the thousandth time, vowed never to let him drive her again.

He raced along Eglinton Avenue, and my mom buckled her seatbelt just as my father slammed on the brakes for a light that had turned red.

My father waited, ready to pounce the second the light turned green. My mother braced herself, as he proved you could be eighty and still cherish the dream of one day becoming a racecar driver.

They arrived with my mother under duress, enlightened by my dad's conspiracy theories, the latest from the old guys at the donut shop, with Two-by-Four, Wrinkly, and Trash getting the most air time. She cursed herself for forgetting her earplugs.

He dropped her off at the secondhand clothing shop and offered to pick her up in a couple of hours. My mom must have had the shortest memory in the world, because she actually contemplated it for a moment. But, remembering she had forgotten her earplugs, she told him not to worry and she would make her own way home.

"But don't forget you have a doctor's appointment tomorrow, so pick me up at eleven," she said.

My father's doctor wouldn't write any more prescriptions for him unless he got a blood test. He had refused for months, convinced that they were selling his blood. Finally, Vesna asked for an empty vial, poured water into it, and showed him how little blood they were taking. This calmed him, and he agreed to go the next day. Whenever my sisters were working, my mother kindly went with him and reported back.

"Fine. I'll be there at eleven," he said, with my mom knowing full well he would show up shortly after 10:30.

"And don't wear that jacket, Picasso, or I will not go in with you," my mom threatened. Though he had dozens of new jackets, this one was his favorite and it showed, because the latest paint color he'd used was splattered on it. "It looks like your children have robbed you and taken all of your money."

He laughed at her exaggeration but promised to clean his jacket.

In the morning he arrived early and got mad when my mom was on time. With my father already out the door, it wasn't until he peeled out of the parking lot that she noticed his jacket.

"What the hell?" she asked.

In his defense, he *had* attempted to clean the jacket. He'd forgotten to put it in the machine last night, so this morning he took a bottle of Windex to it. Now dried, it had left large splotches. Looking at them, even he admitted that perhaps this wasn't the best solution.

"Couldn't you have taken one of the many other jackets you have?" my mom asked.

He remained silent but obeyed when my mom insisted they buy him a new one before she would go to the doctor's office. Because he was running out of some prescriptions, he obliged. Thanks to my dad being early, they had time to buy three jackets for him and one for my mom, and both happily left the store.

My father anxiously waited to see the doctor, then, once in her office, anxiously waited to leave. He got his prescriptions and promised to go for blood work soon—one of the rare times he wouldn't be in a hurry.

"Lifetime Warranty"

by Ivanka Di Felice

Tata and Vesna had returned from a one-week cruise aboard Royal Caribbean's largest ship. The vastness of the vessel had worn out my father, as well as Vesna, and both seemed to be in need of a vacation.

Judging from people's T-shirts boasting various states, my father realized there were too many Americans on board. Thus, he'd had to invent an alternate career, fearing that he might meet people from Florida while bragging about his funeral home empire there. This time it was safer being a real estate mogul in Toronto. Only in Cuba could he discuss his funeral empire.

I called my dad from Italy to see how he liked the cruise, and he laughed. "I can die now. I've been on the world's biggest ship."

"Stop joking like that!" I said. Though my father seemed virtually indestructible, he would be eighty-one in December.

A few months ago, he'd purchased a brand-new, shiny blue VW Jetta and even got the sunroof. He bought a new hammer to keep in the glove box, still not trusting automatic windows. He loved driving his new car, especially because he could tell people that "it came with a lifetime warranty." He always laughed heartily afterward, while it took everyone a minute to join in the laughter.

"I've been looking at condos," he said. "I'm tired of tenants."

I was shocked, because although he seemed glad that Vesna and my mom had moved into a condo, I never imagined him wanting to live in one. But at his age, any tenants, never mind the lot he currently had, could be a handful.

I reflected back over the years on all of the tenants who'd come into our lives and then left, some to our delight. The SWAT team that entered in stealth mode, clearing out room by room, before storming and apprehending the suspect who had been using his dwelling to store all of his heavy-duty weapons.

Then there was Roger, who had grown accustomed to his high-end, High Park address and thus refused to go to an old age home. Instead, he sneaked his way into my sister's third-floor apartment and turned her into a full-time nurse, as he lay incontinent on her couch for days. Finally, she was able to convince him to go to a facility where he could get proper care. Mirko was gleeful, because although he felt confident that *he* brightened up our day, he didn't feel the same way about One-Eyed Roger.

My father used to like hanging out with the tenants, yet he didn't need the money, and because he no longer drank, this crowd proved far less entertaining. Perhaps it was time to give up his career as landlord. My parents had done what they had to do to buy this house, but now it was too much.

"As long as that's what you want, that's great," I said. "Find something nice. But remember, no roommates."

"Don't worry. And I'll look for a condo that gives me a lifetime warranty on the workmanship," he said, laughing.

CRUISING SOUTH AMERICA

by Ivanka Di Felice

M Y FATHER REALLY MUST NOT have been feeling well, because when Vesna proposed that they go to the emergency room at St. Joseph's Hospital, he agreed, even though he hated waiting, even for possible life-saving treatments. On a previous visit to the ER, despite finding himself a stretcher and lying down, he realized he was more comfortable at his place and had many more TV channels. Though he could barely walk, he told the nurse that he was going home and to please call him when the doctor had time to see him.

Vesna ensured that none of the tenants were watching when she and my dad slowly made their way to the porch to wait for the ambulance. Andy stumbled by, but in his current state he wouldn't remember anything by the time the other tenants came home. My father shouldn't have been too concerned, because whenever Andy and Mirko spoke, they could barely understand a word the other one said.

The ambulance arrived in record time and the EMTs placed my father on the stretcher and strapped him in. As the last strap was secured, he panicked and refused to go via ambulance. So they helped him into Vesna's van, and she kept up with the speeding ambulance, making my father proud.

It was December 24th, and most people in Toronto were out doing last-minute shopping. Because it was early in the day, the hospital wasn't yet full of people who'd overindulged in celebrating. My father was admitted quickly and given a room. They did a series of tests. My dad waited for the results impatiently, while my sisters waited for them anxiously.

One thing that living in Italy had taught me was the importance of family. At times like these, being so far away was difficult, and I waited both impatiently and anxiously. The wait grew more unbearable by the hour.

My father and I had become closer during the last few years—despite his visiting me regularly. His antics made me laugh. Whenever I took him to another charming Tuscan hilltop town, where everyone in the world aspired to go, and he asked, "Is this just another old town?" I realized he was unique. I smiled, because I doubted that anyone else in the entire city of Toronto could boast of having a custom built-in raccoon trap. Not that anyone else would want one, but that's beside the point.

While in his hospital bed, Tata discovered soccer on the Internet and watched his favorite games over and over. He chose his preferred teams based on whatever country supported Croatian independence. As he watched his beloved teams win repeatedly, he was in good spirits and cracked jokes. The nurses all loved him and treated him well.

Since he had an accent, a young nurse, still not jaded from choosing a difficult profession, showed personal interest and asked, "Where are you from?"

"Uganda," my father responded, his round brown eyes serious.

Assuming she must have misheard, she said, "Uganda?"

"Yes, Uganda," he said, as she looked at him, puzzled.

She took his blood pressure and left, no doubt telling people that she'd had a senile patient that day who thought he was from Uganda. Meanwhile, my mischievous father laughed uncontrollably. On other occasions, when people looked at him curiously after he said, "Uganda," he explained, "It's in South America, not far from Brazil," and had an additional reason for laughter as they walked away suspiciously.

***

The test results came back, and they were not good. He had cancer, and they gave him months or, at the most, a year. They sent him home and made appointments with a hospital that specialized in cancer treatment.

We were all devastated. David and I decided to return to Canada to be with my father and family.

At the Rome airport, I took the pink pills the doctor had prescribed to me for flying—or driving on the highway with my husband, which, with his Italian blood, amounted to the same thing. I woke up ten hours later in Toronto. I profusely thanked each flight attendant, letting everyone know "This was the best flight I've ever had."

In my current state, they could have fed me sand, ignored my pleas for water, and kicked me each time they walked down the aisle. But as I continued to compliment them, David whisked me away. They smiled, none the wiser that I said that after every flight, while still under the influence of my pink pill.

We arrived in Canada to some wonderful news. A surgeon said that he could remove the tumors and that based on my father's health in general, he would be fine. He should be able to resume his "normal activities" of meeting Two-by-Four, Wrinkly, and Vermin at the donut shop within a few weeks.

We felt ecstatic—but also confused because the other two oncologists had given him just months to live and, with that news, had no doubt taken years off our lives. Regardless, we were thrilled and immediately made arrangements for the surgery.

The first few days in Canada, David and I smelled of cheese, because we'd packed our suitcases with a few clothes surrounding several liters of olive oil, assorted pecorino cheeses, and specialty pasta. I thought back on how I'd laughed at my dad with his moss-green suitcase full of beer and orange juice, and now I laughed at myself.

Vesna had planned a two-week cruise to South America a year ago, and my father encouraged her to nonetheless take it. She wanted to cancel, but my father insisted she go.

"You are not the surgeon," he said. "Go on your trip!"

Thus, she reluctantly did.

We checked my father in on the scheduled date, and he was given a room in the new wing of the hospital. My father's mood soared when David set up the Internet, and he watched, for the umpteenth time, the match between Brazil and Germany, in which Germany, Croatia's ally for years, won.

His disposition was still upbeat, and he laughed as the night nurse walked away, wondering whether he really was Ugandan.

David and I, as well as my sister Kathy, came early to be with my father before his surgery. But due to an emergency room full of urgent situations, the surgeon couldn't perform the operation as scheduled. We all got a little anxious, not because of the delay, but because we knew my father hated waiting. This went on for several days; they withheld his breakfast, only to show up several hours later with it, informing him he would not be operated on that day. Surprisingly, he took it well, and we thanked the Germans for winning that match.

As we returned to his house each day, we ran into tenants inquiring where my father was. He'd given us strict instructions not to mention his whereabouts, so we dodged the questions. Thanks to the short attention spans of my father's tenants, it didn't even prove to be difficult, and we never compromised our integrity by lying.

My father, meanwhile, intently memorized Vesna's cruise itinerary. He followed her progress each day, giving us facts and figures about each country she visited as if he were there. She emailed us pictures of her with the penguins in the Falkland Islands, and Tata devised elaborate details about all of the places *he had been* and all of the stories he would tell back at the donut shop. He had picked his favorite country on his trip. If he'd had anything other than cancer, I'm sure he would have had us take him to a tanning salon.

Given his circumstances, he was calm and cheerful, as he studied maps of the many places in South America he would need to be familiar with.

We heard a knock on the door, and a priest peeked in. "Would you like a visit?" he asked.

Suddenly, my father panicked. "Tell him no thanks. If I let him in, it's a sure sign that I will die the next day."

The day of the operation arrived. The surgeons entered the room, and I sadly realized that I'd reached an age where doctors were younger than I was. Yet even though, or maybe because, they were young, they were optimistic, and they let us go as far as the operating room with my father. We kissed him and reassured him. Though I tried not to cry, I couldn't manage not to. My sister flashed me a disapproving look. My dad sat in the wheelchair, wearing a hair net, and smiled and waved. He was brave. We stayed with him until the very last second when they wheeled him away. Once he was gone, the floodgates opened. I prayed, hoping all would go well. Though he didn't show it, Tata must have also been nervous, because he hadn't made any "lifetime warranty" jokes since his diagnosis.

I looked at the clock and then stared out the window, watching snowflakes like cotton balls gently float to the ground. I checked the clock again and worried about my father. As the snow accumulated, I worried about the drive home. I was no longer accustomed to snow, because in our part of Italy we hadn't had any in years. David, meanwhile, calmly watched a movie. Sometimes it had to be nice to be a man.

After what seemed like forever, they wheeled my father into the room. Though he was groggy, he looked up and smiled at us, and we were told the surgery had gone well. I held his hand, grateful he had pulled through.

He slept peacefully. At least, he would be safe that night.

The following day, the surgeon and his assistant met with us and were positive. "The surgery went well. We got all the cancer."

We felt great relief.

The assistant surgeon added, "Your dad is a miracle."

The generous Croatian in my father quickly came out, because as soon as the surgeons were gone, my father told us, "Go buy them a bottle of cognac—a very good bottle."

"I promise we'll get them a very good one," I said.

The nurse entered and reminded my father to squeeze his pain pump as required. "Don't worry, you can't overdose," she said.

He thanked her, and she left.

Several hours later Tata was in pain. I jumped up to show him how to squeeze the pump, but because he didn't like to be babied, he adamantly said, "I know how to do it."

"Okay, I was just making sure," I said.

"I know," he repeated for emphasis. So I left it to him to manage his pain. Only David knew how to fluff his pillow correctly, so I was absolved of even that task.

My mother came, so that David and I could take a break. My dad said that he was in pain. My mother called the nurse, who showed my father the *actual* button he needed to press for pain management. He had been squeezing some other button the entire time. Even he laughed at himself.

Within a few days, he had improved greatly, because he was back to studying Vesna's itinerary. "If anyone asks what was my favorite place on the trip, I will say it has to be . . ."

He would probably remember more from Vesna's trip than Vesna herself would.

Much to the chagrin of the nurses, he had managed to put his fleece sweater over his IV and pain drip.

He asked me to pick up the weekly Croatian newspaper and reminded me that if the store owner asked, "Where is your dad?" to tell him that due to the bad weather, he was unable to go out. He was covering all of his bases.

My sister brought two bottles of expensive Italian wine for the surgeons: an aged Amarone and a Brunello. The surgeons were pleased, because they recognized the labels. I figured that surgeons could afford to drink such wine often.

Tata gradually began to eat normally, and the doctors talked about releasing him soon. I spent several hours cleaning his house, preparing for his return.

David took my father's things and left to get the car, while I walked with my dad.

"Don't worry, walk slowly," I said.

He looked at me, bewildered. "What do you mean, just walk slow? I'm walking as fast as I can!"

I slowed the pace even further.

We reached home and ensured that none of the tenants were around to ask him where he'd been, for though he had been practicing all week, he was too tired to brag about his trip.

He took a long nap, while I prepared dinner.

Mirko came home from work and entered the kitchen. He heard the TV in my dad's room—in his mind, a signal to come and say hello. On catching sight of me, he was eager to show us his latest acquisitions.

My father tried to watch tennis, while Mirko provided more commentary than the sportscasters and, for David's benefit, threw in some Italian with English and Croatian.

Mirko had left the kitchen door open, and George, the elderly tenant from the second floor, heard the commotion and joined us. He insisted that he needed his rent receipt for the previous month and he needed it right that second. Perhaps all elderly people felt that "time is of the essence."

My father was in no mood to issue receipts and accused George of fraud.

Mirko joined my father's rampage and said, "George has never worked a day in his life."

Because the comment was pretty much true, George ignored it and again asked for his rent receipt. The uproar reached Andy downstairs, and he, too, made an appearance. With no income from catching raccoons lately, Andy was getting desperate for some extra cash. Thus, amid the chaos, he provided my father with a report on how many garbage bins he had cleaned that week.

My father wasn't on enough medication to filter out these three, and David noticed, so he directed them out of the room, as each tenant rambled on about something on his way to the kitchen.

David calmed George, promising we'd check into getting him a receipt.

My dad looked toward the kitchen and rolled his eyes. "I need to rest up—"

"Of course, you do," I said.

He finished, "So that I can go and buy some lottery tickets later today."

My dad wasn't giving up on any dreams. I smiled and let him try to sleep with the racket now in the kitchen.

Mirko was engaged in preparing dinner. A huge silver metal bowl sat on the table, and Mirko shredded a whole loaf of white bread into it, then poured half a gallon of hot milk over it. Once the bread was saturated, he shoveled the "meal" into his mouth with a huge spoon.

On seeing me, he disappeared and in the blink of an eye reappeared with a plaster statue of the Virgin Mary, insisting I take her home. I declined for the umpteenth time, so he shifted his efforts to convincing David of our need for a saint.

I finished making the chicken soup and took it to my father.

"David, would you like some almonds?" my father asked.

"Sure," said David.

I headed into the kitchen and returned. "I couldn't find them."

"They're in the bathroom," said my dad, as if it was completely normal to keep nuts among the shaving supplies and the toilet paper. "Mirko kept eating them, so now I keep them in the bathroom."

David flashed me a frightened look, no longer eager to snack on almonds stored in a bathroom.

***

We showed my father the many pictures Vesna had emailed, and he smiled as he stared at each one for a long while.

Vesna returned from her trip and confessed that she hadn't been able to enjoy herself because of worrying about my dad. Every free minute she had, she spent with him, and my father was glad to have her back. Now they just had to coordinate their stories.

My father felt well enough, so we treated him to breakfast at the restaurant he and my sisters enjoyed going to in High Park. He ate a quarter of what he normally did and then fed the remainder to the birds outside.

Vesna took him to his appointment with the surgeon.

I was eager to hear the report, and Tata filled me in. "I asked the surgeon if I can drink beer now. His reply was, 'Only Fosters!'"

I was taken aback and wondered how the surgeon even knew what my dad's favorite beer was. I looked at my dad and his broad smile. Of course, he was joking—and I felt happy to see that he could.

His health had improved, and I tearfully prepared to go back to Italy. They took us to the airport, and my dad thanked us for coming.

"You are fortunate you have children to care for you," Vesna said. "Some people have no children."

"No. I am fortunate to have *good* children," he said. "Many with children still have no one to look after them."

This time he wasn't joking, and I was in shock. This was the nicest compliment my father had ever paid us. I even detected a tear in his eye and several in mine.

Too Young to Die Old

by Ivanka Di Felice

TOWARD THE END OF MAY, my father felt extremely weak, so my sisters rushed him to the emergency room. He underwent a week of tests, which confirmed our worst fear—the cancer had returned. He insisted on knowing how long he had, and the doctors, though reluctant to say, after much pressing told him not long—weeks or months.

He took the news well, much better than we did, though with sadness acknowledged, "I guess I won't be able to go back to Croatia."

He insisted this be kept from me, because he didn't want me to worry. Regardless, my sisters gave me the diagnosis, and David and I returned to Canada. As soon as we cleared customs, we made a beeline for the hospital. My father saw us and smiled. He was relatively happy, given his circumstances. In fact, his main source of unhappiness at the moment wasn't the cancer but rather his roommate.

An elderly Scottish man, Mr. Finlay, had been trying to befriend my father, who was not taking applications at this stage of his life. As we entered the room, Mr. Finlay opened the curtain and introduced himself. My father quickly closed it. Not having finished the introductions, Mr. Finlay opened the curtain again.

Although Mr. Finlay hoped to make friends, he was also trying to reduce a painful outlay of capital and wanted us to plead his case. "Your father likes football, and so do I. So we could share his television. No need for both of us to pay for one."

My father swore, albeit in Croatian, and pulled the curtain with even more resolve. I had to laugh, as I imagined the entire curtain and its track crashing down, leaving us under it and in close confines with Mr. Finlay.

My father, with his usual habit of referring to others not by their Christian names but rather by some character flaw he had discovered or imagined, said, "Yesterday, Lunatic tried to get into bed with me so we could watch soccer together. That cheap—"

My father had heard a joke or two about the Scottish being stingy.

Tata lay back in bed and adjusted the touch screen with his foot, a feature he enjoyed. He found a soccer game but turned the volume low, hoping to keep his roommate at bay.

Mr. Finlay had good ears, for soon we saw his hand on the curtain. David nipped this in the bud and pulled the curtain back, much to Tata's delight. We updated him on life in Italy and didn't discuss the cancer. If he'd wanted to talk about it, we would have, but for the time being we let him enjoy the soccer game, while David stood guard.

***

I came alone the following morning and was greeted first by Mr. Finlay, then by my father. Though happy to see me, every few minutes my dad asked for David. I told him that mom was making soup for him, and David was waiting for it to be done. He made a remark about how my mom liked to sleep late, and he didn't have time to wait for the soup.

The hospital allowed patients to leave for a few hours, and though he felt very weak, he wanted to go home. As his vomiting became ever more violent, I worried about the wisdom of leaving the hospital. I encouraged him to rest until David came.

He was about to fall asleep when Mr. Finlay made an appearance. My father suddenly got a burst of energy and yelled. I then worried about the wisdom of leaving him *in* the hospital.

David arrived with my mom and the soup. Of the three, my father was only glad to see David, blaming my mom and the soup for his current predicament. He ordered David to get the wheelchair, and David obeyed, assuming my father wanted to go to the lounge.

David came back in no time, frantic, because my father had demanded that David take him home. David wasn't sure what to do, but my father settled it when he said, "If you don't take me home, I'm calling a taxi."

David shrugged, so I grabbed the medical supplies and other items we would need for the day and followed them.

Once home, my dad turned on the soccer channel with the remote, lay down on the couch, and instantly fell asleep. Despite being so sick, he looked quite good, with his skin a healthy tanned color, and his shirt matched his pants, evidence that my sister and my mother had purchased and packed his clothes for the hospital.

My mom noticed how nice he looked and, wanting to take advantage of senior's discount day, said she was going out to buy more shirts for him.

My dad, though near his final demise, said in a feeble voice, "Make sure to buy me at least a dozen." He laughed and fell back asleep. He hadn't lost his sense of humor.

My mother returned with several shirts. The store had honored her with the designation of senior long before she became one, and despite her integral honesty, if they were to insult her, then she could in good conscience console herself by accepting 20 percent off.

Tata carefully examined them and, with renewed vigor, found fault with each one. "No pocket, no deal." He handed it back. He didn't like the color of the second one and repeated, "No deal." With a mischievous grin, he rejected all of the shirts she'd purchased,

"Don't worry, I'll exchange them," she said.

My father gave up, laughing, and realized that nothing could stop her, apparently not even imminent death.

We took my father back to the hospital for the night, where Mr. Finlay eagerly awaited.

"Hello," he said, pulling open the curtain.

My father rolled his eyes and asked for his sleeping pill.

Tomorrow Tata would be transferred to the hospice, but we would continue to bring him home each day for as long as we could.

We were told to pack my father's personal items, and we searched his drawers, but everything, including his prescription eyeglasses and false teeth, was missing. Mr. Finlay had gone for some tests, so my father couldn't interrogate him. We informed the head nurse, who checked Mr. Finlay's stuff, and, sure enough, all of my father's things were there.

We packed up, and I left a note for Mr. Finlay, wishing him well and gifting him a new pair of socks, as he had requested and already helped himself to.

We arrived at the hospice and met the doctor.

"Do you know why you are here?" the doctor asked my father.

For someone smart, this was the dumbest question I had ever heard. Did she think we'd wrestled my father past security, against his will, and dropped him off in this bed for the three square meals a day?

My father looked at her, also surprised by the question but smiling, and answered, "My future is not bright." He said this not in the resigned tone of a man about to die but in a matter-of-fact voice.

At that moment I saw how strong he was and because I had to leave, unable to hold back my flood of tears, how gutless I was.

After the facility determined that we hadn't kidnapped my father and brought him here, he was given his medicine, and we took him to my mother's house. He felt weak but, miraculously, still in good spirits.

It was a warm, sunny day, and we sat together on their large balcony. My father lay in the sun, sleeping, while I made lunch.

I brought a plate of food to him, and he examined it before asking, "Ivanka, when you have people over for dinner, do you go around the table and mash the food on everyone's plate?"

I burst out laughing. So did he, and after that, I stopped mashing his food.

My sister Kathy called him from work, and they chatted. I heard him say, "Kathy, I want to go home and catch one more. Just one more."

And while I was happy to take Tata to his house, I feared his days of catching and releasing raccoons had ended—though Andy would still have encouraged it, because he desperately missed the "good old days" when he profited $5 per raccoon caught.

I had to leave the room, because I couldn't stop crying. I imagined Kathy was, too, on the other end of the line.

My mom took this moment to encourage my father. She quoted a scripture to him from Psalms, about the earth being transformed into a paradise. She added, "People will be perfect then. Maybe you and I can even get remarried."

He looked her in the eye, all serious, and said, "In that case, I'd rather go straight to hell!"

Then he burst out laughing, as did the rest of us. The cancer hadn't affected his impious sense of humor.

***

We picked him up every day and brought him back to the hospice at the latest possible hour. Though he got more fragile, if I was a couple of minutes late, my phone rang and he asked, "When are you coming?"

We brought him to his house on Saturday, and all of us stayed there with him.

"I want Kentucky Fried Chicken for lunch," my dad said.

Though we feared for him—and for us—eating this again, Vesna hopped into her van and headed out to buy a bucket of Kentucky Fried Chicken.

After a long while, I called her to see where she was.

"I had to drive downtown," she said. "I'll be there soon."

She returned home and placed the original bucket of Kentucky Fried Chicken, five cans of Crush Red Cream soda, and two bars of Kit Kat on the kitchen table—the same table we'd sat at more than forty years earlier. Memories of 2 a.m. snacks flooded back.

She whispered to me that she'd had to drive all over the city to get this bucket, because most locations now served only the healthy version. Yet in honor of old times, she had to get the unhealthy version and in a bucket, at that, for my dad. The salespeople, perplexed, kept pointing out the new and improved menu, while she insisted she didn't want the healthier version.

My father took a thigh, insisting, "I know you kids like the drumsticks, so I left them for you."

We sat at the table with my dad, as happy as we could be, given the circumstances. We dined on the unhealthy version of KFC, along with french fries, the mint-green stuff they tried to pass off as coleslaw, and a macaroni salad that would have made Italians sue KFC for using the word *macaroni*.

After lunch, my dad wasn't feeling well and lay down. For years, he used to massage Vesna's feet whenever he came over for coffee, believing it had healing effects. Now Vesna massaged his, as he lay on the couch. When her hands got tired, I took over.

We let him sleep for a long while; even a healthy person would have needed time to digest the food we'd eaten today. Though we felt sad, we couldn't help but smile, as we put away the bucket and threw out the empty cans of cream soda and the Kit Kat wrappers.

NO WEDDINGS AND A FUNERAL

by Ivanka Di Felice

MY FATHER HAD PLENTY OF opportunities to marry after he and my mom divorced. Several women were interested, but my dad never found the perfect woman, as defined by him: "one who is not interested in my money." So he remained a happy confirmed bachelor right up to the end.

Most people needed six pallbearers. We had to choose eight: six original ones and two backups, in case Mirko showed up tipsy and Andy high.

Kathy insisted my father would have wanted Andy and Mirko as pallbearers, because they had been tenants for the last twenty years. Though it could be argued that trapping raccoons together brought a measure of closeness, I was concerned that being high and being a foot and a half shorter than all of the other pallbearers wouldn't be a good combination. And while Mirko would always offer you a drink, that didn't guarantee he wouldn't offer himself several before the funeral. His generous pouring of wine knew no bounds, especially when his glass was concerned.

Unless a miracle occurred, Vesna and I worried that these two couldn't carry the coffin in their "normal" state. Yet

Kathy felt strongly that we should allow Andy and Mirko to be pallbearers, as long as we had two others as backups, so we all agreed on these arrangements.

We lingered over photographs for many hours, putting together the photo board, choosing pictures for the TV screen, and deciding which ones would go on the website. My father would have been proud. I wrote up the blurb for the bookmarks that people could keep as souvenirs: "My father traveled to many places." Then I recalled him memorizing Vesna's cruise itinerary, and I wanted to add, "Not as many as he'd claimed to, but still to many places."

We had our hands full, choosing an outfit to put on my father. Just as my grandma had requested not to be buried in shoes, we knew my father hated suits. Yet because his suit was the only article of clothing he had never painted in, we debated. I searched his drawers and closets and found an abundance of virtually brand-new, beautiful jackets and pants, all of which inevitably had a couple of spots of paint. The concept of work clothes or work shoes was clearly not something my dad had ever grasped.

He loved baseball caps and was particularly fond of one that had a beer opener under the peak, telling everyone it was a GPS tracker for old people. He had bought my husband a matching one, and, much to my chagrin, David wore it faithfully around Tuscany. So we chose a baseball cap and found a jacket that had only a tiny spot of paint. We could have purchased a new jacket but put this one on him, knowing he would have wanted it that way.

The good news was that Mirko and Andy both showed up sober, and the bad news was that they both showed up sober. The other four pallbearers were family, dressed in crisp white shirts with somber ties and dark suits. They were also very tall, hovering several inches over six feet. Andy, already standing out as a foot and a half shorter than everyone, was dressed as if he'd just left a Caribbean resort, and Mirko, too, with his black leather cap, brought a more casual approach to pall bearing. Yet they were sober and respectful, and maybe my father himself would have chuckled if he'd been able to see them.

Instead of taking the dark limousine the funeral home provided, David drove us three girls and my mom to the cemetery in my father's virtually new, shiny, bright-blue VW Jetta. We knew my father would have been glad.

We followed the hearse to the cemetery where my brother was buried. Tata's body would be laid to rest near Steven's.

David inherited my father's Timex watch, with numbers so big he was prepared for old age, and his unfortunately indestructible Chinese flip-flops—the only "made in China" item that was durable. They were an ode to every paint color my dad had ever used. Every time David wore them, I cried—for more than one reason.

LEAST LIKELY TO SUCCEED

by Ivanka Di Felice

DESPITE A LIFETIME OF TENANTS, some good, but most rather unusual, for more than one fleeting moment, I contemplated keeping the house. I sent Scott McGillivray of *Income Property* an appeal for help, stating it could be his most challenging house; he could rename that episode **Extreme** *Income Property*. I sent him pictures but never heard back. Perhaps I shouldn't have showed him the built-in raccoon trap. Maybe that scared off even the usually intrepid Scott McGillivray.

I then appealed to Jonathan and Drew Scott of *The Property Brothers*, but again, I foolishly included a photo of the raccoon trap and, not surprisingly, never heard back from them either.

I stared at the grand staircase and began to dream . . . until Mirko came home and once again tried to give me a statue of a saint. Andy next showed up, slurring his words. I looked at them and at the ceiling my father had wallpapered, then sprayed, which now was peeling, making the house appear near collapse. Even though I hadn't had a drink, I sobered up and realized the landlord business in this house was too much for me. Apparently, I didn't possess enough vision or the sense of adventure my father had.

For more than a brief moment, Kathy also contemplated keeping the house, but once again, thanks to Mirko, Andy, and George, coupled with a sharp memory, she, too, let the nostalgia go and decided to purchase a luxury condo.

The real estate agents prepared to leave, but as we chatted on the front steps, an elderly man across the street lugged his garbage out with great effort.

"There's your next prospect," I said and winked. Their eyes conveyed shock, but I caught a smile cross the agent's face.

As I walked back into the house, the humor was gone, and I cried. The realization of what was taking place hit me hard. I was suddenly aware of the emptiness and wondered, "Where did life go? Where did the last twenty years go?"

The agents said the property would be easier to sell if there were no tenants in it, and they hadn't even met them. Other buyers had been turning this type of house into single-family units, so the new owners would most likely, and legally, give notice to the tenants. On hearing this, my sister said that it was "our moral duty to help them find a new place." We could assist them and help them save for it by not charging rent.

I had to laugh, for as weeks passed I realized that "our" moral duty was mainly "my" moral duty. Because the majority of the tenants were the sort who would have been voted least likely to succeed and had exceeded expectations, finding them housing wouldn't be easy—especially if anyone asked me for a reference. I simply couldn't in good conscience provide the glowing report my father would have.

Now that my dad had passed away and, with him, Andy's greatest source of extra income, Andy devised work projects for himself around the house, in the hopes that I would pay him.

He mangled my name, despite knowing me twenty years. "Hi, Bianca. I moved some wood from the back of the house to the front."

Knowing that his rent money had already "gone up in smoke," I said, "Thanks."

After an uncomfortable pause, Andy asked, "Can I borrow two dollars? I only have enough for one beer but not for two."

In his mind, this was a logical reason for why I should part with my hard-earned funds. I gave him the money, knowing that he would use the same line when my sister came home. He assured me he was actively searching for a place. I wanted to believe him, but judging by his stagger, the only place he had found lately was the Beer Store.

Mirko came home from work, thus was sober, and we discussed plans for his move. Matter-of-factly, he said, "I knew that I'd eventually have to move. It won't be hard to find a place."

Given that he'd lived in the shed for five years, with the sound of fermenting wine and percolating cabbage lulling him to sleep, perhaps he had a point. Still, it would be best if he kept that "address" off his list of previous residences.

Mirko, about sixty, didn't own a phone and had no access to the Internet. Despite this, with steady employment, he was the best candidate of the lot for placement. He had several numbers of rooms for rent a workmate had printed for him.

I called the first one. After the landlord heard his age, the response was an adamant no. I made several more attempts, but it was unmistakable that preference was given to students. I exhausted every telephone number on the list and was no further ahead by the end. I began to worry; if I couldn't find Mirko, the best of them, a place to live, what would we do with the others?

That evening I scoured the Internet. Almost everyone preferred students or professionals, and the closest I got to a room within Mirko's budget was one ad where "clothes are optional." Maybe I'd have to filter my keyword search to "shed for rent."

None of the tenants felt concerned about where their next known whereabouts would be, and some suggested that the prospective buyers would welcome, even appreciate, having tenants come with the house. The man with the large snake in his little room was certain he wouldn't have any problem finding a place. I worried enough for all of them and said I would have to look outside their preferred neighborhood, but they all objected.

To help them understand, I said, "Even I can't afford to live in this neighborhood."

But that argument was lost on them, because *they had* been able to afford it, thanks to my dad charging half of the going market value for the last twenty or so years—so too bad for me if I couldn't find a similar bargain.

I feared I was in over my head but then felt a glimmer of hope. A lady with a room above a store on St. Clair Avenue agreed to meet Mirko. We made an appointment for the following day, and David and I picked up Mirko and drove him over. We found the address and entered the video store. A Vietnamese lady standing behind the counter did not look up. We announced who we were, and, still looking down, she said, "I already rented the room."

"Why didn't you call us? We wasted our morning coming here."

"That's not my problem," she said.

Mirko wanted to slug her and shouted, while David held him back. We both led Mirko out of the store, still yelling, and back into the van.

I picked up the dozens of sheets of paper with addresses and numbers and proceeded to call each one. With Mirko cursing in the background, I could barely hear one after the other say, "Too old." I handed the phone to David to make the next call, while I tried to calm Mirko down. David was making progress, and the Chinese man on the other end asked if tomorrow would be okay to see the place.

"Tomorrow, what day is it tomorrow?" David asked.

"Saturday," said Mirko, supposedly the crazy one of us three. Despite this, we made an arrangement. We dropped Mirko off at home and reminded him of the drill for tomorrow: "Remember, clean and sober."

Though the room was not in his preferred neighborhood, Mirko agreed to go. Thankfully, due to his mangling of three languages, as well as the landlord's limited understanding of English, the man couldn't understand Mirko and deemed him fit. One tenant down, six more to go.

GEORGE—THE HUMAN BOOMERANG

by Ivanka Di Felice

MY DAD HAD MET HIM two years earlier in the donut shop. At the time, George was living on an unheated porch and paying four hundred dollars per month. My dad felt pity for him, a fellow countryman, thus rented him a room on the second floor.

It didn't take long for us to realize that someone who had been living on a porch in Toronto for the last decade would be somewhat unusual. Yet at the same time, considering he had hardly worked a day in his life and had made it to age seventy-eight, he wasn't stupid, either.

George was tall and thin and always wore a dark suit jacket and a baseball cap. He spent his days in High Park, watching the old men play chess. He confessed, though, that he never liked to play the game himself, for it required discipline, a quality he admitted he'd never acquired. In the European fashion, each day he waddled up the street to the corner store run by a Chinese family, to pick up his meals. Unlike the

Europeans, though, George picked up a "fresh" can of food each day.

Similar to the other tenants, George didn't own a cell phone, didn't have access to the Internet, and had no real motivation to move. I would have to take matters into my own hands.

Each morning over coffee, I combed the latest want ads. I made call after call on behalf of the tenants, but none of them possessed the particular attributes that landlords look for—namely, a steady job, and preferably youth. If our tenants were rejected *before* anyone even met them, I worried whether we would be able to pawn them off on anyone *after* people met them.

It was sad, but no one wanted to rent a room to George, at seventy-eight. I made inquiries about accommodations in an old age home. Some were willing to accept him, and I shared the good news with George, but he didn't embrace the news with the same enthusiasm I had. According to him, at seventy-eight, he wasn't old. You only became old at eighty; therefore, he was too young for an old age home.

"Well, you can't stay here," I said. "The new owners will ask you to leave, so we want to help you while we can."

"Your sister Kathy is a good person. She also needs to move, so I will move in with her. She can get a two bedroom, and I don't even need the bigger room. She can have it. I will give her five hundred a month."

As an added incentive, he mentioned that he didn't own a car, so if her place came with a garage, she could have exclusive use of that.

Kathy was kindhearted, but there were limits to her charity. Besides, I knew that she could hardly cope with living one floor above George, so his moving in with her was not an option. I tried to break this to him as gently as possible.

"Fine, then I will move back to Croatia," George said.

This seemed rather drastic to me, so I offered to drive him to at least look at a few old age residences.

"I was going to move back in October anyway, so I may as well go a month earlier," he said.

I was thrilled—the hardest tenant to find a room for, and he had a contingency plan. I offered to drive him to the travel agent, but this conversation had worn George out. He promised to let me take him tomorrow.

David and I arrived right on time at 10 a.m. I knocked several times on George's door, and he finally answered.

"Okay, I'm here," I said. "Are you ready to go?"

George looked at me, perplexed. "Go where?"

"To the travel agent!" I responded.

George shook his head adamantly. "No, I just shaved. I need to rest."

"Fine. I'll be back in a half hour," I said, and David and I left. We took a final walk through the pretty, almost completely yuppified neighborhood, sad that we couldn't afford to keep the house.

When we came back, Andy and his friend were outside. I overheard the friend remark that we should clean up the front of the house, which incidentally was littered with Andy's junk. Then he asked me in a suspicious tone, "Are you looking for someone?"

"We are the owners," I said.

I knocked on George's door. He had rested, but now he wasn't in the mood to go to the travel agency. I explained that one didn't need to be in a mood to go to a travel agency. One was not performing. "You just get in the car and you go."

"I need air, so I don't want to go in the car," he said.

I told him I could open all of the windows or strap him to the roof rack, if he preferred, but he was coming with me. After a half hour of gentle nudging, George decided conclusively that he wouldn't be going today. He simply wasn't in the mood and felt too tired.

I stormed downstairs into my dad's kitchen, about to cry, when I heard steps. George was tiptoeing down the stairs, covering the side of his face with his baseball cap and assuming I wouldn't recognize him.

"You got a sudden burst of energy, did you?" I said.

He kept walking, holding the baseball cap. I gave up.

"I'll be back tomorrow morning," I said, before he exited the house.

Vesna and I came back the next day, only to find that George had changed his mind. He would check out the "residence for mature people," as I now called it. We put him in the van, buckled his seatbelt, and opened all of the windows.

Much like an anxious child, every few minutes he asked, "Are we there yet?"

I tried to make conversation with George, while Vesna was unusually quiet. She felt uneasy, as if we were kidnapping someone. The guilty expression on her face made me wonder whether we were. George noticed her silence but was obviously not a multi-tasker, for he said, "Vesna cannot talk, because she has to pay attention to the road."

I asked him if he'd ever been married, and he replied, "Empty pockets don't attract women. Three dresses cost a thousand dollars."

He seemed to know more about the price of dresses than I did these days. To his credit, he was the only person I knew who was honest enough to admit to being too lazy to keep a job. He tried five times and determined that work wasn't for him.

"Are we there yet?" George asked, as we pulled into the driveway.

A tall Jamaican man named Donavan greeted us as we entered. Immediately, George became suspicious as he saw several older people amble by.

Reaffirming his youth, seventy-eight-year-old George told Donovan, "When you get over eighty, *then* you are old."

Donavan kindly explained how the facility operated and showed George what I hoped would become his room.

George peeked in and quickly exited. Donavan next showed us the kitchen and the dining room, and his wife greeted us.

George looked at her and at the food she was preparing and said, "You do know that the African kitchen is really not the best cuisine?"

I smiled and pretended George's dementia was kicking in.

I was ready to discuss further details, whereas George was ready to wrap things up.

He shook Donavan's hand and said to this jovial Caribbean man, "You are a good person. I spent two years in Africa during the Second World War."

What next? I rolled my eyes, thinking George was trying to form a comradeship by making up stories about living in Africa.

As we left, George concluded, "By law, I cannot live on the street, so take me to the travel agent."

On the way home, now that he had decided to move back to Croatia after all, George was chatty and had a lot to say about industrial heat patterns in Toronto and how Europe's heat would be better for him. I didn't know what he was talking about, but if it would make him purchase a ticket back to Croatia, then I was grateful for Toronto's industrial heat.

He also told us that he had learned ten thousand English words and appeared determined to use all of them on the ride home.

We entered the travel agency with George, and Vesna's demeanor made me feel like a deportation officer.

Suddenly, George wanted the first ticket to Croatia. Though relieved he would be moving out, I didn't want to be responsible for Vesna's ultimate nervous breakdown or, possibly, George's. Yet he insisted.

The agent stared at us suspiciously, confirmed whether this was George's idea or ours, and finally found a flight with SkyGreece, which flew once a week on Mondays. The agent booked a ticket on a plane departing in two weeks, satisfied that George would have enough time to settle all of his affairs.

George didn't want to pay for the ticket today but would return on his own the following morning.

At noon, I called the travel agent to see if George had come by. He hadn't. I called every day until at long last, at the end of the week, George was well rested enough and in the right mood to pay the travel agent. His flight was confirmed for Monday, August 17th. I offered to drive him to the airport, as a goodwill gesture (and also to ensure that he left), but he had made other plans.

On Tuesday, August 18th, I called my sister, who was still living at the house, to see whether George had gotten off okay the previous night. According to the other tenants, George had left that afternoon, with a small shopping bag in hand.

I was stunned! He'd gotten the day wrong. I'd reminded him each time I'd dropped by the house. Positive he would be coming back, we left his room unlocked. He would feel completely at home, because he had left the room exactly as it was when he lived there. In fact, it appeared as if he'd walked out in the middle of lunch. Food remained on the table, and clothes, shoes, and hundreds of plastic bags he carried his cans in each day were strewn around. Sure enough, George returned home soon after 10 p.m.

The following afternoon, George was again seen leaving the house with a small shopping bag and then again returned to the house after 10 p.m. I wondered what type of stunt George was trying to pull, when a news headline stated, "Passengers Stranded after SkyGreece Delays Flights Several Days."

I called the travel agent, and she calmly said, "They are waiting for a part," as if waiting days for a part was a routine matter in airline travel. I wanted to suggest they could get the piece flown in. George was like a human boomerang, going to the airport each day and coming back soon thereafter.

On Thursday, with great relief, I read, "SkyGreece Plane Takes Flight after 4-Day Delay at Toronto Pearson Airport."

After learning that SkyGreece had only one plane, a commentator said, "They only have one jet? One? Why does a Greek airline with one jet even offer service to a destination on the other side of the planet?"

We now wondered the same.

With all of this drama, I wouldn't believe he had officially moved out until the plane landed in Croatia (after it landed in Athens). I had visions of a wing falling off, and as long as they were in Canadian airspace, the plane might turn around and come back to Toronto to order another wing—with George subsequently moving back into his room. As it turned out, George was on the last departing flight before the airline ceased operations and declared bankruptcy soon thereafter.

A week passed, and with George officially gone, I had one less tenant to worry about. Oddly, sadness overcame me, and I wished him the best and hoped he would be okay. The sadness quickly left as we embarked on the colossal task of emptying and cleaning his room.

BEER CAN FLOOR PLAN

by Ivanka Di Felice

WITH GEORGE FINALLY GONE, THINGS seemed to be lining up. I had seen Jeff, a tenant on the second floor, just days prior, and we had amicably chatted, with him assuring me all was going per schedule and that a moving truck would come either Wednesday or Thursday. With Jeff being the most capable of the lot, he was the least of my worries. He was moving out a few days later than we had agreed on, but we could live with that.

Saturday morning my sister called me, in tears. Wednesday had come and gone with no moving truck, then Thursday had come and gone, and Friday was more of the same. Today was Saturday, and still no moving truck. Instead, only Jeff had come and gone.

"You cannot believe the mess!" she said, in between sobs.

Because my sister could be excitable, I assumed she was overreacting. Our plane back to Italy would leave in a couple of days, and we still had much to do. Yet despite this, I got a few garbage bags and rubber gloves, and David and I headed over to my dad's house, certain we would be back soon.

I marched up to the second floor to find that several others had already joined the disaster relief effort and greeted me wearing masks and gloves. Andy, despite the early hour and already himself somewhat of a disaster, was there to help. I should have guessed the situation was dire when I saw the shovels in their hands. They rushed me to Jeff's apartment, awaiting my reaction.

As the kitchen door opened, I screamed. As the living room door opened, I screamed even louder, and when the bedroom door flew open, I almost collapsed. Even though I had watched several episodes of *Hoarders* on TV, nothing could have prepared me for what I saw. Jeff shared even his bed with dozens of empty beer cans. Remember, Jeff appeared the most normal of the lot, and he probably still was. Days ago, he had looked me straight in the eye and told me the moving truck was coming.

Each room was littered two feet high with clothes, garbage, cigarette butts, and beer cans. And to beer snobs, it was particularly disturbing, because they were all American beer cans: Pabst Blue Ribbon.

I peered into the fridge. Jeff had proved that one could survive almost exclusively on beer.

The rampant mice problem might have been solved earlier had my sister worded the question differently when she'd recently asked Jeff, "Have you *seen* any mice?"

Andy couldn't contain his disgust—not so much for the condition of the place but rather because Jeff had discontinued giving him empty beer cans to return for deposit.

"Jeff used to give me his empties and then stopped. When I asked him about it, he said he didn't have any."

Betrayed, Andy shook his head in disbelief and looked at me for sympathy. Even worse, though returning a few cans at a time on his bike was easy, now Andy would have to take back so many at once. It would be especially difficult to ride back and forth, because after he returned the empties, the funds would be directly invested back into the Beer Store.

David and I had to scratch our heads at this surreal conversation with Andy. We put on masks and gloves and each tackled a room. I put many books in a bag, among them *How to Win Friends and Influence People*, Dale Carnegie's *Lifetime Plan for Success*, and a host of other self-help books, which apparently didn't work. If only I'd found the recent best-seller *The Life-Changing Magic of Tidying Up*, that would have been the icing on the cake.

With the house going up for sale soon, we needed to move fast. We lugged out furniture and every sort of item imaginable, and soon the entire lawn filled up. In no time, a crowd gathered and began rummaging through everything.

An Indian lady dug through the garbage bags and, as if I were a clerk in a store, asked, "Do you have any kitchen pots?"

My sister overheard her, went inside, and brought her some pots.

Gratified, the Indian lady again viewed us as her personal shoppers, saying, "I'm looking for some art. Preferably with some red or blue in it."

She appeared quite upset when we had none. She studied Kathy, then disapprovingly said, "I'm also looking for some clothes, but you're too fat."

On that note, we left her to rummage on her own.

It was hot and humid, and Andy had taken off his shirt, revealing pants that hung way too low on his waist. He frantically ran up and down the stairs, trying to rescue as many empties as he could.

Six of us worked for several hours and hardly made a dent. Thus, furniture was no longer carefully carried down the steps but was thrown over the balcony. The real estate agent would be coming that afternoon to suggest last-minute touches. I feared these might include arson.

The rest of us were tiring out, while Andy had picked up the pace—having discovered that underneath all of the garbage and beer cans lay hundreds of dollars in loose change.

Ironically, amid all of the filth Jeff had the largest collection of soaps and cleaning products ever to be found in a single man's house.

A team of us worked all day and almost emptied the apartment. However, now the front porch and the lawn were littered several feet deep with garbage, furniture, and the occasional beer can Andy had neglected to squirrel away. A waste disposal bin would arrive on Tuesday, the same day we'd leave for Italy. I imagined I would smell like rotting garbage on the ten-hour flight home. I just hoped Italian customs wouldn't ask me about any recent contact with vermin or infectious diseases.

THE CLEAN TEAM

by Ivanka Di Felice

I ARRIVED THE FOLLOWING DAY after lunch. The cleaning crew my sister had gathered looked like carousers in an alternative bar, after last call. I introduced myself to everyone and discovered that the hefty blond man was a gay bartender from down the street, the woman with burgundy hair was a mother of two from Utah who was into Goth, the petite lady was a Russian intellectual, and joining this motley crew was Andy. Others came merely to observe—and for the free beer.

Everyone took a floor of the house and began cleaning. The bartender asked me what I would like him to do, and I asked whether he was a lugger or a cleaner. He readily picked "lugger," so I enlisted his help in clearing the backyard of debris that had been thrown over Jeff's balcony the previous day.

Daniel, the neighbor, must have been anxious as he saw couches, filing cabinets, and the like raining down from the sky and just missing, by inches, the good neighbor fence he had installed. Poor Daniel, he'd moved into this high-end neighborhood about ten years ago, assuming his neighbors would be professionals such as himself. Instead, he had

Mirko, who at the supermarket told a cashier, "I'm crazy for you."

She sized him up right when she replied, "You are crazy without me, too."

No wonder Daniel had built the fence.

"Lugger," as I called the bartender, was strong and hurled even the heaviest objects into the wheelbarrow with ease. He carted them onto the front lawn, in clear view of Daniel sitting on his front porch.

Tearfully, Kathy grabbed an axe and began smashing the raccoon trap attached to the house. We had asked the real estate agents what should we do with it, and they advised removing it. They gently and tactfully said that while it might have deep sentimental value to us, perhaps potential buyers would find it weird. As Kathy attempted to destroy the unbreakable contraption, we feared the new owners might inherit it. Perhaps it could be advertised as a bonus feature. But Kathy, motivated to sell the house, took one last hard swing, and the door flew off. She continued, and eventually the raccoon trap was in pieces. So were we.

Andy now almost exclusively spent his time in Kathy's apartment—the only unit we weren't cleaning, but where the beer and the wine were kept. He took a break from drinking only when two of his friends showed up and headed to the backyard. I wanted to scream, as I lugged garbage from the back to the front, watching the three of them smoke marijuana. I finally broke up their party, insisting my father wouldn't have approved. Andy was respectful and instructed the men to leave. They did, all the while muttering under their breath. Andy returned to the third floor.

The rest of us worked hard and soon discovered that there was good news and bad news: the good news was that the floors were finally clean, and the bad news was that they didn't look much different than they had before. "Staging" would have to be taken to a new level.

The kind Goth lady had vigorously cleaned Mirko's room, and although it smelled better, it, too, looked no better. The room was originally part of a wide, grand entryway, prior to my father having discovered the miracles of drywall. Its windows had the original leaded glass and rich oak casings. The prized oak trim had been painted years ago by a crazed tenant in a color I imagined was called "Black Tar." To add to the avant-garde for the insane look, light gray was splattered on top.

Meanwhile, Mirko, continuing with the madman theme, had perfected the art of making a ceiling look as if it were about to collapse. He'd applied large globs of plaster to the ceiling, in what must have been an attempt to add plaster crown molding to this tiny room. What we really needed was a wrecking ball.

***

Vesna came by a few days before the house would go up for sale. Kathy had gone to work but had hired two new cleaners, after firing the last one. These two again confirmed that hiring people was not her forte. One was male and the other female; they appeared to have either failed or escaped re-hab. They were supposed to be cleaning the basement but had a problem following directions, because Vesna found them on the third floor—coincidentally, where the beer and the wine were. Apparently, they'd discovered the third floor ages ago, and they had very little interest in going back to the basement.

They sat casually and let Vesna in on their entrepreneurial ideas. They assured her that this cleaning gig wasn't what they intended to do forever. Judging by the state of the basement, Vesna felt relieved for them and for any potential clients.

"The real way to make money cleaning is to do it in your underwear."

They could see that Vesna was taken aback and assumed that she had misheard the word *underwear*.

Thus, the guy defined it: "You know, undergarments, not naked, but just in underwear. And there would always be two of us, so it's safe."

Vesna had not misheard but couldn't believe that they felt they had a future in cleaning—either in underwear or without it. Granted, anyone who called their service probably wouldn't be too concerned with the vacuuming skills of these two weirdoes and would be more interested in other talents they might possess.

Vesna shook her head in disbelief and pity and left them discussing their get-rich-quick scheme. They poured themselves another glass of wine, while *she* went to the basement, fully clothed, to finish cleaning Andy's place.

Although Andy was appalled at the state Jeff had left his place in, his own was only marginally better, because, naturally, he'd taken all of his empties with him. He had left a note taped to the back of his door: "Dubba chek the stove is off before leeving." He'd hung this reminder after he once fell asleep with a pot on the stove and almost set the house on fire.

Having determined that cleaning Andy's fridge and stove weren't worth the effort, Vesna headed outside, where she got better cell phone reception, to phone someone to pick up the appliances.

Fortuitously, as she was dialing, a truck collecting scrap metal happened to drive along the street. She flagged it down, and out stepped two Jamaican men. They readily agreed to take any scrap metal she offered and followed her down to the basement.

She suggested taking the handrail off the stairs, and one of the guys, the brute force behind the operation, grabbed a nearby hammer and proceeded to whack the handrail. He chipped a portion of it, and Vesna yelled, "Stop! I meant remove the three screws and take it off."

315

They carried the fridge up to the landing of the narrow staircase. Then somehow Vesna, who was trying to direct them, got trapped between the fridge and the stairs carpeted in my dad's red-and-orange leopard print. They couldn't figure out how to move the fridge to free Vesna and became quite worried. Vesna was more concerned that after this setback, they wouldn't want to take the stove out. Though her poor back was already twisted by severe scoliosis, she contorted it even more and told them not to fret over her.

"What we gonna do, mahn?" one asked the other.

"Dun know," he said.

Vesna wasn't worried about herself. The real estate agents would be there any day now, so she told the men not to panic. They didn't take instructions well, because they continued to wriggle the fridge, with Vesna underneath it. Jamaicans were known for being laid back and for moving slowly, and Vesna had found the only two exceptions. They struggled with the heavy fridge, but, thankfully, Vesna's body supported most of the weight. They finally un-wedged it, and Vesna escaped, slightly thinner but wider.

"Are you Portuguese?" one man asked her.

"No. I'm Croatian," Vesna said.

"You are so strong. Like a Portuguese woman," he said.

Though curious about what type of encounter this man had had with a Portuguese woman, Vesna said, "The Portuguese women got nothing on us Croatian women."

After the events of that day, I believed she was right.

With only one tenant left in the house, Vesna fought her last battle, as she begged him, "Before the open house, can you please remove the snake from your room?"

We had found new homes for most of the tenants, the place was as clean as it would get, and the snake would be relocating. After months of manpower, expense, planning, pleading, beer, and wine, we felt good about our progress. The photographer arrived, decked out in designer clothing, and Vesna asked him whether we should adjust anything to make the place look even better.

He rolled his eyes and, in an effeminate drawl, waved his arms and said, "Dear, *nothing* will make this place look better!"

Perhaps arson would have been our best bet.

THE LAST TENANT

by Ivanka Di Felice

RETURNING TO CROATIA, I FELT heartbroken to be in the land my father had so loved.

We drove through the forested hillside, with purple cyclamen bursting through the fallen leaves, scenting the air. Memories returned, of hours I'd spent wandering through the forest during summer vacations. I'd picked these flowers for my grandma, who put them in a drinking glass on the table, as their perfume wafted through the little kitchen.

We arrived at the two-room, two-story cottage, its white stucco silhouette contrasting with the vibrant green hill in the vineyard. From afar, the house appeared to be in better shape than I'd expected. I felt happy that we would give the little vineyard cottage to my mom's cousin Ivanka. So many years ago, when she was only six, she'd run four miles in the cold to get a ride back in my father's Ford Galaxy XL. Despite the divorce, my cousin had remained close to all of us over the years, and we knew giving her the cottage would have pleased my father.

We parked and walked down the stone steps to the entrance. Adorning the outside door was a red mesh bag of onions, along with a large bag of potatoes, several pots, and many empty beer bottles. Laundry hung haphazardly on the gate, on the railing, and on top of the bushes. Two sturdy twigs shoved into the ground each had a black rubber boot hung upside-down on it, drying.

I had come to ask my dad's final "tenant" to move out. I felt bad about this, but he had a house and had moved into the vineyard cottage not out of necessity but rather to escape daily battles with his gypsy wife.

We knocked, but no one answered. His bicycle was gone; hence, he must have ventured into the village. We turned to go when a short, dark-haired man, who looked as if he had led a rough life, pulled up.

He looked at me, and I introduced myself as Steve's daughter. Rather than extending condolences, he said with surprise, "You're pretty."

I laughed and made a mental note to tell David he had competition.

I explained the circumstances, and he asked, "How much time do I have?"

We agreed on two weeks, leaving him plenty of time to cart his belongings on his bicycle back to his house, not far away.

My dad had been kind to let him live there rent free for the last ten years. He would need to patch things up with the gypsy woman. He might have to learn not to flirt with other women, though, because he once more said, "You really are pretty."

I laughed again, but as I said goodbye, I began to cry. He consoled me by shrugging his shoulders and saying, "That's life."

My mom's cousin Ivanka took one more look at the vineyard cottage and smiled. The birds were in full serenade. It was nicer than she'd recalled, and she would be happy to escape to a place in the countryside in the summer heat.

We hadn't seen the inside and feared to, because a neighbor had informed us that the interior room was the color of his jacket: black. Apparently, the tenant had brought in a wood stove to heat the house, the only problem being there was no chimney. My father seemed to attract only indestructible tenants who flaunted logic and reason.

In two weeks, Ivanka would find out exactly what awaited. The girls and I sent her money to pay for the paint and cover other expenses to get the place in order.

My mom had made many sacrifices to go abroad, leaving behind a loving family and all things familiar. Although life hadn't delivered what she expected, she had it much easier than her family in Croatia. Pensions were small, and work was hard to come by. Many building projects had been halted and would probably stay that way for years.

In the end, not much had changed from the time my mother had left, when "some had and a lot didn't." Regardless, our family was happy. Though life was simple, they proved one can be content without a granite or quartz countertop. And my mom's cousin Ivanka, despite having rickety, decades-old kitchen cupboards hung crookedly in a tiny kitchen, dished out the most amazing meals, served with love.

Fortunately, my mother's sacrifices benefited not only her but also her entire family. To this day, she is busy squirreling away barrels full of clothes, tablecloths and pretty knickknacks for them. Her family members are the most grateful and appreciative recipients of her generosity.

My father's house, with all of his visions of grandeur, was sold (to someone who didn't mind prodigious amounts of caulking), while the vineyard cottage would remain in the family and would always affectionately be called "Tata's."

I returned to Florence, and David was waiting for me with flowers. We celebrated a belated anniversary, as I reminded him to treat me well, because other men still found me pretty.

I was told that the last of Tata's tenants was actually sober on that occasion.

"Rich"

by Anica Blažanin

So I was one of the followers, stalkers, and worshippers of
the legendary 1964 Ford Galaxy XL. Then I met the man in
it, Steve, and what followed proved that on occasion, reality
was stranger than fiction. We lived together for fifteen years,
sometimes happily but more often unhappily. We had four
wonderful children whom both of us loved and cared for,
each in the way that we knew how, which I now know wasn't
always the best for them. They have forgiven both of us and
are happier for it.

Ivanka taught me how to look on the funny side of life—
not that all occasions could be viewed that way, but many
could, and why not focus on those? As someone said,
"Holding onto anger is like drinking poison and expecting the
other person to die." It's much better to try to find humor in
the situations we encounter.

After the divorce—not right away, but a few years
afterward—I began to view my ex as a sort of relative whom
you don't necessarily have tender affection for, but you
wouldn't like to see anything bad happen to him. I felt that

we were relatives through the children. They loved him, so, for their sake, I became kind of a second cousin to Steve.

Of course, he never remarried, and neither did I, which made our relationship, as it was, possible. He was willing to drive me to the doctor's or shopping. Most of the time, we had some kind of disagreement while driving. Lights that turned red or a man lollygagging across a pedestrian crosswalk occurred merely to spite him. Bus drivers were bullies who pulled into his lane, despite the fact that they had the right of way. When traffic wasn't out to get him, he took that opportunity to curse at politicians.

Each time I swore that I would rather trudge through snow and sleet than call him again for a ride. I stuck to my decision, until I froze at the bus stop and got splashed with dirty sleet. Then I caved, but I equipped myself with the most soundproof earplugs on the market.

One day, Steve saw me smiling, while he was eviscerating yet another victim. He turned to me and yelled, "Are you deaf?" Then he noticed the bright orange earplugs.

I immediately blamed the draft as my reason for wearing them. That worked, because in Croatia a draft is the cause of all dreadful illnesses, from acne to typhoid. The unforeseen result was that after this, he spoke a lot louder.

That was how it was, on and off, for the last few decades until his death last year. I helped the children care for him right up to the end. I was sad and cried when he died.

I am almost seventy now. How do I feel about my life? If I could describe myself in one word, what would it be? I thought about it and came up with *rich*. Not materially rich, though. My life in Canada is far from what I had dreamed. I did briefly get the large house, but even in my wildest imagination, it had never been shared with eccentric and, on occasion, dangerous people. Nor did the bank own most of it. Life was very hard, yet full and never boring.A river of people always streamed through my life. I have hundreds of pictures of friends eating meals in the little house we moved to in the poorer part of town. Our tiny kitchen had a picnic table with two benches that we stained ourselves—and not very well. It served as our dining set, because it was what we could afford. We would pack eight people or more around it, but everything we needed for dinner would have to be taken out of the fridge or the cupboards ahead of time. If we forgot anything, the entire row of people would have to stand up and tuck the bench under the table, so we could open the door of the fridge or the cupboard.

I don't remember many really unhappy times, just hard times—except for the tragedy of losing my son, Steven. The pain tore at our family like a ferocious beast for a long time. I thank God for lessening the pain over the years. I believe I will see Steven again, but I miss him so, even now after twenty-three years. He was so charming and so very special. Everyone felt this way about him—not just me, his mom. And even with his license suspended, he made a much better chauffeur than my ex-husband.

People say, "Oh, if I could be young again!" They can have it. Our life course depends on the decisions we make. What could guarantee that I would make better choices the second time around? Would I be willing to give up all of my experiences or the people in my life now or the ones I cling to in my memory? These people and experiences make me feel rich. I would never want to trade my children for my youth. Now I know what happiness is, but I've also learned what it is not. I can enjoy it in my seventies and eighties and on. When visiting many sick friends and relatives, I observe that they can enjoy a measure of happiness by seeing that their loved ones care for them. I trust that I am among such people who take care of one another.

Wondering "what if I had, if I did, if I didn't?" is a source of discontent. One will never know what would have happened if one had, one did, or one didn't. Frank Sinatra and Edith Piaf sang about having no regrets. Do I have any regrets? I have regrets for any of my actions that have hurt others, be they my children or my friends. I never planned to hurt anybody, but through ignorance, pain, insecurity, and sometimes pride, I have managed to. And for that, I repent. But how could I regret the choices that brought me to Canada, without denying the many joys that came as a result?

TIME AND OTHER FOES

by Ivanka Di Felice

NORA EPHRON SAID THAT AFTER a certain age, "If your elbows faced forward, you would kill yourself." My mother is no less encouraging when she maintains that "after a certain age, your goal is just to still look human." With these two women doling out "advice" on aging, it's a wonder *I* have not killed myself.

During this same period in my life, every manufacturer has conspired by making the font much smaller on all packaging. All of the elderly people I know have begun to compliment my weight gain, which, according to my new passport picture, is all below my neck and not in any desirable places, as confirmed by Canada Customs.

On a recent trip, one of the officers searched me. She patted me down and asked me to lift up my sweater to see what I was "hiding" beneath it. I did, but that only proved I had eaten too much pasta over the years, and it chose to settle not on my bust, but on my belly. She was frightfully apologetic, and whisked me through to avoid further embarrassment.

So Catherine Deneuve was wrong when she said that "At a certain age, a woman must choose between her face or her 'buttocks.'" I have not been offered this choice; my thighs and my stomach increase in size, while *at the same time* my face gets thinner. It seems my only option is to sleep upside-down, imploring gravity to reverse its effects.

Worse yet, certain friends my age now claim that pants "fit better if you turn them backward."

Renewing my passport after the age of forty-five was a traumatic event. For, previously unbeknownst to me, gravity had cruelly imposed its force since my last passport picture, a mere five years ago. I now believe a passport for women my age should have a mandatory one-year expiration date. Taking photos five years apart is simply cruel. As I look at my new passport photo, I console myself that in five years, this current picture will be considered a great one.

I have my own suggestions on coping with aging: Only look in the mirror without your glasses on, and hence accept poor eyesight as a small blessing. Exclusively attend art galleries that feature Renaissance women. And if I am considered middle aged at forty-nine, then that means I should live to almost one hundred. If you don't have a sense of humor, then get one—it helps immensely.

With the passing of years, although my large eyes are getting smaller, they see more. Of course, I see my physical changes (thankfully, less without glasses on), but I also see that life is no longer carefree, as I'd felt it was not that long ago. When you don't have children, as I don't, your parents and siblings are your nuclear family, and perhaps this made us even closer. But my small eyes clearly see that I have to face up to the fact that my brother was not invincible, my father was not indestructible, and my mom is not the pillar of physical strength she once was. And that despite all of our teasing, my dad was right: "Time is of the essence."

I believe in the power of forgiveness, the resolve to try to understand why people do what they do, and this not for the sake of others, but for our own sake. With Tata gone, there is one less person for me to share my joys with—one fewer who cares, anyway. As my doctor said, I will always have a small hole in my heart, and my dad deserves that. There are two holes now: one for Steven and one for him.

As I sat awake with my dad during his last night, never letting go of his hand, I got strength from deep within to do things I never imagined I could. I thanked him for all he had done for us, and he replied, "Thank God." I don't fear death itself, but, after this experience, I do fear going through the process of dying.

Tata's was a story of "rags to riches." Not "riches" as defined by many today, but, like my mom, he was rich, in that he left behind three girls who dearly love him and miss him. I'm sorry he isn't around to know exactly how much. Tata did his best, and in the end, isn't that all we can ask of ourselves and of others? By writing this book, I felt as if I had him with me that much longer, and the many humorous situations he created brought a smile to my face.

From a material standpoint—from the kid voted poorest in the class, hence given a pair of shoes, to leaving his daughters a house in swanky High Park in a world-class city, albeit full of eccentric tenants—Tata did well. He left us with many fond memories and also left his son-in-law David with those indestructible Chinese flip-flops that he wears each day and swears by.

I miss my dad more than I ever could have imagined—though I am quite sure the raccoons don't.

It's been a year since he passed away, and I still pick up the phone to call him. Often, in our youth, we don't take the time to find out about our parents' history. But when we get older and we start to care, we may no longer have the opportunity. So for those of you with parents still alive, appreciate them while you can.

I miss the house and even the tenants.

I miss Mirko, who, if he were not crazy, would be very normal. And I will always appreciate his generosity in pouring bad wine in almost-clean glasses.

I often think of George, the human boomerang, and hope he is okay in Croatia. I heard he reunited with his family after forty years. With his pension coming in monthly from abroad, three times the salary of your average Croatian, I am positive they will keep him healthy and themselves wealthy.

I found out that George wasn't making up stories but did live in Africa during World War II. Many women and children from Dalmatia, Croatia, had escaped the war and been transferred to refugee camps in El Shatt, Egypt. I hope the Caribbean man at the old age home appreciated this bit of "comradeship" that George shared with him.

Andy will no doubt also be fine, now that the government of Canada is changing the laws on marijuana possession. Though without his earning extra income from trapping raccoons with my dad, the timing is off.

I contemplate the many lives lived in the house we grew up in and wish I had chronicled each of the tenant's stories, certain something could be learned from every one.

Yet I can glean lessons from those whose lives I do know. Vesna, despite her bad health and the pain she endures every day, has a positive outlook. Thinking back to our childhood, she says, "My greatest privilege is to have grown up underprivileged." I agree. Many children today have everything but appreciate nothing, whereas having done without lets you feel deep gratitude once you do get something. We're so happy to have grown up poor, even in a rich neighborhood.

Would I change anything? We all make mistakes and, given the opportunity, would do some things differently. But I wouldn't change all of the bad; it's what made us who we are today. It's what taught us to be grateful for even small things, to be empathetic, and to always ask tenants for references.

Though we cannot change the past, I do want to apologize to all of the Chinese men to whom I sold shoes that were far too big.

My last thought is, don't bother imploring gravity to show mercy on you by sleeping upside-down. It does nothing at all.

And I'm delighted to report that David and I are still happily married, after eighteen years, proving my mom's teary-eyed aunt wrong.

Years ago, my friend Leah showed me a list of things that made her happy. She kept it in her pocket for when she needed it. I made my own list, and on days when I felt blue, I reflected on the many things that made me happy. I revise this list, as the years pass. It's still a substantial one, though a few frivolous things have been replaced by precious memories.

My mom would sum up her life by saying, "I feel rich. Very, very rich." If a woman who grew up in poverty, married a stranger, struggled in a foreign land, worked long, hard hours to provide the basics, tragically lost a son, and is now in bad health can say that she feels rich, then her example is one to be imitated. Her secret: she lives by the belief that there is "more happiness in giving than in receiving." And dwell on the good, rather than on the evil, for the challenges will come, but they will also go.

She proves that despite life not always delivering what we'd dreamed of, we can still be very happy. And if she can feel that way, then marrying for the Ford Galaxy XL was worth it, resulting in a zany but wonderful life.

Dear Reader,

Reviews are important to a novel's success and will help other readers find *My Zany Life: Growing Up in a Rooming House*. If you enjoyed our book, please leave a review wherever you purchased it. Thank you.

I am always delighted to receive email from readers: Ivanka.DiFelice@outlook.com

Happy reading.

ACKNOWLEDGMENTS

I WANT TO THANK PATTI Waldygo for her superb editing once again and Jim Shepard at Octagon Lab for his great cover design.

Hvala od srca ("heartfelt thanks") to my Italian prince, David, for his support and love for me and my family over the years. My father gave him the highest compliment when he said, "Even though he's Italian, he's better than any Croatian!"

Special thanks to my *mama*, Anica, for her love of books and the humorous stories she wrote during her interesting life and for encouraging me to do the same.

Much love and, unfortunately, belated thanks to my father for providing endless inspiration for my stories, as well as making us smile on many occasions with his antics. I thank him for having taught us Croatian, thus broadening our horizons and enabling us to know our family in Croatia. I could rely on my father to help us out in any way needed, and it gave him great pleasure to do so. I will miss Kentucky Fried Chicken during our next renovation. I miss my father.

Thanks to my family, whom I love dearly.

My deep appreciation goes to Filomena Becker, for her invaluable input and enthusiasm. Whether it was sincere or not, it greatly inspired me.

Congratulations are also in order *to me*, for the patience I mustered up while trying to decipher my mother's notes and for partnering with probably the last known author to still use pen and paper and write in a painful scribble. My mother, well aware that English is not phonetic, applied her "more is more" theory and, just in case, added an extra vowel or consonant to each word. She demonstrated her creativity with each draft she sent me, and she challenged my math. Sentences were written vertically and horizontally, and pages were randomly numbered, rarely in order. Celebrate the completion of this book with us, for it is nothing short of a miracle!

Yet as a final note, I want to thank my mom for being who she is and for having taught us the valuable lessons she did.

58522529R00209

Made in the USA
Lexington, KY
12 December 2016